THE
HOME
STRETCH

THE
HOME
STRETCH

Why It's Time to Come Clean
About Who Does the Dishes

SALLY HOWARD

Atlantic Books
London

First published in hardback in Great Britain in 2020 by Atlantic Books,
an imprint of Atlantic Books Ltd.

10 9 8 7 6 5 4 3 2 1

A CIP catalogue record for this book is available from the British Library.

Hardback ISBN 978 1 78649 757 4
Trade paperback ISBN 978 1 83895 056 9
E-book ISBN 978 1 78649 758 1

Printed in Great Britain

Atlantic Books
An Imprint of Atlantic Books Ltd
Ormond House
26-27 Boswell Street
London
WC1N 3JZ

www.atlantic-books.co.uk

For Ginny and Mary

Contents

Introduction

After nine months of sobriety and two and a half months on a gruelling 24-hour regime of two-hourly baby feeds, I was on my first night out as a new mother: an office Christmas party. I had expressed the bottle of breast milk with the electric expresser that moistly exhaled, *shoot-pffft-shoot-pffffttt*, like a breathless retriever (I'd grown to hate that machine). The sleeping bag was washed and laid beside the baby sleepsuit. I'd blow-dried my weirdly thinning hair – who knew fistfuls of hair fell out postpartum? – squeezed my new moonscape of a midriff into a festive red dress, and left Leo in Tim's charge.

I was two inches into an unpleasant but welcome glass of London-pub Pinot when the messages started to arrive.

When you say warm it up do you mean put it in boiled water? The whole bottle in boiled water? Or is boiled water too hot?

Does he wear these tiny trousers in bed? [picture enclosed] Or are these tiny trousers tights?

In the midnight confidences of early intimacy, my partner Tim and I would laugh about the 'honeydos'. These were our parents' generation's wifely domestic instructions and corrections to their husbands: 'Honey do you think you could empty the bins?' 'Honey do you mind putting the crumble in the oven?' Tim amusedly speculated that his aunt's honeydos had deskilled a male family member to the extent that, when left to fend for himself, he would spend half an hour trying to remember whether peas were cooked with water or without, before ordering a takeaway balti.

Somehow, despite my feminist ambitions of an egalitarian division of domestic labour, here Tim and I were, a few months into parenthood, with an expectation that I'd keep the domestic show on the road by knowing what was needed and when, and how these needs could be met. I knew the temperature the milk had to be. I knew if we owned enough of those maddeningly poppered babygros in the right size and if they'd been washed. I knew what we'd feed Leo for his first meal, that it couldn't include salt or honey, and where he stood on the baby-weight percentiles (92nd down from 4th at birth, as a prize marrow to a prawn). I knew to whom we owed thank-you cards for that teetering pile of too-small bootees (childless friends always buy you bootees). In short, both the emotional and mental labour of keeping the family alive and thriving fell on my (aching) shoulders.

It's a strange feature of new motherhood that your own childhood is suddenly, vividly brought back to life. And so it was for me: snapshots of my smiling mother handing an earthenware pot of casserole through the kitchen hatch, and of swift embraces and gentle scoldings. Awake in the small hours, scrolling through the list of social obligations to my partner's family and friends, or pureeing endless sweet potato for Leo's weaning menu because my partner declared himself incapable of performing a culinary task without a recipe to follow, I wondered how different the emotional and domestic battles I faced were to my mother's and grandmother's.

What was so perplexing was that, on the face of it, Tim and I had entered into parenthood with a genuine willingness to share domestic tasks equally. We'd talked about our ambition of being a truly fair family, in which chores would be allotted equably rather than with an eye to gendered norms. I took comfort in Tim's long pre-parental record of knocking out Jamie Oliver 30-minute meals in 45 minutes. He cleaned more assiduously than I did and attended to some domestic touches I'd never notice: smoothing the bottom creases from the sofa cushions at night, for example, and moving the newly bought provisions to the back of the fridge so we didn't end up with three circulating tubs of half-eaten Lurpak.

Yet, somewhere along the line, Tim had resigned domestic administration to me. And somewhere along the line, barely noticing it, I had accepted that this was the natural order of things. I was the one with whom the domestic buck stopped, however many bottles Tim sterilized, or milk stains he sponged.

It was during a bleak night of insomnia brought on by six months of shifting night feeds that I discovered an essay written by Judy Brady for Gloria Steinem's *Ms.* magazine in 1971. Titled 'I Want a Wife',[1] it spoke poetically of the invisible role women/ wives/mothers perform in the smooth running of family lives. Brady opens by explaining that a newly divorced male friend is on the hunt for a brand-new wife, and it had occurred to her that she could do with a wife of her own. With a wife, she could return to her studies, become better qualified, get a new job and become financially independent, while her wife committed all of her energies to making Brady's life as pleasant as possible.

I want a wife who knows that sometimes I need a night out by myself...

I want a wife who will take care of the details of my social life... [and] the baby-sitting arrangements...

I want a wife to keep track of the children's doctor and dentist appointments...

I want a wife who takes care of the children when they are sick...

3

My wife must arrange to lose time at work and not lose her job.

This 47-year-old essay, it struck me, had barely aged. In it I heard the voices of the harried women I'd met through mothering classes who'd found themselves sidelined in the workplace after maternity leave; friends who'd been forced into freelance work to keep up with their children's schools' growing demands for attending concerts and fundraisers and, in the words of a North London single-mum acquaintance, 'knocking up fucking Victoria sponges with a day's notice'. Women who juggled these swelling domestic demands with all the finesse of a drunk unicyclist and had slowly, inexorably, begun to despise their other halves. Brady's essay speaks to domestic labour,[2] but also the smoothing and facilitating labour that women in heterosexual unions disproportionately undertake. To be Brady's 'wife' is to be a sponge: wives absorb every problem, obstacle and distraction, and ensure that a husband/partner's path to success and self-fulfilment is set in a smooth, straight line.

Around the same time, I read about the work of 1970s feminist activists Wages for Housework. In 1972, at the height of Second Wave feminism, an international collective of feminists from Italy, England and the USA gathered in Padua to give voice to women's daily grind. The campaign that came out of that conference positioned housework as an issue of capitalist abuse. It was capitalism, they argued, that most profited from women's unpaid labour – on their backs, on their knees – in the patriarchal home. In the language of the Marxist left, from which Wages for Housework had sprung, these activists declared women 'double proletariats': abused by a capitalist-patriarchal system that underpaid them in the workforce (in 1972, working women earned on average 58 per cent of the male wage[*]) at the same time as their labours at home were

---

* Rich-world average.

relegated to the status of 'nonwork', ascribed to them on the basis of the shape of their genitals and expected to be conducted out of love. Well, they said, let's put an end to 'cooking, smiling and fucking'[3] for capital — women should organize and REVOLT! It was heady talk, and tens of thousands of women joined the cause, in the US, UK and across Europe.

Today, Wages for Housework is a curio remembered by few other than feminist historians. By the 1980s, the postmodernist turn refocused attentions in popular and academic feminism:* on gender as a social construction; on popular cultural representations of women; and, vitally, on white feminism's erasure of the lived experiences of women of colour and the way in which oppressions through race, class and gender inform each other. The preoccupations of these 1970s socialist feminists became stuffy artefacts, relegated to history alongside symbolic bra-burning (a gesture that was always more caricatured than practised). The work the Second Wave feminists had undertaken for years on behalf of women and homemakers had become, in a bitter irony, as invisible as the labour itself.

Somehow, in the short generation from the 1970s to the 2010s, the era in which I came of age, the emancipating feminist pronouncement 'Girls can do anything!' was mangled into the edict 'Women must do everything'. This was when, as Barbara Ehrenreich puts it, feminism — after a few concessions — suffered its 'micro-defeat' in the home.

Of course, the labour these Second Wave feminists had theorized had gone nowhere. Bottoms still needed to be wiped and toilet bowls cleaned, and the hand that pushed the sponge and thrust the brush was still, invariably, female. From the mid-1980s in the UK, as elsewhere in the rich world, it was as likely to be the hand of a lowly paid migrant woman as that of an unpaid spouse. The 'problem' of the gendered attribution of domestic labour was offloaded down a classed and

---

* Then Women's Studies — now, broadly, Gender Studies.

racialized female labour line, and liberal feminism opened a new door for women: the servant's entrance.

Many men, of course, do much more housework and childcare than they did in the 1970s. In the UK's Office for National Statistics 2016 Time Use Survey,* British men reported putting in an average of 18 hours a week of domestic effort, including laundry, cooking and cleaning; compared to the average 1 hour and 20 minutes of a 1971 man. Yet these efforts fall far below the 36 hours a week that female Britons contribute to household chores.

British men's scanty efforts on the home front garner them a cool five extra hours of leisure time, compared to women, each week.[4] The picture is similarly lopsided elsewhere. In the US, men contribute 7 hours a week to women's 17; French men 10 to French women's 20; and Australian women 15 hours to an Australian male's 5 hours. Meanwhile, women in Italy devote 24.5 hours a week to men's 3.5, and men in Portugal manage to rouse themselves for less than 3 hours a week (to Portuguese women's 22). Even in Sweden – where gender equality is a government project – women put in 45 minutes a day more, on average, than their male counterparts.

And these figures, of course, do not account for the many extra hours women spend on those 'silent' categories of domestic labour: the mental load of assuming the responsibility of running a home; chivvying unwilling partners; or the wearing emotional labour of keeping everyone happy and maintaining extended family relationships.

Delve deeper and the statistics are more baffling. After a decade of slow gains from the early 1970s to the mid-1980s, in many rich nations the domestic labour gap stopped narrowing at some point in the 1990s.** Indeed, in the US and UK, male contributions have gone into reverse, with today's

---

* The last available.
** In the UK the gap stopped narrowing in 1986; in the US it was 1988.

30- and 40-something British men putting in almost two fewer hours per week of core housework (excluding care) than their similarly aged counterparts in 1998,[5] and their US counterparts reducing their inputs by an hour a week.[6] Clearly, the increasing entrance of women into the paid workforce, a trend that took flight in the 1980s across the West, hasn't influenced these asymmetries in the way we had hoped. In heterosexual households where the woman is the main breadwinner, the more the woman earns, the less her partner will contribute — proportionally — to household chores.[7]

So what happened to the promise of egalitarian households the Second Wave feminists held so dear? Why have gains women have made in the public domain (a quadrupling of women CEOs of US Fortune 500 companies since 1995; the narrowing of the gender pay gap by 20 per cent since 1980; a global doubling of female parliamentarians since the mid-1990s[8]) been met with backsliding on the home front? 'Everybody's in favour of equal pay, but nobody's in favour of doing the dishes,' said activist Mary Jo Bane, of the Wellesley Women's Research Center, in 1977. Little, apparently, has changed.

But the answer is not as simple as blaming a nation of heterosexist jerks who feel entitled to glug beer and watch *Top Gear* rather than scour the pans, although such jerks definitely exist. As we'll see, the roots of this stalled feminist revolution reach deep: the stories we tell ourselves about masculinity and femininity; the gender norms that pervade our homes like the aroma of cheap fabric softener; the intergenerational patterning from our mothers and grandmothers, fathers and grandfathers. They arise from the Parent Labour Trap: the fact that economic and structural forces discipline many of us, however much we hope or struggle to avoid it, into traditional gendered roles when kids arrive on the scene. Childless young women often think these battles have been won, but — as we'll see — the blitheness with which we celebrate feminism's achievements masks myriad stubborn realities behind the closed doors of family homes.

In 1963's *The Feminine Mystique*, American journalist Betty Friedan portrayed the quiet, pill-popping desperation of a nation of women in thrall to the post-war cult of feminine domesticity. Her book – based on a survey conducted amongst fellow alumni of the all-female Smith College – articulated the 'problem with no name': that the exclusively wife-and-mother role prescribed as the route to post-war feminine fulfilment was a lie and a trap. In 2020, cultural messaging no longer tells women that their sole route to feminine fulfilment is through the wiping of runny toddlers' noses and the rustling up of soufflés for husbands commuting home from 9-to-5s. But the cult of the domestic feminine has, nevertheless, proved surprisingly plastic, metamorphosing into the cultural tropes of 'yummy mummies', domestic goddesses and have-it-all mums on whom falls the expectation of being 'super' both at work and at home, and at the same time performing the 'aesthetic labour' of being easy on the eye. Our survey* finds that 59 per cent of women, and 76 per cent of heterosexual women, still consider a clean and tidy home to be a marker of their self-worth. Friedan's problem with no name, as feminist essayist Katha Pollitt puts it, has become the 'no-problem problem'.

There are more pressing reasons to address the domestic labour gap than our pursuit of fair and harmonious households. Recent studies point to a raft of implications arising from these asymmetries, from higher anxiety levels amongst the children of rowing heterosexual couples, to the damaging effects of double-shifting on women's physical and mental health. Moreover, the fact that women in the West earn 20 per cent less than men, for all of national governments' attempts to shame employers into tackling the issue upstream, is in large part down to the Double Day of motherhood. The woman who leaves work

---

* An anonymous questionnaire of 1,081 partnered individuals between the ages of 17 and 70, in Europe, the USA, the Antipodes and South Asia. See p. 10 for methodology.

because her son is sick is the woman who's passed over for a promotion, while the man who marries sees his income and status rise. Gendered labour inequalities at home reproduce gender inequalities in the workplace, in an ever-increasing circle of rising anxiety and dwindling time. As one feminist wit puts it: 'It's not a glass ceiling, it's the sticky floor, stupid.'

Feminist theory gives us new terms for the myriad invisible tasks that fall to modern women: Arlie Hochschild's 'emotional labour' for the feminized work of smiling and soothing, of easing intergenerational family relationships and managing our own emotions according to social rules; 'mental load' for the work of taking responsibility that's in part captured by that old formation 'good housekeeping', and which I like to call (wo)management.

From domestic violence to everyday sexism, the glass ceiling and systematic wartime rape, the coining of concepts is often the first step in calling attention to injustices. But – much as feminists might hope for this – we can't simply rely on the trickle-down of feminist ideas to effect real change in our material lives. And the devaluation of the work of washing and wiping – of, more broadly, the labour of caring for the young, the ill and elderly - is something that intimately affects us all, even for those of us who have managed to escape the Double Day.

Second Wave feminism gave us the insight that household labour is invisible in two ways: as an expression of male privilege and as work. But they – we – left a job half done: our revolutionary pots half washed, our ironing pile in disarray.

Our challenge, and it's a moral as well as a feminist one, is to bring politics back to the kitchen sink.

A Note on Survey Methodology

Some of the data that forms this book came from an anonymous questionnaire of 1,081 partnered individuals aged between the ages of 17 and 70 in Europe, the USA, the Antipodes and South Asia. This was, by design, a qualitative rather than quantitative study, with large text fields designed principally to gather anecdotal, rather than statistical, information about respondents' intimate domestic experience. Although this voluntarily reported qualitative survey disproportionately attracted heterosexual mothers, I corrected for this bias, to a limited extent, by reaching out to groups that were under- or unrepresented (notably older gay males).

Despite such attempts, this survey can only be a partial and imperfect reflection of the intimate domestic realities in these global contexts at our point of time, and I make all due apologies for these shortcomings. The questions used in the questionnaire and a full description of methodology can be found online.[9] Throughout, the material derived from the survey is marked in *italics*.

1

Coming Clean

My grandmother Mary was the first woman in her West Yorkshire village to abandon wartime tweeds for Dior's New Look. The arrival of nipped waists and full-skirted crinolines marked more than an end to fabric rationing; Mary's womanly silhouette embodied a cultural mood that sought to reposition Britain's wartime ambulance drivers, shopkeepers and munitions workers in their rightful place: tending hearth and home.

Mary was a trendsetter for another reason – she was the first to own one of the 'twin tub' washing machines which, in their whirring, boxy white form, signalled one of technology's answers to the perennial slog of keeping house in the 1950s. Soon, the Yorkshire-built mangle that sat by the outdoor coal scuttle disappeared, and with it the copper pot that doubled, at Christmas time, as a steamer of suet puddings, carefully wrapped in sheaths of muslin. Food rationing still had four years to run – the bananas that formed the centrepiece of Mary's 1960s trifles were yet to arrive, and carrots still bulked up her Christmas fruit cake – but for the Greatest Generation, a brave new world had arrived on the doorstep in the form of electric carpet sweepers, skittering twin tubs and Morphy Richards electric steam irons.

It only fleetingly occurred to Mary, as she carefully pressed the turn-ups into my grandfather's tweeds, that she missed the day-to-day conviviality of the munitions factory line in York.

Life, after all, was tangibly easier for her than it had been for her mother Elsie. At Mary's age, Elsie was struggling to maintain a household of small children at a time when husbands and sons returned wounded and shell-shocked from the First World War. One bright morning in 1921, three years after her husband Percival had returned from the Front, Elsie walked out onto the moorland surrounding the family's Yorkshire-stone farmhouse at Blackmoorfoot, slipped the cool barrel of Percival's shotgun into her mouth, and pulled the trigger. The poacher who discovered her body would remark to a local newspaper on the shade of her hair: a glowing auburn that echoed the late-blooming heather on which she fell.

When pressed, in later years, about her mother's death, my grandmother would softly repeat the family adage that Elsie's was 'a mother's trouble'.

A mother's trouble. I remember grappling, as a child, with this phrase, redolent as it was of things-between-women and gynaecological discomfort. It took me until adulthood to understand that my grandmother Mary had in mind two specific troubles: the episodic mental illness we'd now call postpartum depression, and the drudgery of keeping a young family fed and warm with a generation of men unable to work for a wage.

The Lost Generation's lot on the home front was as brutal as it was on the deathly battlefields of France. Many of the young men who'd left in Kitchener's Pals battalions for the Front — which included 1,659 men from Elsie and Percival's small quarter of West Yorkshire — would never return home. Of those that did, many were broken by their experience: wheezing from chlorine gas attacks, haunted by the daily horror movie of nightmares and flashbacks. Amongst the young women of Elsie's generation who were single at the outbreak of the First World War, only one in ten would marry.[10] It fell to these 'silent widows' and 'surplus women' to hold domestic life together — and care for the sick and wounded — on a shoestring.

In 1921, only 6 per cent of British homes were wired for

electricity. Coal-gas lighting – a feature found in 40 per cent of London working-class homes by 1937 – was a big breakthrough, putting paid to the laborious and ancient task of 'lighting up', but only a fraction of rural homes benefited from piped coal-gas in the 1920s. Homes such as Elsie's made do with paraffin lamps, the filling and cleaning of which was a labour-intensive job: lamps needed to be kept half-filled to maintain a flame, and were vulnerable to being extinguished by the draughts that plagued rural dwellings. Cleaning equipment – mops made of old rags, brushes from pigs' bristles, and birch-handled brooms – had barely changed since the 1600s, and washing up, in the era before modern surfactant detergents, was performed with soda flakes, which left hands cracked and raw. Particularly onerous was the effort to keep homes warm. Cleaning coal-fire grates, setting coal fires and disposing of staining and blackening coal-dust was a never-ending task, particularly in the regions, such as Elsie's, that burned ash-producing, non-bituminous coal. Meanwhile, laundry day – traditionally Monday – was just that: extending through hours of backbreaking wringing and scrubbing, little aided by technology such as the 'dolly' (a wooden, three-legged fabric-twisting device) and ridged wooden scrubbing boards.

In her 1967 *Fenland Chronicle,* Sybil Marshall enumerates the labour that fell to women such as Elsie in the agricultural regions of Britain at the turn of the 20th century. Up at dawn to sweep, clean and set fires, these women were often called upon to work in the fields between their cooking, food production, washing-up, fire-setting, lighting-up and laundry duties. With menfolk relaxing at nightfall, it fell to women to prepare and clean up after the evening meal, put the children to bed, and make or mend clothes and spin yarn by candle- or lamplight. Women's working days began when they rose and ended at bedtime. Leisure, for women, was non-existent.

In her 1982 history of housework in the British Isles, *A Woman's Work Is Never Done*, Caroline Davidson notes the weighty domestic labour burden that, until the late 20th century, fell upon country women such as Elsie. Unlike city-dwellers, country women typically kept animals and cottage gardens, adding food processing to their list of chores – alongside the production from scratch of goods that could be bought readymade in the city, such as tallow or rush candles and lye, a detergent extracted from wood or plant ashes. Laundry services to 'put out'* the weekly wash, common in cities by the 1920s, were unknown in the British countryside, and fuel was often harder to come by than in cities and suburbs, where horse-and-cart coal delivery men plied their wares.

The spectre of social attitudes will also have haunted Elsie's daily grind. Even if the men at Blackmoorfoot had been willing to alleviate the domestic labour burden, in the 1920s the taboo of male involvement would have been a powerful inhibitor.

In Elsie's day, the first Housework Cult held sway. The 19th century had spelled the end of the pre-industrial 'family economy', in which most labour was conducted in and around the family dwelling. With the arrival of industrial capitalism, work was divided into two categories: that which was undertaken for a wage and conducted outside of the home; and that which was unpaid and conducted at home. The latter became a new occupational category of nonwork – or 'Occupation: Housewife', as the census records termed it. Emerging as a by-product of this development and reaching its zenith in the 1880s – but persisting well into the 20th century – the Victorian Housework Cult invented the term 'housework' as we understand it today: a specific set of tasks ascribed to women that were carried out within the home or on its periphery, unpaid and (supposedly) discrete to the male domain of productive labour. Although men and women seldom shared housework on an equal basis, diaries from the 17th and 18th centuries talk of a climate in which men pitched in at home. The diaries of Nicholas Blundell

---

* Sending it out to be washed by a paid laundress.

of Little Crosby, Lancashire, written in the early 1700s, describe the author laying the Christmas table, dressing decorative flower pots for chimneys, making preserves, managing servants and keeping household accounts to make life easier for his wife Frances, who bore him two children in quick succession.

By the 1890s, however, a rigid gendered division of labour had been established in much of the West. In his 1935 memoir, *Yorkshire Days and Yorkshire Ways,* J. Fairfax-Blakeborough paints a picture of late-Victorian rural Yorkshire in which it was a marker of household honour that men did not lift a finger at home. Wives were expected to address their husbands as 'master' and serve them obsequiously – even, as Fairfax-Blakeborough describes it, within days of giving birth. Husbands compelled by character or sympathy to help out on the home front often did so in secret: Caroline Davidson notes that husbands in 1890s Manchester who were caught in the act of pitching in domestically were mocked as 'mop rags' and 'diddy men'.*

The Housework Cult led to the extreme and neurotic state of affairs encapsulated in *Mrs Beeton's Book of Household Management,* a strange and despotic advisory that prescribes, amongst other pointless tasks, the washing of stair bannisters daily and the zestful 'shaking' of curtains. Amongst the middle classes of this era, domestic femininity was frequently performed through the collection and maintenance of dust-gathering lace and knick-knacks (signalling a woman's ability to afford and manage servants).

Similarly, for working-class women good housekeeping was performed through the propriety and outward appearance of their family's front step. Styles of doorstep finish varied from region to region – in Salford a substance called 'blue mould' was popular; in Wales, chalk was in vogue; and orange-red ruddlestone found favour in the West Yorkshire region where Elsie lived. What united these women was the

---

* 'Diddy' = foolish.

effort of donning their aprons and getting down on hands and knees with buckets and brushes, to scrub away the thankless muck and grime of industrial streets. In the 1950s, according to historian Virginia Nicholson,[11] visitors to working-class terraces would still be greeted by the sight of crouching women scrubbing and chalking their stoops, a space, as Nicholson describes it, where working-class women found happy camaraderie. As late as the 1970s, my grandmother's neighbour Hilda, in my mother's recollection, got down on her knees to soap and ruddlestone her Yorkshire-stone threshold. 'She was set on getting it to what she called a "clean fettle",' my mother recalls. 'She did it into her eighties and I suppose her knees held up because she'd rub them with liniment afterwards.'

Working-class women's step-scrubbing, in historian Robert Roberts's interpretation, was designed to broadcast 'the image of a spotless household into the world at large' – a spotlessness that was intimately associated with religious and moral virtue. 'Cleanliness is close to godliness', the motto of the 19th-century sanitary reformers,* was accepted wisdom, with dirt and sin the twin moral battlegrounds of the respectable home.

My grandmother Mary and her husband Thomas were brought together, in part, by a cruel coincidence. Six years after Elsie's suicide and barely two miles east, 33-year-old Hilda Barker had knelt on the cool flagstones of her kitchen floor as her seven-year-old twins Tom and Bob ran errands for customers in the family's grocery shop downstairs and her newborn son John, the shop pet, giggled on her sister's hip. The same sister, with an animal scream that her nephew Thomas could still recall as an old man, discovered Hilda an hour later: her head drooping into the oven drawer of the new coal-gas range.

Thomas and Mary married 15 years after Hilda's death and a few months after Thomas's return from the front at El

---

* Who tackled the conditions that led to deadly outbreaks of cholera throughout the mid-1800s.

Alamein, where he'd been an army engineer. Home life during early marriage, she told me as a child as she reminisced over orange-hued photographs, was happy. Through 50 years of marriage, my grandmother kept more-or-less patient house, tolerant of Thomas's muddy boots and expressing bright gratitude when he made her a cup of tea; and he rose at 6 a.m. to build the tower of twisted-newspaper kindle to light the coal fire that warmed their 18th-century stone cottage. Thomas served sherry at Saturday-afternoon gatherings with extended family, when they'd put wood shavings down on the floor of the 'lean-to' garage and dance to the strains of the new 16-inch gramophone.

Twenty-five years after her mother took delivery of that gleaming twin-tub, my mother Anne, a Home Economics teacher with a good line in sausage plaits, embraced the domestic vogues of the 1970s: the chest-freezer cookbook and the backyard chicken coop. The Home Economics syllabus at the

Anne in the chicken coop with Hen, Holly, Sammy and Hilda, 1983

Church of England girls' school where she taught included 'family egg dishes' as well as crafting tasks such as crocheting oven gloves and hand-beading dinner-party napkin rings. At home, she baked hemp-seed biscuits with her hand-reared eggs; rustled up fine salads with the blushing tomatoes that fruited, too briefly, on our suntrap patio; filled the freezer with single portions of *coq au vin*; and made homemade vanilla yoghurt that my brother and I would steal from the back of the fridge, unscrewing the little yellow jar tops to guiltily eat the contents with our tongues.

It didn't matter that our chickens Hen, Holly, Sammy and Hilda (and their several avian successors) were cruelly torn apart, limb by limb, by suburban foxes; their carcasses melancholically strewn across box hedges and pampas grass. The coop, and the neatly serried rows of spring beans, were my mother's bid for the Good Life. If my grandmother's pocket advisory was *Housekeeping Monthly*, my mother's was John Seymour's *Self-Sufficiency*, the suburban smallholders' bible that advised how to press cheese, spin flax and properly construct a goat coop (at a wise distance, apparently, from the caprine peril of the rhododendron bush). Anne's ambition was her generation's: to return to a largely imagined British Golden Age of allotments, buttered spuds and hand-reared cattle stock. Much of this misty-eyed nostalgia was, as we'll see, a backlash to the pace of social change: to British women abandoning the kitchen for the workplace, and all of the anxieties that provoked around how – and by whom – families would be clothed and fed. Keen-eyed feminist readers won't miss the irony of a generation who'd never had it so good in terms of domestic comforts and technology, and in which men were beginning – however half-heartedly – to pitch in on the domestic front, nostalgically harking back to the 'natural living' of an Edwardian era that had been, for many, back-breaking and hard.

Yet my mother hummed as she vacuumed the hessian matting around our ginger Habitat scoop chairs with her upright Electrolux, relieved that the inefficient carpet sweepers had gone the way of her great-aunt Lily's punishing corsets. She viewed her life, as did many of her contemporaries, with mixed grace. Following a package holiday to the Tarragona resort town of Salou, my father Kenneth had started to produce Friday-night suppers of half-collapsed egg scrambles he optimistically called 'Spanish' omelettes. Kenneth also made a stab at the nightly washing-up, tapping Condor Ready Rubbed pipe ash into the gathering suds. He offered a then-generous three hours a week to the labours required to maintain our three-bed semi in the least posh part of Solihull. That said, my mum wouldn't – as she tells me now – have called herself a feminist. She liked her padded bras with their cups like the Great Pyramid of Giza, and she vaguely imagined feminism might deny her the benefits of her Maybelline Great Lash mascara. Feminism was for other – metropolitan – women.

These days, women of my generation have three times as many gadgets to ease household burdens as my mother did, and five times as many as my grandmother enjoyed.[12] We have gadgets to automatically vacuum overnight, or to shush a screaming baby with a mimic of her mother's heartbeat or by rocking her according to the pitch of her wails; we have technology that controls the heating in individual rooms and warms the oven for our return from work. And it's easy to swallow the spiel that technology is the answer to our domestic woes. For a few deranged few months of early parenthood, for example, Tim and I became obsessed with the promise of technology to help us survive our newborn's non-stop, eardrum-punishing screams. We bought Shaun the Sheep, a bulbous ovine that glows red and plays a soundtrack of heartbeats, and, memorably, a Fisher-Price Rock 'n Play that promised 'the perfect calming combo for your little one' but which we rechristened the 'vom box'. None of these gadgets stopped our newborn son from screaming, for three hours daily, at a pitch reminiscent of a beauty salon's worth of nails being dragged across a chalkboard.

On the surface, my domestic fate is very different to that of the women who preceded me. My mother was too late, for all of her awareness of its arrival, to reap the full benefits of Second Wave feminism, which started to ripple out into the suburbs in the 1970s. However, thanks to the rallies, the activism and the sheer recalcitrance of these women, I grew up in different times: through the Thatcher years of the woman with a baby on her hip and a briefcase in her hand; through the feminism-lite of the Spice Girls and Britpop, when emancipation was restyled as being able to drink the boys under the table and reclaiming female promiscuity as empowerment. So, through my teens and much of my twenties, I naively believed that some, if not all (of course not all), of the feminist battles had been won. If not on the streets – where, as a teenager, I'd been repeatedly wolf-whistled, flashed and groped – then behind domestic closed doors, in the houses of middle-class grown-ups to which I'd graduate when I was done with swilling alcopops and falling off my patent black platform boots into the nearest roadside bush. Yes, we women were still objectified and sexualized, under-represented and underpaid. But we weren't scrubbing the old man's Y-fronts over the kitchen sink, were we? Or, at least – not yet being *in loco maternis* myself – I confidently hoped. I hazily pictured my future life-partner in a long line of progress from Neanderthal man to *Homo sapiens*: from my workboot-shining grandfather, via my omelette-cobbling dad, to the man I'd end up with, who was as unlikely to step out of his underpants on the bedroom floor as slap my bottom and call me 'toots'.

Elsie and Hilda, Mary and Anne's lived experiences are the familial recent histories of many of us in the West – women navigating the impacts of Christian cleanliness doctrines, gendered ideologies and the forces of capitalism on the private processes of the home. Many of our great-grandmothers lived hardscrabble lives, while our grandmothers performed domesticity under the shadow of the second, post-war Housework Cult and our mothers were torn between home and productive work. For those of us from non-white and working-class backgrounds, our grandmothers might also have been expected to work for a wage even as they bore the weight of the domestic load. The domestic expectations of patriarchal capitalism might have pressed more heavily on some generations, and some classes of women, but these forces are at work on all of us: disciplining us, forming ideals and inheritances against which we live our gendered home lives.

In recent years, feminists have articulated invisible forms of domestic labour that we might call the Triple Day or 'third shift': emotional and mental labour. Coined in 1983 in Arlie Hochschild's book *The Managed Heart*, 'emotional labour' refers to the work that women are expected to perform in order to smooth relationships and keep the show on the road. These feminized expectations are at play in the working world, of course: feminist academic Silvia Federici calls jobs that expect emotional labour of women – smiling and flirting; complimenting clients – 'perfume jobs'. However, it's at home that these 'womanly skills' come into their own, with women world-wide working overtime to 'make nice': keeping kids happy, putting on a smiling face against the drudgery of day-to-day living, and keeping extended family on side.

'Emotional labour' is now sometimes used to mean another distinct aspect of women's third shift: mental load, or mental labour. The concept of the mental load was neatly captured in the feminist cartoon that went viral in 2017: *Fallait demander*, or *You Should've Asked*. Authored by a French web designer who goes by the name 'Emma', it begins with a scene in which a woman arrives for dinner at her male colleague's family home. The mother of the household bids her a cheery hello as she simultaneously looks after two warring kids, tidies up the kitchen and cooks a casserole; her husband sits down and enjoys a bottle of wine with their guest. When the pot overflows because his wife is performing three tasks simultaneously, the husband races over with an '*Ohlala*, what have you done?'

'What have I done?' screams the red-faced wife as their guest looks on. 'I've done everything!'

'But,' the husband responds, 'you should've asked! I would've helped!'

The comic struck a chord with the hundreds of thousands of women in heterosexual relationships who shared the cartoon on social media, reading in the telling cluelessness of the phrase their own daily experiences of being expected to be the micromanager of their own homes and having to apportion labour to their other half – of bearing the full mental effort of knowing what needs to be done and when.

'I knew that I would never do ironing for my husband, and that we would share tasks such as cleaning and cooking. I didn't anticipate that I would need to ask/remind him to do chores, though.' Woman aged 33–45, UK

'My dad never did any household chores. That said, my husband is unaware of what to do – I have to "coach" him!' Woman aged 25–33, Australia

The terminology may be new, but this (wo)management work has a heritage in much earlier feminist thought. In *Feeding the Family*,[13] first published in 1991, feminist theorist Marjorie DeVault terms the wifely labour of juggling and managing (and knocking up fucking Victoria sponges with a day's notice) the 'feminine production of normalcy'. Feeding and household management, in DeVault's view, are ways in which women are schooled to express their identities. Through tasks such as planning my son's teething meals and picking up my partner's strewn underwear – the latter being married women's top domestic complaint in a thread on website Mumsnet – I reaffirm both my relationship to the world and my identity as a gendered individual. I make sense of myself in a value system that I've internalized, and which measures my worth through the performance of care. Girls, DeVault argues, are early on recruited into these womanly domestic activities through an expectation placed upon them to be responsible and attentive. As a child, I knew if my younger brother's nose was wiped or his homework was done (they rarely were); today, I know there's tea and biscuits in the cupboard in case the in-laws pop round, and that a birthday card and stamps have been bought for my partner's cousin's son. Because if there's no milk for the Assam or the card goes unsent, it's me – not their blood relation – who will be judged. Through the day-in, day-out repetition of domestic activities, I 'fix' the meaning – to me and to the world – of what it is to be a woman.

In 1985's *The Gender Factory*, which looked at the distribution of work in US households, Sarah Fenstermaker Berk similarly offers a 'gender performance'-based explanation for the fact that, even in two-paycheque families, women consistently put in more work to maintain households than men. Berk argues that 'gendered identity formation' takes precedence, in both household and society, over economic efficiency or even fairness: in short, the sense that husbands and wives being 'good' men or women trumps a rational approach to division of household labour, even in households with egalitarian aspirations. For Berk, this work that women are expected to do to achieve 'womanliness', or for love, is necessarily unremitting. There's never enough time to satisfy a (largely imagined) hunger for the productions of expert mothering: organic home-cooked food; interior decor to a hotel standard; hand-stencilled depictions of the Serengeti on your toddler's bedroom walls. In Berk's take, it's these naturalized expectations – from others, from society and from ourselves – that are the real job women have to take on.

Berk's model also makes sense of another impediment to my own ambition of setting up a truly egalitarian household: Tim's unexamined notion of the 'manliness' of allotted tasks. He will cook one-pot dishes with a flourish, but will never bake. He'll happily stroll about the park with baby, Leo's feet bouncing in a BabyBjörn sling, yet he's embarrassed to attend any of the proliferating baby-and-parent singing, raving and 'sensory development' events peopled by knackered middle-class mothers. He refuses to carry the nappy bag because 'it looks a bit like a handbag', but is first to volunteer to change the baby in the cramped bathroom of a London boozer. These hard-wired gendered taboos around masculine and unmasculine tasks are something we all – Tim and I included – need to interrogate (as we will in Chapter Three).

I meet Silvia Federici in the Brooklyn apartment she's lived in for 40 years. Spring sunshine slants through the window blinds onto books and campaign materials that are piled as high as the Manhattan skyline: the material remnants of four decades of front-line feminist activism. During our two-hour chat, Federici – an elfin 70-something who dresses in top-to-toe black – periodically leaps up to rootle about in the piles' lower storeys, for an arcane document from the 1970s or a well-thumbed book. 'No, no, ah! No...' she says. 'It's here somewhere, here somewhere... But where?'

Federici is not, she says, at all surprised by my household's domestic impasse. Then she inhales a draught of the strong black filter coffee she plies me with from her permanently bubbling stovetop pot. After half a cup, I'm so wired that my left eye has started twitching involuntarily.

'Women, I am sorry to say it, are in a sad position,' she explains. 'What capitalism and patriarchy expect from women everywhere in the world is an impossibility: working for less and less pay, and also performing all of the reproductive labour. This is an impossible situation.'

The co-founder of Wages for Housework, Federici was a leading light in the feminist movement that sought to make sense of the interplay of work and capital, as understood by the left from a feminist perspective. Importantly, Federici added the dimension of reproduction to Marx's construction of productive labour, or the work capitalism extracts from the worker to derive profit. For Federici, the subordinate status of women hung on this hidden exploitation of women by capital and patriarchy in the home.

In *Revolution at Point Zero*, a collection of Federici's essays dating from the 1970s up to 2012, she talks of a 'lightbulb' moment in which she realized that something deeper than patriarchy was at work in the nuclear family home: 'Through my involvement in the [1960s and '70s] women's movement I realized that the reproduction of human beings is the foundation of every economic and political system, and that the immense amount of aid and unpaid domestic work done by women in the home is what keeps the world moving.'

What happened to Federici's insights? It's something I'd been wondering about since reading Judy Brady's essay, 'I Want a Wife'. The Second Wave feminists voiced their ire against the intimate oppressions of the home. They went on strike. They demanded wages. Then the issue evaporated as feminism moved on to how gender was relational, slippery and performed; and, in the 1980s and 1990s, to its Damascene moment of race consciousness, as theorists such as Kimberlé Crenshaw called out white feminism's erasure of classed and black experiences.

Only, domestic labour didn't disappear. Women continued to disproportionately carry the can and wash and dry the can.

The difference today is that fewer women campaign about it. We complain about it in the merest whimper: in polite *Woman's Hour* reports on the 'Chore Wars', or private moans between harried mums.

Federici knows what happened.

'Well, in a sense, it was our fault as feminists,' she says. 'This idea came about that waged work would be the path to women's liberation. Of course, that didn't work out, as neither the state — in the form of free universal childcare — or men stepped in to fill the shoes vacated by the full-time housewife. Decades of evidence shows us that in fact the opposite of what we hoped is true: female work outside the home increases the exploitation of women both in the home and the workplace. So the working mother stretches herself ever thinner. And you get this family housework crisis. And white feminists forget their solidarity with women of colour and start to pay other women simply to get things done.'

This, I realize as I head out into the sunshine of Prospect Park, legs twitching with caffeine and my arms heavy with books and pamphlets, is the stark difference between my grandmother's and my mother's time and mine. In those brief decades, capitalism has gone from relying on the scaffolding labour of the nuclear family to both relying upon and com-modifying it. Modern capitalism has responded to women's arrival in the paid workplace by seeking profit in our domestic crises, with market solutions to the domestic labour gap that range from babysitting apps to cleaning agencies staffed by migrant women labourers.

We tell ourselves stories in order to live. Making do in heter-osexual relationships in which even the best-intentioned men fail to pull their weight often requires, at least for women, a storytelling facility that would make a Booker shortlister proud. Through these we make sense of, say, the problem of living with a man who is simultaneously a loving partner and unable to take a bath without leaving pubic hairs embedded in the soap. Or of the Good Dad who's happy to be congratulated for looking after his son but can't be arsed to fill the fridge. Maybe, we tell ourselves, it's fair that he does the outside, the leaf-sweeping and the dog bowl, while we do the inside: all of the cooking, most of the childcare, the cleaning and the management work that goes into maintaining family life. But many of these mollifying tales – of incompetent dad and 'super' capable mum; of toddlers that 'just need their mums more' or women's more exacting standards ('I just notice if the hoovering's not done *properly*,' as one survey respondent put it) or natural-born skills at 'multitasking'[14] – are in fact inaccurate, and a distraction from the necessary work of changing the structures that keep women overburdened and on their feet. These fictions offer the second-shifting mum the comfort of imagining other women in the same boat, but they don't offer a solution. Part of the problem, it's not unfeminist to admit, is ourselves.

Oh, and on women's main complaint – men's strewn underpants – Tim, for one, tells me that he steps out of his pants on the bedroom floor, leaving them in a concertina of soiled fabric, because he needs to be ready to step into them in case of 'midnight burglarization'.

'Whereas you just kick yours across the room to the laundry basket with your toe,' he points out, 'like Sophia Loren.'

I'd never admit it to him, but he has a point.

2

Battles on the Home Front, a Recent History

1944, Deritend, Birmingham; Virginia is 22

Rosie the Riveter wartime propaganda poster, 1941

Modern Homemaker, 1945

efore she died, I visited my paternal grandmother in her wind-scoured granite cottage in the Cornish village she'd returned to after 50 years of urban misery in Birmingham. Virginia 'Ginny' Trembath had been a bright grammar-school girl who'd given up a place at an Oxford college to work in a nursery during the Second World War. In 1945 she married Sidney, a handsome and unintellectual navy man she'd met after they'd both lost their wartime sweet-hearts to Blitz bombs.

During my time in Pendeen, Virginia and I went to the Radjel Inn, the sort of pub where locals scrutinize you for signs of effete 'up country' behaviours (such as ordering a G&T or a beer with a lemonade top). There, sitting primly on a bar stool in her half-mast pop socks, her hair a golden, hairsprayed orb and a menthol cigarette glowing in an ashtray nearby, she matter-of-factly recounted the story of her first meeting with her future Brummie in-laws. It was late 1944, and Sidney was on leave from the Allied naval campaigns that would eventually capture southern France. The affianced pair had travelled together to Small Heath, the smoke-blackened Birmingham suburb in which Sidney's publican grandfather Frances had, two generations before, served pints of warm stout to the notorious local gangsters, the Peaky Blinders.

As would later become typical of their 49-year marriage, Virginia was left at home with her soon-to-be mother-in-law while Sidney, his father and five brothers visited a nearby pub to play dominoes and get 'in their oil tot', a local saying that referred to the tradition of working men drinking a tot of oil in the belief it would line their stomachs before getting very drunk indeed.

'They'd been out late morning and I heard them come in at 5 p.m., caterwauling,' Ginny recalled. 'Frankie, the oldest of the brothers, was singing "Ten Green Bottles", Sid was behind him, and the father Frank came stamping in with a black face on him. He turned to his wife, May, who was threading one of those old rag rugs that we used to put by the hearth. We were sitting in the small parlour waiting for the men. Frank yelled: "Where's dinner, you old cow?" She was a strong woman, May Howard, but you wouldn't argue with Frank in that mood. She walked into the kitchen to finish dinner and he followed her in there, took the cooking roast out of the oven and threw it, the sizzling fat and everything, all over his wife. That was my first meeting with my in-laws.'

Ginny died shortly after my visit in 2001. Perhaps knowing that her time to share such stories was limited, she'd divulged to me many of the Howards' and the Trembaths' darkest secrets: the Trembath who'd murdered someone down Boscaswell Mine; the story of her father, a Methodist minister who left his Cornish wife and eight children in poverty for a new life in Canada, married bigamously and never looked back. But it was the story of this flash of connubial violence that stayed with me, with aching clarity.

A few years later, writing social affairs stories for British newspapers, I became aware of the correlations between domestic labour and domestic violence. According to Women's Aid, 30 per cent of the incidents of domestic violence that bring women to the charity's refuges are provoked by domestic labour:[15] by coercive partners deeming their wife's performance of domestic tasks to be inadequate; and by the intimate control abusive men exact through expectations of domestic behaviour and access to household resources. Through the 19th and until the late 20th century, mealtime punctuality was central to the performance of good housekeeping, with few women defying their husband's expectation of, as historian Virginia Nicholson puts it, 'a piping-hot meal at 6 p.m. sharp'.

In *The Revaluation of Women's Work*,[16] feminist theorist Sheila Lewenhak speaks of a 'chain of abuse' of capitalism that manifests as intimate partner violence in the heterosexual family home: 'The more the outside world, with its devaluation of blue-collar labour, chips away at male machismo, the more the man is allowed to recover his ego at his partner's expense,' she writes. 'He gets bossed around, so he bosses his wife around. Legal systems which fail to adequately prosecute domestic abusers in effect condone this outlet.'

Predictably, Ginny suffered her own share of domestic traumas. Sidney would spend his weekends at the boozer, returning late, confused and inebriated. She told me that the two miscarriages she suffered in the late 1950s were endured at home alone, with Sidney refusing to come back from the pub. Yet Ginny was, unquestionably, a feminist. She worked as a teacher at a primary school and kept her finances strictly separate from Sidney's earnings as a market butcher. She spoke of the need for female financial independence and lamented the end of the Second World War and what it meant for young women like her, who had tasted the freedoms that came from productive work and female camaraderie. Little wonder she intuitively held current wisdom's belief that financial independence is the first precondition for avoiding domestic violence.

Flo Sergeant, now 96, was one of the 'tilly girls' (the 1940s argot for Brummie lasses) in my grandmother's branch of the British Women's Auxiliary Army Corps. Still alive and living in a care home in Torbay, Devon, we met at her granddaughter's Paignton home in 2009. Over tea and garibaldi biscuits, she recalled her WAAC training at a camp in North Wales and the excitement she and Ginny had both felt in signing up. Flo was billeted in barracks in Chatham as a staff driver for the first few years of the war, before being posted as a night-rota ambulance driver in the Blackout. She and my grandmother stayed in touch through long years and difficult marriages, up until Ginny's death.

'I learned to love the work,' Flo told me, 'even though we were often on a night-call rota. It was pretty grim, picking up seriously ill people during the Blackout, especially as air raids often threatened. But it was the best time of my life. Life was all in Technicolor somehow, as what you did every day was so vital. And we were treated with respect by all the men we worked with.'

Like Ginny, Flo lost a young sweetheart – 'Blondie' – to

fighting in France. By the war's end, she'd met and married a 'Red Cap'* named Ted. Six months after her wedding, she was told she had been released from the WAAC, in a two-line letter. 'By then it was clear we'd won the war and the married girls were first out,' she said. 'I was heartbroken about leaving a job I loved and going back to civvy street.'

During the summer months of 1945, 3 million women drivers, mechanics, aircraft welders and sheet-metal assemblers were demobilized to 'civvy street'. Many of these young women went on to contribute to the post-war boom in marriage and childbirth, which peaked with the more than 400,000 weddings that took place in 1947 alone (the year of Elizabeth Windsor's marriage to Philip Mountbatten). Others found that their experiences of exercising autonomy and initiative prevented them from easily stepping back into women's constrictive pre-war social and economic roles. Flo was amongst them.

'I did my duty and returned to the kitchen,' she told me. 'It was our new duty, we were told, after our war duties, to rebuild Britain through raising children, and raising them well, and keeping a clean and orderly home. I never did get to sit behind the wheel again, though I'd have loved to.' She smiled ruefully. 'I have been in the passenger seat ever since.'

In the immediate post-war period, acute social pressure was applied to demobilized women to turn away from the world of productive labour and become, if not the wives they were pre-war, then 'modern homemakers'. The agent of wartime propaganda, Rosie the Riveter – who had been featured in posters dressed in a boiler suit, flexing her muscles – was retired, and everywhere, from popular culture to politics, powerful voices urged women to leave productive jobs to returning servicemen, despite the fact that the jobs many women held at the war's close were jobs that had not existed

---

* The nickname for members of the Royal Military Police.

before the outbreak of war, and many returning servicemen had not, in fact, regularly worked for wages in the depressed 1930s. As one social historian wittily puts it, 'Rosie the Riveter was abandoned to the less-than-riveting fate of keeping her lace curtains clean'.[17]

Polls of female war workers found that many of the 37 per cent of working-age women in the workforce at the war's end wanted to remain there. Typical of this cohort was Phyllis Noble of South East London, who saw the prospect of embracing homemaking as unwelcome and infantalizing.

'It's ridiculous to be forced to live like a schoolgirl at the age of twenty-four,' she recounted in her diary in May 1947. 'The war pulled me out of Lee [a London suburb], and now I must make my own road. There is no doubt in my mind that I must get "a room of my own".'

However not all women felt like Phyllis. When Prime Minister Clement Attlee suggested, in 1947, that young married women might be the solution to a shortage of manpower, mainstream magazine *Woman* reacted with shock, with a February op-ed crying: 'Attlee calling up women? Surely not now. Surely not.'[18]

After six years of bombs and make-do-and-mend, the drive to reposition women in the domestic sphere tapped, as Virginia Nicholson notes, into a very real yearning for the feminine graces of a bygone era.[19] This is the pent-up hunger for family and home that Betty Friedan explored in *The Feminine Mystique*: returning US servicemen pining for the imagined certainties of picket fences and the smiling wives they'd fought for.

For Flo, too, there was an appeal in this glamorous depiction of feminine domesticity after six years of mess-hall dining and reused teabags. 'It was all centred on this young queen somehow: a pretty young woman with two bonny kids. Never mind the fact that she wasn't boiling ham for her own tea.'

The trope of the Modern Homemaker – a fantasy of efficient stay-at-home motherhood facilitated by new labour-saving technology – emerged within a few short years of the end of the Second World War. In Muriel Goaman's 1947 *Judy's Book of Housework*, we meet the titular housewife who – in a pinafore dress and neat roller-set hairdo – sings this cheerful ditty as she folds perfect hospital corners into bedsheets:

> *First the toe, and then the head*
> *That's the way to make the bed!*

Judy has new carpet-sweeping devices and detergents as her domestic helpmeets, but she isn't afraid, schools Goaman, of applying her wartime gusto to 'two parts elbow grease and one part of polish'.

By 1953, the Modern Homemaker had merged with her glamorous American correlate, the Perfect Wife, with my grandmother's *Good Housekeeping* magazine advising housewives, in spring 1953, how to 'plan a good time': 'Make soufflés and jellies the day before, heat up patties and bouchées on the day, and wear a slim dress in kitten-soft charcoal angora.'

In the years from the end of the war to the early 1960s, British women dropped three dress sizes and 30 per cent of us took to bleaching our hair blonde. Soon, the Perfect Wife would be the hegemonic feminine ideal, with the memory of the Second World War's riveters, ambulance drivers and engineers apparently lost. Although, not quite. The template the war years had offered for alternative ways of thinking about sexuality and social roles was not, in fact, forgotten. The collective memory of women's productive contribution to the wartime effort would fire the equality crusades – from civil rights to women's rights and workers' rights – that would take centre stage in Second Wave feminism's 'big bang'.

1972, South Birmingham suburbs; Anne is 22

Spare Rib magazine, 1972

In 1972, with David Bowie topping the UK charts in gender-bending spandex, it remained legal to require a female employee to submit herself to sterilization as a condition of the offer of work. In this same year, 43 per cent of British women between the ages of 18 and 60 listed their occupation as 'homemaker' in the national census. But seismic changes were about to shake the foundations of the British family home.

By 1980, 60 per cent of British women of working age would be in paid labour, a trend that reversed, in a mere handful of years, wartime women's retreat to the kitchen. It was echoed across the West, with 71 per cent of American women aged 25–44 in the workforce in 1985, compared to just 10 per cent of this age group in the 1950s. By 1988, 65 per cent of Australian women aged 35–44 were part of the workforce, compared to 23 per cent in 1954.

Meanwhile, the Second Wave feminist tsunami had arrived in Middle Britain's living rooms. It did so not with bra-burnings or feminist consciousness-raising groups, but with that very British mode of protest: a handful of flour and stink bombs. The event was the 1970 Miss World beauty pageant, held at the Royal Albert Hall – which in that era was primetime television, attracting up to 10 million viewers. Toting placards and rattles, the members of the Women's Liberation Movement who disrupted the pageant were taking aim not just at the inherent sexism of parading bikini-clad girls' vital statistics, but at a mainstream culture that traded on such casual sexism. That night, 6.5 million British TV viewers saw toupee-wearing host Bob Hope almost knocked for six by a flour bomb.* And everything changed.

My mum was too timid to buy a copy of the feminist mag *Spare Rib* in 1972 to find out what all the fuss was about; although bolder friends, including her flatmate Janet, bought theirs from a hippy-run stall at a street market in Moseley, Birmingham's student district. The radical periodical had been launched that year, and early editorials looked at the household drudgery that was naturalized as a woman's role.

In 'Family Everafter', a feature in *Spare Rib*'s fifth issue, Michelene Wandor asked whether the limited world of the '70s housewife – 'home and shopping' – slowly undermined her ability to deal with the outside world and led to her dominating in the only available arena. This miserable woman might become, in short, 'bossy, hen-pecking, [and] encourage her husband's helplessness… If in fact he *did* offer to share the housework completely, she would lose what little control she had, and be made redundant, and at some level she is aware of this.'[20]

---

* Hope had just priapically admired a contestant's legs.

In a feature in Issue 60, 'Portrait of the Artist as Housewife', we meet Sally Gollop, an artist resisting the drudgery of house-work through art. Her pieces, fabulously, include a to-scale miniature model of a home in which the kitchen dresser is shelved with prison bars, and human hands and a brain hang from the crockery rack. Meanwhile, in Issue 26, Catherine Hall surveys 'The History of the Housewife' in Britain, from the 1400s 'feudal housewife' up to the 1970s, via the 18th-century 'housewifisation'* of the middle classes. In conclusion, Hall pines for the better world that had been glimpsed during the war, and for an expansion of women's worlds that neither over-sells the 'male capitalist' importance of paid work, nor makes domestic labour wholly women's own:

> It is only when the capitalist economy needs women in large numbers on the labour market that the mystifica-tions of the idealised wife and mother disappear and a new note is introduced... society can organise creches and canteens and substantially reduce the need for privatised domestic activity as can be clearly seen from the experience of two world wars.

My mum's room-mate hid her issues of *Spare Rib* in the bed springs at their Edgbaston flat when parents came to visit. Mary and Thomas would arrive in their Ford Consul with its tan paintwork and wind-down windows, my grandad parping peremptorily at city traffic and my grandma bearing northern survival supplies of Kendal mint cake and Schweppes yellow lemonade.

'Back home in Yorkshire, women's libbers were both a talking point and the target of mockery,' my mum remembers. One elderly uncle, a fusty man who even in the 1970s wore a 1930s getup of trilby and braces, memorably interrupted a

---

* As Maria Mies memorably terms this historical process.

Christmas parlour game with a red-faced complaint about how 'they'll be bloody asking for dog liberation next'.

In his essay 'The Great Women's Liberation Issue: Setting It Straight', Murray N. Rothbard voiced an opinion typical of the contemporary press as he scowled at feminists' complaint of discrimination on the basis of unfair division of labour: 'The women's libs claim that men are the masters because they [the women] are doing most of the world's work. But, if we look back at the society of the slave South, who indeed did the work? It is always the slaves who do the work, while the masters live in relative idleness off the fruits of their labor. To the extent that husbands work and support the family, while wives enjoy a kept status, who then are the masters?'

The 'domestic labour debate' became one of the pressing concerns of 1970s feminist intellectuals. The arguments had begun to take shape in the 1960s, as an attempt by feminists who'd emerged from the political left to theorize the oppression of women in capitalist societies. Marxist theories, which dominated the political left at the time, understood structures of capitalist oppression through hierarchies of class. Marx broadly distinguished between the 'haves' and the 'have-nots' in capitalist society: those who possess private property and the means to accrue wealth; and those who possess little or nothing. To Marxist thinkers, the site of workers' exploitation was crystal clear: it was the capitalists' extraction of the profits of their labour. Waged work under capitalism was the root of their oppression.

The problem, leftist feminists were quick to note,[21] was Marxist theory's neglect of women.[22] Or, more pointedly, the work of women: those many thankless hours of cooking, cleaning and caring that were unwaged. Were these labours not then oppressive? What of this half of the population who divested their energies in the unwaged work of housework and childrearing – and, when they did work for waged labour, did so in more exploitative conditions than men.

In the 1960s, with the North American women's liberation movement in full swing, Canadians Margaret Benston and Peggy Morton published two influential essays. In 1969's 'What Defines Women?', Benston argues that, whatever their involvement in the waged labour arena, unwaged domestic labour determines women's identity as a group, and is key to their emancipation. The family, to Benston, should above all be seen as an economic unit in Marxist terms, in which the products of women's labour – childcare, meal preparation, laundry – are consumed. She then calls for an end to this material basis for discrimination through the socialization of housework and childcare.

In her 1970 essay, 'A Woman's Work Is Never Done', Peggy Morton expands on Benston's theory of the material oppression of women through domestic work. Morton describes the family unit, maintained by women's unpaid labour, as having the principal function of 'reproducing' labour for capitalism, i.e. breeding, rearing and feeding the workers upon which capitalism relies. In Morton's argument, women are central – rather than peripheral – to the waged economy, making possible the functioning of low-waged capitalism. If a 'man' does not need to feed and clothe himself or care for his children, he is thus 'freed' to work longer hours for a subsistence wage. Are women, in the Marxist notion, then, a class? asks Morton. And, if so, should women organize for the purpose of revolutionary emancipation, through this, their designation as domestic workers?[23]

In a paper that would light a fire under the feminist housework debates, Mariarosa Dalla Costa developed these arguments further. 'Women and the Subversion of the Community', published simultaneously in the USA and Italy in 1972, takes the position that women are in fact exploited workers in the strictest Marxist sense, producing a form of value in the capacity of future workers, which is then appropriated by capital. As Dalla Costa sees it, the haves pay a wage to the working-class male, which he then uses to secure women's exploitation: 'The woman is the slave of a wage slave, and her slavery ensures the slavery of her man.' All women are 'housewives' under capitalism, and women's struggle against the exploitative capitalist construct of family, to Dalla Costa, is, therefore, essential:

> we must discover forms of struggle which immediately break the whole structure of domestic work, rejecting it absolutely, rejecting our role as housewives and the home as the ghetto of our existence, since the problem is not only to stop doing this work, but to smash the entire role of the housewife.

Dalla Costa argues against socializing housework (or making it a shared or co-operative enterprise). Instead, she suggests, we should socialize the struggle against domestic labour, and mobilize women, particularly working-class women, around issues such as community, the suppression of women's sexuality within the nuclear family and, crucially, the wagelessness of housework.

At the 1972 International Feminist Collective conference in Padua, Dalla Costa's call to action became a revolutionary roar. Wages for Housework grew out of this fated meeting, taking its impetus from the workerist movement that had grown up around the Northern Italian factory strikes of the 'Hot Autumn' of 1969–70.[24] In a manifesto drawn up after the conference, activist Giuliana Pompei distilled what the movement was calling for: women's strikes on a global scale; financial transfers from the state to account for women's unpaid domestic labour; and a voluble rejection of the 'deforming, suffocating… "shit work"… known as housework'.

In her 1975 essay 'Wages Against Housework', Silvia Federici – one of the architects of Wages for Housework, alongside activists Selma James, Brigitte Galtier and Mariarosa Dalla

Costa – developed the movement's political demands: 'To say that we want wages for housework is to expose the fact that housework is already money for capital, that capital has made and makes money out of our cooking, smiling, fucking. At the same time, [the demand] shows that we have cooked, smiled and fucked throughout the years... because we did not have any other choice.'

No more Mrs Nice Housewife, railed Federici – not least because 'niceness' was one of the confidence tricks the system played on women in order to discipline them into unpaid labour as an act of natural womanly love. Play 'nice', work with smiling self-negation, and society whispered its approval: *Yes, darling, you are a real woman.* To Federici, demands for paid childcare, equal pay and free laundromats were all well and good, but none of these surface fixes for women's domestic burden addressed the cancer of women's naturalized 'work'. Wages were required to compensate women for their many roles as 'housemaids, prostitutes, nurses, [and] shrinks'.

By 1975 Wages for Housework activist groups had sprung up across the US, Canada and Europe. The Wages for Housework Committee, established in Brooklyn that year by Federici, handed out flyers across New York calling for all women to join the cause, regardless of marital status, nationality, sexual orientation, number of children or employment status. Meanwhile, International Black Women for Wages for Housework, founded by Margaret Prescod and Wilmette Brown in New York in 1974, focused not only on politicizing domestic labour but also the call for reparations for 'slavery, imperialism and neo-colonialism'.

Soon, Wages for Housework representatives embarked on speaking tours across the US, and the campaign achieved a degree of popular notoriety. 'Charge Housework is $wept Under the Rug', read a 1976 write-up in the *New York Daily News*, which patronizingly referred to Wages for Housework's older members as 'old gals'. The *Tallahassee Democrat* was forced to issue a correction after a 3 March 1977 story confusedly mangled Wages for Housework's demands into the charge that 'women are underappreciated prostitutes' who 'ought to charge their husbands for sexual favors'.

In the UK, a Wages for Housework chapter launched in 1975 – followed in short order by Wages Due Lesbians, a group calling for wages for housework along with extra wages for lesbians to account for 'the additional physical and emotional housework of surviving in a hostile and prejudiced society'.[25]

British press responses were often cutting. '[They] come over like Jehovah's Witnesses,' complained a May 1976 op-ed in the *Guardian*. 'Open any door marked Liberation and behind it is a woman with a Wages for Housework badge on her bosom, ten thousand leaflets in her hand, a fanatical gleam in her eye and her foot wedged firmly in the jamb.' To the author of the op-ed, a working woman keen to 'get out of the home... to do something more fulfilling than housework', these 'sister enthusiasts' did little more than 'harangue conferences, shout from soapboxes, gesticulate on television, burn with a strange fever'.

The work of the Women for Housework collective was part of a broader ecosystem of 1970s feminist activism that took on the unquestioned ascription of household chores to women. On 26 August 1970, women across the US boycotted cooking, cleaning and care responsibilities to strike for equality. With the rallying slogan 'Don't Iron While the Strike Is Hot!', women marched to demand free abortion on demand, equal opportunity in jobs and education, and free 24-hour childcare as a right. Activists across the West lobbied for laws and policies that would provide social security to unpaid workers in the home and, in the UK and US, full labour rights for domestic workers. Everywhere in the Western World, feminists struggled to get the social and fiscal value of housework recognized and to slay the assumption that this work was by its nature unpaid and accorded to women. In Iceland, these movements even bloomed into a 1975 women's general strike that brought Reykjavík to a standstill.

Now seen as a seminal moment in Second Wave feminism, these radical activist movements in fact got a mixed reception among contemporary feminists. Some felt that Wages for Housework would help the cause of making visible the importance of domestic work; others thought that it reinforced the idea that domestic labour was 'women's work' rather than men's, and hindered the idea of overturning this naturalized expectation. Allegations of 'economism', or an obsessive fixation on money, were also rife. Many demurring Marxist feminists thought it preferable to urge women to join the paid workforce and trade unions, and in that way change the status quo; a criticism that Federici explicitly addressed in 'Wages Against Housework': 'The second job not only increases our exploitation, but simply reproduces our role [as nurses, maids, secretaries] in different forms.'

Feminist interrogations of the domestic sphere also fired the utopian imagination. Inspired by their insights into the nature of housework as oppression, members of the Women's Movement began to experiment in new communities; some women left their traditional heterosexual marriages, or looked at new ways to share and socialize domestic labour.

The more extreme advocated 'separatism' (or physical separation of the genders) as a way of life. Separatism advocated that women prioritize relationships with other women over men, in partnerships, communities and businesses. Writing in 1983, feminist theorist Marilyn Frye described separatist feminism as 'separation of various sorts or modes from men and from institutions, relationships, roles and activities that are male-defined, male-dominated, and operating for the benefit of males and the maintenance of male privilege – this separation being initiated or maintained, at will, *by women*'.

Rather than continue to struggle against men, separatists saw separation from men and all forms of patriarchy as the fastest and most creative route to emancipation. In Chapter Ten we will meet the most ambitious of these separatists, the 'land dykes', who set up rural communities based on a belief in separatism and tactical lesbianism as a radical response to patriarchal capitalism.

Others, meanwhile, sought to include men in creative solutions such as communal living, in which several families lived together and domestic duties, including childcare, were shared between everyone. California-born Kathleen, 68, lived in a gender-inclusive feminist commune in Northern California in the early 1970s.

'On the one hand, we had this altar to Artemis and everyone went on about the spiritual maternal,' she recalls. 'But we also had rotas. Endless freakin' rotas. And someone was always pissed that someone had slept with their lover. But not as pissed as when the four men in the commune skipped their rota duties, as they always did. The theory was fine, the practice of anti-patriarchy less so. You couldn't just will it into being.'

Before my brother and I came along, my mother toyed with the idea of joining a commune that she'd heard of in Moseley, a quarter of Birmingham whose Victorian townhouses had been colonized in the late 1960s by self-sufficiency communities and cottage-gardening co-ops. In the end, she came nowhere near following through on the plan.

'It was a bit sad cooking meals for one on a Baby Belling cooker,' she tells me on the phone from Yorkshire, in the middle of changing my stepfather's incontinence pad. But she knew a girl who joined one of the Moseley houses where they kept bees, and she spent all of her time making chicory coffees for the men. However, in the end it was more the fact that it was improper to cohabit, as a young unmarried woman, with men

— rather than a fear of drudgery — that put her off. 'Though, of course, drudgery was something of a badge of honour for young women back then.'

For all of this, Wages for Housework — and the social movements that arose alongside it — made real gains. It was thanks in part to their demands that laws were instituted, in the late 1970s, to criminalize discrimination against married women and to give women financial rights within marriage and access to legal representation and mortgages,[26] as well as the recognition of a homemaker's contribution in the division of marital property in the case of divorce. It was also thanks to these social movements that British families gained the right to universal family allowance, later replaced by child allowance, and low-income women in the US gained access to food stamps (in 1964, thanks to the activism of women of colour). Across the West, social security and insurance programmes moved towards models based on need rather than male-earner workforce participation. But many of Wages for Housework's demands, of course, remain unresolved to this day. Notably their call for recognition of the worth of the unpaid work of caring in the service of capitalism, and the challenge this call represented to the structure and oppressions of the patriarchal family.

During my visit to Federici at her apartment in springtime Brooklyn, as the coffee pot put-putted beside us, she had sagged a little in her chair when I asked her if she believed that Wages for Housework was fundamentally misunderstood.

'Yes,' she replied. 'Wages for housework was not a condemnation to live in the kitchen, as some people seemed to understand it. It did not mean we would rather be at home washing the dishes. It was an attack on capital's abuse of our bodies and love. We still need these arguments.'

The decade that began with advertisements advocating KitchenAid devices as the answer to wifely hysteria would end with a baffled advertising world coming to terms with the mainstreaming of the Women's Movement on the domestic front, in conceits of muscle-bound women 'liberating' themselves from the ignominy of doing dishes.

1969 and 1979: advertising for domestic appliances and cleaning products co-opt Women's Lib and — in this Rosie the Riveter pose — Second World War propaganda

The academic feminism of the decade would end with 1980's *Gender and Class Consciousness*,[27] a depiction of a nation in which women's work was changing, even as the stories men (and women) told themselves about the natural domestic lot of the genders remained resistant to change.

In the book we meet Gladys and her husband Ted, in their terraced home in a mining village in Staffordshire. 'He would never wheel a pram out,' says Gladys. 'He would say, "Take these children out, and everything will be done when you get back". And the house would be like a new pin… *But*, he'd stop when he got as far as the back door step; that was that, because he wouldn't want nobody to see him with a scrubbing brush and mop, or a bucket or whatever in his hand.' How much progress, we have to ask, had there been since the emasculated 'mop rags' and 'diddy men' we met in the 19th century?

My mother, who at the start of the 1970s was living in a Birmingham bedsit and wearing Laura Ashley high-necked Edwardian revival, ended the decade as a working mother with a sleek power bob, juggling the demands of work and home. By 1980, capitalist economies had – with astonishing efficiency – co-opted women's lib, responding to the feminist rejection of prescribed domesticity by increasing the number of women in the workforce. As male domestic efforts failed to keep pace with this formalization of female labour – British women in the early 1980s worked on average 22 hours more per week than British men* – the Double Day (or 'second shift', as coined by Berkeley sociologist Arlie Hochschild in her prescient portrait of California's harried working mothers) became the norm across the West.

The 1980s gave us the go-getting careerist 'super mum' – or as Hochschild memorably put it in *The Second Shift*, 'the woman with the flying hair – briefcase in one hand and child in the other' (the reality of a working mother's lot, of course,

---

* When you factor in paid and unpaid labour.

was more accurately bags under the eyes and jacket striated with snot). This was the era in which Prime Minister Margaret Thatcher, all fierce shoulder pads and immovable hairdo, relaxed after a long day in the Commons by ironing husband Denis's shirts in the Houses of Parliament's Ladies Room.

Back in 1978, *Ms.* magazine editor Letty Cottin Pogrebin defined this new cultural turn as the 'have it all' hype. The dream of the perfect post-feminist life was 'the three-ball juggling act: job, marriage, children. Voila! You've got it all!'

The first 50/50 or 'fair' families arrived in this era, most of them couples who'd met in the heady 1960s civil rights movements. They strove to construct home lives based on their egalitarian and feminist principles. But as women flooded the workplace, the call for a wholesale revolution in domestic labour was lost in the suds. Women's willingness to go out to work and simultaneously carry the can at home became, as Federici puts it, a 'golden opportunity' for capital.

Furthermore, the legacy of Second Wave feminism was under attack. Its exponents had always contended that sharing work at home was as integral to equality as equal opportunity at work. Yet, in a cruel irony, the ignominies suffered by housewives – the thanklessness and devaluation of their vital labour – came, at least in some quarters, to be laid at the door of Second Wave feminists. It was they who had volubly challenged society's disregard for housewives' worth and labour and asked for recognition of this vital work as work. Yet defenders of the status quo effectively recast feminism as the source of housewives' woes.

And these messages resounded with housewives on the street. A divorced American homemaker, Pat, had accepted that Second Wave feminism was, in part, her enemy. As she told a journalist:

> I'm in favour of the movement, but women like me, we can also see how the movement has been used against us. I don't mean by the feminists, but by our ex-husbands

who say go out and get liberated and get a job so we don't have to support you.[28]

In the Third Wave of feminism, beginning in the early 1990s, liberal feminism was predominant. Liberal feminism had developed under Reagan and Thatcher's political agendas and concerned itself with the extension of political rights for women through legislation and specific reproductive issues such as the right to abortion.[29] Federici told me that she regrets that, as the liberal feminist doctrine took hold, feminism forgot its old allyships: 'White feminists shouted for access to abortion, but where were white feminists when their black sisters were being sterilized by the state, or drafted in to clean white women's homes on a starvation wage? In the '60s and '70s this was all one argument. There's no other way to see this than as a betrayal.'

My mother, with good grace, cleaned the rubberized cheese remains out of the Breville sandwich toaster as I added to the domestic load in a bedroom three inches deep in Bourbon biscuit crumbs. Madness's 'Our House' blared out of my tape recorder, portraying a world in which:

Father gets up late for work
Mother has to iron his shirt
Then she sends the kids to school...

Largely immune to mother's efforts, I lay on my suburban bed, blinding myself with aquamarine eyeshadow.

That jolt of woman-to-woman recognition would come 25 years later, as I woke at 6 a.m. for the fifth day in a row to pick my way across a landscape of discarded underpants and unravel my baby son from his urine-soaked sleep sack as Tim snored. It would come on the day I realized that childcare costs had reduced my take-home income to pin money. And it would come on the day I decided I couldn't square paying my

Bulgarian* cleaning lady to tidy up my newborn's toys as her children grew up 2,000 miles away; their memory of her, she told me, guilelessly, was fading every day.

And it would come on the day my mother picked the phone up when I called at 5 a.m., neglecting the thankless shifts of care work for my disabled stepfather so she could comfort my post-natal terrors.

1997, Reading University house share; Sally is 20

'Freshening up feminism for the '90s!'

With that talent for cruel nicknames for which young people excel, I called them the 'Little Miss Mops'. The Little Miss Mops were the girls that cleaned their university boyfriend's grotty student houseshares out of a sense of feminine duty – or, God forbid, a perverse sense of enjoyment. In one defining incident, an offending Mop tackled the 'second kitchen' in her boyfriend's 12-bedroom houseshare – or rather, the bathtub that had become the dumping ground for the pots and dishes no one could be arsed to wash up, the household long ago having resorted to takeaway kebabs.

I and the other young women in my houseshare were, like most students, wilfully incompetent in our accomplishment of domestic chores. Slugs meandered across the kitchen work-tops, fag butts spilled out of the ashtrays, and used coffee cups hosted weird and wonderful mould colonies. Matters reached an unsavoury pitch when we returned from the Christmas break in our second year to discover that our sleazy landlord had built a meat storage unit on our small patch of garden. It didn't help that we lived next door to a branch of Domino's that offered week-long £5 pizza deals for students. But back then, our laddish squalidness seemed to be in keeping with

---

* Actually Lithuanian (see Chapter Seven).

the mood of the time. In 1996, during my first year at university, Girl Power had exploded into the public consciousness. Via the Spice Girls, a pop band made up of five mouthy performing-arts school graduates, it ushered in what journalist Rachel Giese has since christened 'feminism-lite'.

The Spice Girls' Girl Power — with its platform boots and padded bras, shouty slogans and two-finger salutes — was not a coherent or thought-through feminist ideology. Rather, in the words of feminist academic Katharine Coman, it was a 'jumble of feminist insights and hopes'.

'It's like feminism, but you don't have to burn your bra,' Geri Halliwell told a reporter, in explanation of Girl Power. 'We have come up against a few guys who expect five bimbos. It just means you've got to shout a bit louder to get your way. We're freshening up feminism for the '90s!'

When Virgin published the Spice Girls' official book, its first page bore a legend borrowed from 1970s women's lib — 'The future is female' — against a photographic backdrop of the leather-and-leopard-print-clad Spices. Division of labour became a fleeting war cry. 'No way we're gonna stay at home and do washing up for some man... He can take me out for dinner!' said Melanie Brown, who made capital from being the group's mouthiest member and was dubbed, by *Top of the Pops* magazine (in an epithet that has since been called out by black feminists for its racist overtones), 'Scary Spice'.

A friend of mine — we'll call her Bridget — lived the other '90s Third Wave feminist cliché: 'ladettism'. A wholly British phenomenon, ladettism had unlikely roots in a macho, working-class subculture. The 'new lads' celebrated homosociality and masculinity in a backlash against feminism and the early-'90s 'new man' (the popular name for a largely imagined post-feminist male who pitched in at home and was happy to speak about his feelings). In what was in effect a faux-feminist offshoot of a movement that was itself kicking back against feminism, the ladette swilled beer from pints, hated housework and was unabashedly promiscuous. She was one of the mouthy girls on Channel 4's *The Girlie Show*, or Kate Moss, the sort of young woman who, as one journalist put it, 'pushes aside the humble pie and has another fag instead'. Moss summed up the ethic in a 1999 interview with *Dazed & Confused* magazine: 'My mum used to say to me, "you can't have fun all the time," and I used to say, "why not? Why the fuck can't I have fun all the time?"'

When we recently met up in a resinous old boozer in London's Charing Cross, Bridget ordered the pint of lager that's been her poison since 1993. Taking a lusty gulp, she laughingly recounted her domestic set-up at Edinburgh University. It was a somewhat dystopian take on the division of labour according to aptitude.

'We specialized. I bought drugs, another girl bought the booze, the third planned the parties and we just thought SCREW IT! to the housework and lived in filth,' she said. 'As young women in the early '90s, we thought we were coming out of the Dark Ages. The Berlin Wall had fallen, rave culture was breaking down class barriers. My university friends and I thought we were liberating ourselves from that daft world of '80s femininity, of Princess Diana: all demureness and silly lace necklines. And we didn't need to burn our bras, you know?'

With their unapologetic mouthiness, promiscuity and easy dismissal of the stuffy preoccupations of Second Wave feminists, Girl Power and ladettism did not enquire into the nature of the dynamics of power between the sexes, nor the structures that operated against women in the workplace and home. But, in the summer of 1996, this gobby take on feminism seemed as if it was what so many of us really really wanted. Feminism had entered the mainstream, and no one – I believed, in my teenaged naivety – needed to wash the pots.

December 2017, Geffrye Museum of Domestic Life

Tim and I were both back at work full-time. Or rather, Tim was back at work full-time and I was back at my desk, somewhat

distractedly, four days a week, filling the remainder of my fever-
ish waking hours with nursery pick-ups, family administration and
bulk-cooking freezer meals for a persistently ravenous 15-month-
old Leo. Thanks to my ongoing postnatal insomnia, we'd
decided, last-minute, to stay in London over Christmas. In the
otherworld between Christmas and New Year, when an eerie
peace prevails on London streets and there are seats to be had
in restaurants and on trains, I took Tim and Leo to my favourite
London museum. In a series of period-decorated sitting rooms
that occupy a parade of 18th-century almshouses, the Geffrye
Museum offers an intimate insight into British domestic life from
the 1500s to the 1990s. On the way there, we'd good-humouredly
bickered about a category of household labour that Tim, I
believed, wilfully failed to acknowledge: festive obligations.

'But I don't understand why you *have* to send cards to my
family when I never do,' he said.

'Because they send cards to us – and if we don't send cards
back, it's me who's judged.'

'Well I'm not sending cards and I think you're mad to send
them. It's commercialized… totally crap.'*

After arriving at the museum, we strode, pushchair clattering,
through the centuries as Leo reached across the rope-barriers
to snatch at the period Christmas treats – the olives and sweet
wine of the 1600s; the coloured cordials of the 1750s – that the
museum lays out as its annual tribute to festivities past. In the
mid-20th-century room, Tim stopped and brightened.

'It's the way I remember my grandma's house! Look at that
hostess trolley and hatch, and that five-bar electric fire that
fries your ankles like a doner grill.'

He went on to tell me about his grandma Edith, a pugna-
cious woman from the Welsh Valleys who loved Margaret
Thatcher and was pro capital punishment (her favourite motto

---

* Tim now acknowledges that, in fact, he's a lazy git when it comes to
sending Christmas cards.

being 'I'd pull the rope'), but tended to her husband's domestic wants sweetly and without complaint for the duration of their 50-year marriage. 'Grandad would sit in his easy chair and tap his pipe, and Granny Newport would produce great pies made with suet and lard from the warming tray of her hostess trolley,' Tim nostalgically recalled.

I tell him about the provenance of the heated hostess trolley as a 20th-century solution to the between-wars disappearance of domestic servants into the more promising occupations of factory and shop work – or 'the servant problem', as it was known. Serving hatches, trolleys and novel house layouts were architecture's answer to this first domestic labour gap, as was the onus on good housekeeping as a science in which women could invest their identity and pride. The high-maintenance 1930s semis many Britons still live in – and I grew up in – were designed around the expectation that they would be occupied by a servant-less nuclear family with a stay-at-home wife.*

'Did your grandad ever help out, a bit, with the domestic chores?' I asked Tim.

'No, never. Granny Newport died before Grandad Newport – probably the forty-a-day Benson & Hedges habit – and he was utterly lost: reduced to the Co-op ready meals my aunt would put in his freezer. I always thought that he missed the pies as much as he missed Gran.'

Later I asked Tim's father whether his father, Grandad Newport, had ever sent Christmas cards. 'No, never,' he replied. 'But you know, he always asked who'd sent them. He'd say, "Why have we not heard from such-and-such?" – when he'd never sent a card in his life.'

Then he added, with a laugh, through a mouthful of mince pie: 'Different times…'

---

* In a 1945 issue of *Architectural Review*, American writer Lewis Mumford argued that 'the first consideration of town planning' must be to 'encourage in women of the child-bearing age the impulse to bear and rear children, as an essential attribute of their humanness'.

3

Paint It Pink and Blue: Naturalizing Gendered Chores

Perhaps it's time to ask what we mean by the terms 'housework' and 'domestic labour'... Housework has never been a preoccupation with a fixed definition – it shifts depending on era, technology, changing expectations and levels of prosperity. The laborious tasks of water-collecting and lighting-up that commanded such a high proportion of our forebears' lives have gone, but categories of labour such as digital technology management are new, as are standards of personal cleanliness (in Britain the average 1950s body was washed once a week; the average 21st-century body daily).

In her 2000 exploration of the global politics of domestic labour, *Doing the Dirty Work*, sociologist Bridget Anderson comes up with a handy formulation for what we mean, as feminists, when we talk of domestic labour. For Anderson, domestic labour is a series of processes – cooking and washing, say, and caring for a child – which are necessary for maintaining and nurturing life, and are often performed all at once. The competing nature of the processes is something additional and unique to them, and something, of course, that redoubles their labour.

Yet, as we've seen, domestic labour is much more than the sum of these concurrent manual processes. Central to this labour is the way in which physical work combines with mental and emotional effort: 'If I prepare chicken soup will it cure my daughter's cold?'… 'Will we have enough wine for that tedious dinner party with his workmates if I slug it all into this casserole?' Domestic labour can thus be seen to include three broad types of work: manual, mental/administrative and emotional. 'Reproductive labour', a term gifted by the 1970s Marxist feminists, perhaps most accurately captures these interwoven efforts: of reproducing ourselves and our kin; of supplying our bodily and emotional and intellectual needs, for the next working day.

But even these formulations do not capture the full constellation of domestic labour. For many, including national governments, the work of caring for children and the elderly forms its own discrete category: care work, conducted on and off domestic premises, sometimes performed by employees of the state or by the market in the guise of nurseries, nannies and care homes. Indeed, many analyses of domestic labour exclude care work in computations of time spent on labour and of GDP. For the most part, we'll humour this distinction for statistical clarity* (although, from a feminist point of view, such distinctions are illusory).

Also typically excluded from definitions of domestic labour are cottage industries carried out within the home, such as clothes and food production for the market (or today, net commerce occupations such as e-lancing, or the production of goods to sell on portals such as Etsy).

If this work can, with care, be quantified, can we measure the extent to which its labours are disliked by the women to whom it falls? Key to many feminist theorists' analysis of domestic labour is the fact that these activities are not merely repetitive and routine but generally objected to. Is Wages for

---

* Noting when we also mean the definition to encompass care work.

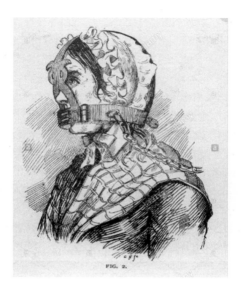

FIG. 2.

Seventeenth-century image of a scold's bridle

Housework's 'shitwork' always thus? Or, to put it another way, were these activities reviled by the women who scrubbed and swept their way through the centuries to the present?

For historian Caroline Davidson there's a clue in the fact that we see few rebels or rebellions against housework until the 1960s, despite centuries of domestic tasks falling to women. However, the cruel methods of suppression of outspoken women that were seen in the 1600s – such as the punitive 'scold's bridle', used to immobilize (and silence) a 'nagging' wife's tongue – would indicate that rebels and rebellions did exist, however small in scale.

But are we doing this work a disservice in designating it menial, dull and hated? One voice amongst my survey respondents, a British woman in the 45–56 age range, struck me: 'I think we should enjoy the work of nurturing each other.' Some would argue that housework, like much work in the paid workplace, is both toilsome and hard but also potentially creative and fulfilling. The many waves of idealized womanly nurturance that we see in popular culture, from the sensual effusions of 'domestic goddess' Nigella Lawson in the 2000s, to the rediscovery of needlepoint and jam-making by city millennials in 2010, and on to the 2019 media phenomena 'organizing expert' Marie Kondo and 'cleanfluencer' Mrs Hinch, would speak of a yearning for fulfilment found in domestic processes.

Does the entrenched Second Wave feminist positioning of housework as shitwork, therefore, deny that something good can come through and from such processes?

One influential theory of human happiness, Self-Determination Theory, enumerates three factors intrinsic to a happy life: autonomy (or a degree of control over one's life); competence (being good at something); and relatedness (interactions with others). Clearly meal preparation – a task in which the worker can both display a skill and forge a loving connection – satisfies our need for competence and relatedness.

I don't disagree that there's pleasure to be found in cooking a meal for one's loved ones and seeing them smile through a mouthful of roast spuds. It's just that such pleasures seem to be unique to a number of specific housework tasks. Survey data would suggest that, for all of the glamorization of the cosy fulfilment of tasks such as cake-baking, gardening and home decoration, most of us agree that the lion's share of domestic labour is, indeed, shitwork: 52 per cent of respondents to a 2008 American Cleaning Institute survey admitted to 'dreading' cleaning the bathroom, with 23 per cent 'hating' cleaning the kitchen and a further 20 per cent finding mopping an unwelcome chore. A 2015 study found that Australians revile oven cleaning above all other household tasks, including taking out the rubbish or rolling up their sleeves and tackling the loo. Meanwhile, in Dan Buettner's study for *National Geographic* of the happiest places on earth, housework was the activity seen to be the greatest impediment to Westerners' day-to-day happiness (above even that common North American complaint: the lengthy work commute).

So, clearly, all housework tasks are not equal when it comes to their agreeableness. And in thankless repetition, even ostensibly pleasurable tasks become odious: a convivial Sunday roast for the family is less of a chore than a pasta dish cooked to the clock with a toddler screaming 'Yucky, yucky don't like that!!!!' as she tries to stick her sleeve into the stove flame.

A 2002 study by the University of Glasgow looked into the effect of housework on mood. In contrast with the serotonin-boosting effects expected of the moderate exercise involved in cleaning and tidying, the study found that housework in fact correlated with low mood. Unlike childcare (at least for men, who often attract praise for the simple act of parenting in public) or the pizzazz of meal preparation (which, as we'll see, can be a special case), cleaning and tidying are boring, repetitive and unrewarding. Nobody notices you've done it or praises you for it, and everything swiftly reverts to mess and filth again.

In this, I tend to side with Simone de Beauvoir, who in her 1949 feminist outcry *The Second Sex* noted that housework's true horror resides in its thankless churn:

Few tasks are more like the torture of Sisyphus than housework, with its endless repetition: the clean becomes soiled, the soiled is made clean, over and over, day after day... Eating, sleeping, cleaning – the years no longer rise up towards heaven, they lie spread out ahead, grey and identical.

What is certain is these domestic processes – unsavoury, thankless, sometimes meaning-giving – have long been ascribed to women.

The Diverting History of the Birth, Life, & Death of John Franks..., a popular comic pamphlet of the 1750s, shows the ironic hero offering to help his womenfolk with the laundry. Rather than rolling up his sleeves or trousers for the task of pounding or trampling the dirt out of the family linens, Franks instead jumps into the tub and takes a shit in it, thus proving himself – as men of the era who countenanced pitching in with domestic labour must have been – an emasculated fool. By the 19th century, the taboo around males doing laundry was so great, and its implications for men's virility so dire, that widowed men too poor to employ a washerwoman would wash clothes in secret in the small hours of the morning, for fear their neighbours would find out.

A widower washing his children's clothes by candlelight as they sleep, in an illustration by George Cruikshank from J. Wight's *Mornings at Bow Street*, 1824

Curiously, it's a masculine laundry taboo that persists in the present day, with British males being the least likely to turn their hand to laundry of all Northern European males, spending an average of four minutes a day on washing and ironing – compared to British women's 23.[30]

Even for heterosexual couples who aspire to egalitarian ideals, the division of household tasks into binarized male and female tasks pertains. In a 2015 study for the *Journal of Men's*

Studies,[31] sociologist Beth Latshaw analysed time-diary data collected from a sample of 30 stay-at-home fathers in the US. She found that certain 'blue work' tasks were readily undertaken by these full-time, stay-at-home dads – including running errands, meal preparation and pet care – but that other tasks remained resolutely 'pink', including ironing, scheduling babysitters and vacuuming. For fathers who had been forced out of economic circumstance – rather than it being their preference – to stay at home to look after their children, the list of 'pink' tasks expanded, to cover laundry, cleaning bathrooms, making beds, picking up toys and grocery shopping.

In his 2012 paper 'Gender Deviance and Household Work: The Role of Occupation', sociologist Daniel Schneider argues, similarly, that household tasks are typically given an agreed-upon societal 'masculine', 'feminine' or 'neutral' designation. Whereas 'female' tasks – such as preparing meals and washing up dishes, cleaning the house and shopping for groceries – are daily, routine and often menial, 'male' tasks (maintenance of outside spaces and cars, for example) are occasional and dispensable. How different is this depiction of gendered labour allocation, we might ask, to Betty Friedan's description of husband Ed, the 'man that does', in a 1954 picture essay for American women's magazine *McCall's*? The essay, published in the ascendancy of the feminine mystique, lists the chores Ed likes. These include making things, painting, selecting furniture and draperies, reading to the children and doing work in the garden. Then there are the tasks that Ed doesn't like. These include dusting, vacuuming, washing pots and pans, taking the babysitter home and picking up after the children. Naturally, Ed does not perform these chores.

In a 2004 study of almost 800 working people in Ohio,[32] researchers were confronted with a puzzle. When women put in more than 10 hours of housework a week, they felt more pressed for time – and, in turn, more depressed. But when men did the same amount of housework, they didn't. A similar pattern emerged for volunteering: men who volunteered more were less depressed, but women became time-stressed and didn't seem to experience as much benefit.

The explanation that the researchers came up with, drawn from interviewees' accounts of how they spent their time, was that men tend to do more enjoyable housework and volunteering. They cut the grass and coach sports teams; they are congratulated and feel a sense of accomplishment. Women, on the other hand, are often occupied with small, repetitive daily chores and service work: less cheering and high-fiving, and more trying not to fall asleep at school meetings. Drudgery, apparently, breeds drudgery.

In 1989's *The Second Shift*, Arlie Hochschild found that the division of household labour into 'pink' and 'blue' or 'girl' and 'boy' jobs is a way many couples make psychological sense of unequal division of labour. In one bleakly amusing passage, Hochschild describes the Holts: a wife with egalitarian ideals who is married to a husband who has a 'traditional' outlook and refuses to pitch in with household chores. The Holts come up with what Hochschild refers to as a jointly devised 'outer cover' for the management of family life: Nancy 'does' the upstairs, and husband Evan the 'downstairs'. The upstairs includes two bedrooms, two bathrooms, a living room, the dining room and kitchen; the downstairs, in the Holts' construction, refers to the garage where Evan stores the tools needed for his hobbies and where the family dog, Max, is fed. 'The dog is all Evan's problem. I don't have to deal with the dog,' Nancy tells Hochschild. The couple's upstairs-downstairs arrangement accommodates Evan's failure to contribute domestically through rhetorical sleight of hand, without upsetting the patriarchal status quo. The problem becomes the 'no-problem' problem.

This naturalized – and often spatial – pinking and blueing of household chores is a well-established trope. In an awkward pre-election interview on BBC's *The One Show* designed to humanize the then British prime minister in the run-up to the catastrophic June 2017 election when she was memorably nicknamed 'Maybot', Theresa May and her financial executive husband Philip lightly addressed their own division of house-hold labour.

'I get to decide when, but not if, to take the bins out,' said Mr May, with an effortful smile. 'I do the traditional boy jobs, by and large.'

'There's boy jobs and girl jobs, you see,' added Mrs May, with a forced chuckle.

Sociologist Sasha Scambler was typical of feminist tweeters in her response to this conspicuous bid to soften the British PM's image: 'Boy jobs and girl jobs. #everydaysexism from the top. Good thing we've got a female prime minister to tackle this. Oh, wait a minute...'

For all of the cultural prominence of the conceit, the explicit division of domestic labour into pink and blue jobs is, on the face of it, rather rarer than these cultural representations might suggest. Of the heterosexual couples we surveyed for this book, only 9 per cent responded in the affirmative to the statement 'Do you divide chores according to pink and blue tasks?' Of these same couples, 25 per cent said that they divided tasks 'according to aptitude'; 27 per cent 'accord-ing to our domestic priorities'; and 30 per cent 'according to who spends most time at home' (these statements having the potential, of course, to conceal a multitude of gendered assumptions). Meanwhile, 62 per cent of coupled gay males and 56 per cent of women in same-sex relationships stated that they divided chores based on aptitude. And 15 per cent of coupled Scandinavians, the highest number of positives by nation for this category, said that they divide chores 'according to the unpleasantness of the task'.

Curiously, agreement with the statement 'we divide labour by areas of the home' was negligible in every context apart from the US, where the adaptive discourses of space highlighted by Hochschild in *The Second Shift* apparently still hold. Eight per cent of coupled heterosexual women in the US said that they divide labour by areas of the home, with elaborations on this point provided by two respondents – both married with children – proving illuminating.

'We divide according to area. I do most of the indoor cleaning and my husband does most of yard work and stuff on the exterior of the house. Husband also does the garden.' Woman aged 25–32, US

'My husband helps out a lot and does the bulk of the outdoor work.' Woman aged 33–45, US

In a 2014 meta-analysis of global literature on housework in heterosexual households,[33] Arnstein Aassve et al explored four hypotheses to account for the unequal division of domestic labour: the relative resources theory (the partner who earns less does the most housework); the time availability theory (the partner who spends less time doing paid work does more housework); the economic dependency model (the partner who contributes proportionally less to the household income does more housework); and the gender ideology theory (beliefs around gender roles influence housework-sharing in a couple).

The results affirm the predominance of gender ideology but with certain caveats. Time availability and relative resources mattered in the most egalitarian countries, such as Sweden and Germany, yet economic dependency was more operative in countries where partners contribute more unevenly to household income, such as Hungary and Russia. But if you live in one of the world's most acutely patriarchal countries, it's probably little solace that you buy yourself out of 30 minutes' mopping with a paid job.

Curiously, the idea that gender ideology might be the principal factor influencing division of household labour, above economic and time availability factors, provoked anger in the breasts of several male survey respondents.

'Women always go on about this but if she works less and I'm stuck with working 60-hour weeks, then she does more. I'd love to work part-time and have it how women have it, but I've got a kid to support and all that pressure.'
Man aged 33–45, UK

And one male on a fathering Facebook group flatly refused to fill in the survey on these grounds: 'She earns less, so she does more. If I earned less, I'd do more. There's nothing more in it.'

Man-Yee Kan and Heather Laurie's 2018 study 'Who Is Doing the Housework in Multicultural Britain?' was the first to look into the comprehensive effects of race on gendered housework allocation. Its intriguing finding was that black men were the outliers of all male groups in Britain; and particularly black Caribbean men – who, after controlling for factors such as income and class, contribute 7.12 hours of housework a week compared to a white British man's 6.06 hours (or 38 per cent of the total compared to 22 per cent). Kan and Laurie speculate that 'matriarchal family structures within Afro-Caribbean cultures' might explain this anomaly. That is, that gender ideologies are the root of Afro-Caribbean males' exceptionality.[34]

For all of the evidence that women in heterosexual-couple households are routinely ascribed the everyday grunt work (laundry and loo roll replacement are carried out by women in 70 per cent of British households) and men the discretionary and non-daily activities such as small repairs and lawn-mowing (in 75 per cent of British households), comparative surveys across nations show that the categories are not as fixed and immutable, pinked and blued, as we might think. Finnish men, for example, are much more willing to cook the nightly meal than Spanish men, and mopping, a task anathema to Italian and Portuguese males, is reframed as a 'male' chore' in Latshaw's study of American stay-at-home dads. More troublingly, a 2019 study in the US found that men avoid domestic tasks considered environmentally friendly, such as recycling or shopping with reusable bags, out of fear their heterosexuality would be called into question, or as US gay magazine *Out* reported it, 'looking gay'.[35]

In my childhood home, there was something approximating a spatial and pinked/blued allocation of labour. My mother took charge of the chores in the sitting room with the pine hatch and nasty moth-eaten floral carpet. She also covered tasks in the kitchen with the faux-cottage units, apart from my father's much-commented-upon efforts at washing up and concocting simple, egg-based meals. (He often made scrambled eggs á la James Bond. Read the recipe: it's basically just scrambled eggs made by James Bond.) My brother and I took indifferent charge of our bedrooms – his was a stinking, Tango can-littered pit for the duration of his teen years. While my mother gardened and tended the veg patch and fatality-prone chickens, the garage was my father's domain. Home to greasy bits of metal in repurposed jam jars, it was where he inexpertly whittled things out of bits of wood as an excuse to drink the cider that would eventually kill him, through cirrhosis of the liver, aged 57.

What of Tim's dismissal – for all of his egalitarian ideals – of certain types of domestic work that I feel compelled to carry out? His is, in particular, a discomfort with the category of domestic labour we can now describe as 'emotion work': keeping relatives sweet; maintaining relationships with the parents of Leo's friends from nursery and NCT[36] group. He also reneges, I'd suggest, on mental labour – frequently citing arguments against overconsumption, for example, as an excuse not to assume the work of keeping our growing son provided with clothes that fit him. He doesn't get the laborious duty I feel compelled to perform (though to be honest, I don't fully get it, either) of 'signalling' thoughtful parenthood, or dressing Leo in clothing bought for him by relatives and friends when we visit those relatives and friends.

Tim and I chatted one night over the chicken casserole I'd inherited from my mum's 1980s repertoire: a comfort blanket of booze and homemade stock that's the edible embodiment of my mum's emotion work. I asked him about his take on 'male' and 'female' labour in our run-of-the-mill middle-class home – organized, as the Marxist feminist theorists would have it, around our reproductive roles as mother and father to our toddler son.

In particular, I said, I had some rubs. Was he aware that keeping a line of communication with his sister-in-law is important if Leo – an only child – is to enjoy a relationship with his young cousins? That his refusal to 'get involved' with playdate-arrangement WhatsApp groups piles yet more management and emotion work onto my plate? What would our son be wearing, I wondered out loud, if we both assumed Tim's convenient stance of not engaging with 'planet-bashing capitalist crap'? Tim's determination to live by principle, after all, consigned me to the neon-lit horror of kids' clothing departments (where I endlessly marvel at why toddlers' trousers have skinny legs when most two-year-olds' limbs have the length and sinuousness of a street bollard).

I'm never on to a winning streak when I mention social media to Tim: one of the few men under the age of 40 who has no online presence and regards the arrival of the internet as the source of all social ills, from parental distraction to the unlikely coolness of nerds. Tim harbours an ongoing fantasy in which he shuts down the internet and returns, via a low-tech time machine, to 1995.

'I think it's all – just, I don't know... superfluous,' Tim explained. 'I'm just not going to piss about sending reams of

Tweets* to people I barely know. It only makes them send you more messages that you have to reply to again. It's a vortex of hell. Basically, I fundamentally disagree with your approach.'

He then added that he wasn't sure what I meant by the mental load: 'It sounds like, I don't know, a bad headache or something.'

On the other hand, how much of the fact that I assume these roles so readily, if resentfully, speaks of my performance of the gender norms I've been socialized into, rather than Tim's failure to pull his equal weight? It's that voice – coaxing, corrective – whispering in my ear, again and again. Let's call her Marla. Or, better yet, let's call her Suzy Shitwork.

Darling, look how well your son is dressed – you're a Real Woman… Darling, your Christmas cards were sent on time with inserted photographs of Leo looking cute in a velour Santa outfit [NB ignore the velour] *– you're a Real Woman…*

By investing self-worth in the fact my son is handsomely attired in clean and appropriately sized (and matching – oh, matching is satisfying!) clothing, am I not playing along with the socialized ideal of the perfect mother I rail against? Or am I, as feminist theorists Judith Butler[37] and West and Zimmerman[38] would have it, responding to these ideals and norms performatively, i.e. *doing gender*?

The 1960s US sitcom *Bewitched*, reruns of which were on UK TV throughout my childhood, follows the domestic misadventures of housewife-cum-witch Samantha Stephens and her husband Darrin, a side-parted mortal who works in advertising. Samantha is frequently depicted caught up in an inner struggle between her feminine domestic identity and supernatural powers. In Season 5's episode 'Is It Magic or Imagination?', in a typical scene, Samantha surveys her disordered living room: sofa cushions scattered about and magazines all over the floor. She should tidy up! She lifts a finger and twitches her nose…

---

* Here he means WhatsApp messages.

'No, no,' she says after a moment's hesitation, finger cocked, 'I'll do it myself.' Samantha, although she could supernaturally zap her housework in a jiffy, is a 'true' woman who chooses not to.

So is Tim like Betty Friedan's Ed, cherry-picking the chores he likes? Or am I Samantha Stephens, acting out my feminine worth by performing a 'womanhood'? Or are all of our unions shaped by a range of gendered identities we adopt or rebel against, and are we in fact neither and both? Are we sometimes traditionals, performing gender norms and ideals, and sometimes rebels, exploding out of prescribed domestic roles as if our aprons were made of the flimsiest tissue paper?

There's another reason to bring these invisible domestic asymmetries and accommodations to the surface: the kids of heterosexual unions are, frankly, not all right. In a 2017 study, Rachel Farr at the University of Massachusetts, Amherst, and Charlotte Patterson at the University of Virginia observed 104 adoptive families: different-sex couples, same-sex couples and lone parents.[39] They assessed how the parents allocated 20 childcare tasks, from feeding to dressing to going to the playground, and found – unsurprisingly – that gay and lesbian couples divided these more equally than their heterosexual counterparts. They also found that heterosexual couples scored markedly higher than other cohorts when it came to negative emotional expressions such as undermining each other and expressing anger and resentment about childcare arrangements. Significantly, dissatisfaction with division of household labour had a pronounced impact on the children of these unions, leading, the authors found, to 'maladjusted childhood behaviours' proportionate to the parents' resentment-displaying behaviours. It's something to think about. If you spend your days in a ground-level war with your other half over who does what and when, chances are you're screwing your kids up as well as souring your romantic union.

Across all of our survey's respondents, 72 per cent agreed with the question 'Does division of labour cause conflict in your household?', with 11 per cent of those answering 'Yes, often' or 'It is the main source of conflict'. This disquiet was more pronounced, predictably, amongst individuals in opposite-sex, cohabiting relationships, with 15 per cent of these survey-takers agreeing that division of household labour was the main source of conflict in their households, compared to 3 per cent of cohabiting lesbian couples.

> *'We often talk about the labour involved in remembering what needs to be done. The majority of this falls to my wife and she resents it... She thinks I should do more.*
>
> *'I feel pressure to ensure that our roles do not make one of us seem more feminine or masculine than the other. This is due to unwelcome perceptions of lesbian relationships as being imitations of heterosexual ones.'* White modern professional woman in same-sex union, aged 33–45, UK

Rather than the jointly devised 'outer cover' of a spatial division of labour seen with North American survey-takers, British and Australian respondents were quick to explain the unfair state of affairs by the fact that women are more domestically competent – or simply better at noticing mess – than men.

> *'I just think I notice dirt and mess where my husband doesn't.'* Mother working part-time, aged 25–32, Australia

Yet repeated studies have in fact found no difference in preferences for cleanliness and tidiness, nor an increased ability to notice cleanliness or tidiness, based on biological sex.[40] Men are not 'dirt blind', as they are often proposed to be.

I often think of Farr and Patterson's research when I'm around those heterosexual parent couples – we all know them – who barely contain their mutual resentment in front of others: rolling their eyes, hissing vituperatively beneath surface smiles.

'WATCH Lee, Mark! WATCH HIM: HE'S ABOUT TO WALK INTO THE EDGE OF THAT FLOWER POT! [A pause. Lee crashes into flower pot.] Oh, for fuck's sake, I can't even have a glass of wine in peace.'

'Yes, Paul did go to Thailand two weeks after Eliza was born, and I have to say I was *surprised* at the time, BUT IT WAS FINE!"

[Paul, brightly, fingers white around the scruff of his beer bottle.] 'Yes, it was fine!'

Raising Eve (or How to Bake a Mum)

I arrived at the nursery one evening to the sight of my two-year-old son and two older boys – who would have been around three – queuing up to take turns with the new addition to the nursery toy section.

The boy currently in command of the hot new acquisition – a dome-headed newborn-baby doll in a wicker bassinet – was lost in happy reverie: rocking and shushing it with his knees softly bent, oblivious to the other boys' impatience. In an opposite corner of the nursery, a new play kitchen was also alive with toddler activity: a three-year-old boy was making 'soup' with a plastic croissant for a girl wearing a *Ghostbusters* T-shirt, and an ironing basket and iron* were witness to a snaking queue of toddlers, occupying themselves with bouts of nose-picking as they eagerly awaited their turns.

'Oooh, mum, they do like baby, she's very popular, mum' said nursery worker Tania with the insincere smile that's demanded of interactions with all of the women they call, simply, 'mum'. My nursery is part of a middle-of-the-road US- and UK-wide chain. In 2018, the shareholders of the US-headquartered company earned a record dividend, whilst

---

* I wasn't sure I fully approved of the iron after Leo's thumb's recent run-in with our Morphy Richards.

the nursery 'nurses' were paid between £13,000 and £17,000 a year. All of its employees are female, and two in three are women of colour.* This guilt-inducing experience costs us £90 a day.

Britain's early-years childcare is the world's most expensive – and one of the financially least efficient – systems. It profits, as all care sectors do, from the devaluation of feminized care labour: women are paid 30 per cent less as childcare workers than an equivalent, non-feminized, entry-level job. The sector that some term 'pink collar' – the beauty industry, nursing, teaching, secretarial work, waitressing and childcare – is underpaid by a factor of up to 40 per cent compared to comparatively skilled fields dominated by men. In this, our nursery is unremarkable in every way.[41]

Despite this, my son's nursery has been influenced by the trickle-down of attitudes towards gender-role socialization. Pioneered by nurseries in Sweden, gender-neutral early-years childcare dispenses with toys designated for 'girls' and 'boys' and encourages gender-neutral play.

Over a hissing Skype line from her office in Chicago, I chatted about Britain's childcare model with Barbara Risman, a leading theorist of gender-role socialization. One of the feminist academics of the 1980s and '90s structuralist school, Risman theorizes gender as a social structure that interacts with other social structures such as race and class. She's clear-eyed as to the familial and institutional agencies that socialize girl children from, as she put it to me in her sing-song voice, 'the get-go'. The primary site of this socialization is, she says,

---

* On a related point, in the course of writing this book I interviewed a male nursery worker at a co-operative nursery in another area of London – a former actor who was much-loved by the children in his care. He reported the stigma he experiences as a male nursery nurse. 'I'm regularly asked if I'm actually going to change nappies,' Bruce told me. 'The implication being that, as I'm a man working as a nursery nurse, I must be a paedophile.'

the family, though state and institutional actors – from Girl Guides to Home Economics – play their part.

'As a white female growing up in 1950s America, I was socialized for motherhood. Women of your generation – and younger – in the West were subjected to some pretty ambiguous socialization: you were taught to desire domesticity through dolls, as well as to pursue careers. So no wonder some of you [Gen Xers and millennials] are, you know, all over the place.

'But for all of that you have to remember that socialization for the domestic bespeaks a certain amount of class privilege. African-American women, for example, have always been socialized to assume the labour of both maintaining a home and paid work. That is these women's gender straitjacket.'

Please share an anecdote about division of household labour in your home; or in your home when you were a child (optional).

'My dad used to joke that women's feet are small so that they can reach the sink. Oh dear.' White woman aged 46-55, UK

As a Home Economics teacher in the 1970s, my mother was an agent for one of the most explicit programmes of state-sponsored gender socialization in history.

The Home Economics Movement began in the US in the 1890s, when scientist Ellen Swallow Richards, the first woman to attend the prestigious science college MIT, entered an exhibit at the 1893 Chicago World's Fair called the Rumford Kitchen. This kitchen, which served hearty meals to fairgoers – including cheese pudding, stewed tripe and beef broth – also provided education about food nutrition and how to plan meals with financial economy in mind (hence the tripe). Over the next decade, Richards and a group of fellow scientists set about turning cost-effective and nutritious cookery into a respected scientific discipline. Richards, surprisingly, resisted the feminization of this new field. She wanted to call the nascent discipline 'oekology', or the science of right living, but 'home economics' was ultimately chosen as the official term.

In 1908, Richards founded the American Home Economics Association. By the 1910s, many American women's colleges boasted 'practice homes' – mock-ups of family homes in which women students lived and took on roles such as budgeting, cooking, cleaning and interior decoration, as well as the care of young children (who were, somewhat alarmingly, 'borrowed' from local orphanages).

By the 1920s, the Home Economics Movement had evolved into a campaign to 'rationalize housework' and train American women to be more efficient and prudent household managers. But it also had political clout. In an era when American housewives were becoming important consumers, the movement assumed the role of communicating homemakers' needs to manufacturers and political leaders. It also brought about the passage of legislation[42] to fund Home Economics demonstrations in rural communities and to develop and teach a Home Economics curriculum on the campuses of state land-grant colleges (agricultural and science colleges). In the UK, Home Economics was taught to girls at state-run schools from the Edwardian era. Its unambivalent syllabus included needlework and cookery, and lapel badges reading 'Future Housewife' were awarded to girls who successfully passed the course.

By the interwar period, Home Economics had become a core requirement in girls' education in the UK, India and Australia. Germany, meanwhile, had Reifenstein schools (for the higher education of rural women with a domestic focus), and South Korea a similar discipline called 'family science', which had been established by Western missionaries in the late 19th century. In the 1950s–1970s, when my miniskirted mother was teaching her reluctant private-schoolgirls, the syllabus covered budget management and nutrition, needle-work, cake-baking and even cordon bleu cookery techniques such as julienning and making roux (aka chopping veg and making white sauce). But by the time I was at school in the 1980s, the subject had evolved into 'domestic science', an odd cobbling-together of basic, untoothsome cookery (NB never consider ingesting a canned-tuna *jalousie*) and advice as to how to cut joints of meat which seemed as dated as the fashion sense of the woman who taught us (the wonderful Mrs Livsey, whose false eyelashes would drop into sponge mixes like suicidal spiders).

In 2014, the UK's Home Economics GCSE was scrapped and, stripped of its gendered connotations, replaced with the new Food Technology course – whose contents, one teacher friend confided, is 'a bit weird. For example, you plan and weigh a pizza topping and then you design a box to stick the pizza in. That's not much use unless you plan to work at a food lab.'

Happily, institutional gender-role socialization – whether it's girls' toy boxes at nurseries, or housewifery-focused Home Economics at secondary school – is increasingly passé. But the general populace, apparently, has mixed feelings about this. A 2017 study conducted by the Pew Research Center in the US found that men were less likely than women to agree that it was a good thing for parents to encourage their kids to play with toys and participate in activities typically associated with the other gender: 71 per cent of men said encouraging girls to undertake activities typically associated with boys was a good thing, compared with 80 per cent of women; 56 per cent of men agreed that it was a good thing for parents to encour-age young boys to play in ways typically associated with girls – rocking babies, playing with toy kitchens – compared with 80 per cent of women.[43]

As my Polish mum-friend Katrin, who is married to a British

man, complained to a mothering WhatsApp group I'm on: 'I think it's OK for my son to play with teddy bears and dolls, and to go to toddler ballet, but my husband thinks it will warp him and make him a sissy. It drives me nuts. How can I explain it to him?'

'Ask him how he'd feel if he had a daughter who played with trucks?' said one mother helpfully. (Although another mother's 'Strangle the dick with a tutu' summed up the general mood.)

A 2018 *Saturday Night Live* skit poked fun at the still-prevailing sense that boys will somehow have their masculinity 'polluted' by coming into contact with the tools of women's labour. Stay-at-home dad Jason Momoa struts and hoists and generally mans around the house with his new 'GE Big Boy Appliances' that give housework 'a butch new makeover': a dishwasher with a 70-pound steel door that it takes a REAL MAN to swing shut, and a six-foot-high washing machine with an 'extremely poor' F-minus (ergo, manly) efficiency rating.

Today's parents also perpetuate gender-role socialization in ways that can be metrically quantified. A 2018 analysis by BusyKid, an allowance-management app, found that of the 10,000 families reviewed, parents pay boys twice as much as girls for doing their weekly chores, with boys receiving an average weekly allowance of $13.80 and girls just $6.71. Findings from a 2018 survey of 10,000 Australian primary and high school students also demonstrated a stark playground pay and effort gap: 60 per cent of girls said they helped out with jobs like cleaning and tidying around the house 'often or a lot', compared to 50 per cent of boys. And Australian girls were most likely to dominate the lowest pocket-money brackets (AUS $5–10) or to not be paid at all. Meanwhile, a 2019 study into teen time-use data in the US found that teenaged girls and boys echo their parents' behaviours, with the time that 15- to 17-year-old girls spend cooking and cleaning in an average day being more than double the time boys of the same age spend on those tasks.[44]

In this way, we're all guilty of perpetuating girls' socialization to unpaid domestic work. And this would be worrying if such training had a profound effect on our readiness to perform this labour in later life. Did my mother's imparting of Home Economics cannelloni recipes to me – rather than my brother – and her patient lessons in sock-darning and needlework predestine me to take on the lion's share of housework in later life?

Of the respondents to our survey (of all sexualities) who were living in situations similar to the home in which they grew up in (cohabiting with a partner, with children), 41 per cent said their household division of labour was 'very similar' to their childhood homes, and 59 per cent said that it was somewhat or completely different. Perhaps unsurprisingly, individuals in same-sex unions were least likely to say that the allocation of housework was very similar to the home they lived in while growing up (23 per cent).

I like to think that Tim and I, with our 2010s aspirant 'fair family', have progressed from the almost-housewife/occasional-helpmeet act that my mum and dad performed, but how true is this? Especially in those moments when I catch myself simulating a 1980s mother: casserole bubbling as I hand-stitch the crotch of Leo's trousers (he's always inexplicably tearing the stitches between his legs, as my mother recounts my brother did*). Or when I assume the responsibility of household management without self-interrogation or complaint. When I come across Tim reorganizing his neatly serried screwdrivers as Leo looks on, I wonder if this, too, is a performance that is passed down through the generations?

---

* She notes that, in adulthood, my brother inexplicably develops sizeable 'pocket holes' that his keys and wallets fall through, a wear-and-tear portrait of masculinity.

A German study, published in 2018, found that domestic gender-role patterning may be most formative between the ages of 8 and 11 years old, and have its profoundest effect on boys. According to Julia Cordero Coma and Gøsta Esping-Andersen's investigation of 2,293 respondents born between 1976 and 1995, the housework division between parents when children were aged 8 to 11 was linked to the likelihood of adult sons participating in such tasks – even after the academics controlled for parental education, the mother's stated desire to be in paid work, and time constraints. That pre-teen boys are most affected by gender-role patterning is intriguing. Does this mean that, five years from now, Tim and I should reappraise our domestic *pas de deux* for signs of slippage into traditional models? Is 2024 the year to mothball Tim's prized screwdriver collection?

In Barbara Risman's view, childhood gender-role socialization is in fact less predictive of division of labour in adult homes than we might think. Weaker in its influences, certainly, than factors such as economics and women's work opportunities. 'Studies show that economic and political conditions produce beliefs and preferences for action that frequently overcome childhood socialization,' she says.

In fact, the biggest predictors, according to Risman, of whether women will lead domestic-focused or work-focused lives, are success in the workforce – i.e. the opportunities women have to pursue paid and satisfying work – and mental stability, with women who suffer mental illness, and therefore find the demands of working life more challenging, more frequently living domestic-focused lives.

Arlie Hochschild makes a related point. According to Hochschild, women shop from a portfolio of gender strategies,* like scrolling through a rack of pink-collar uniforms, in response to the circumstances they find themselves in. We find we're

---

* As do men.

lacking opportunities in the workplace? We might base our womanly identity on family and home. We have egalitarian ideals but find our partner traditional? We adopt a gender strategy that makes us feel as if we're living our feminist lives whilst shouldering the lion's share of the domestic work. In this way, we toggle between versions of femininity – our childhood patterning and contemporary role models – and find the blouse, suit or straitjacket that fits.

If there's anyone placed to call bullshit on gender socialization it's my friend Adrianne. A trans woman, Adrianne was raised Adrian in the working-class Liverpool of the 1970s, where 'men were men and men were dockers' – until the docks closed and the dockers became angry ex-dockers. Now married to a trans man, Michael, Adrianne works and lives in Belfast, where she's a railway engineer by day and an enthusiastic amateur ballerina by night.

I met Adrianne when I interviewed her about her experience coming into her trans identity as an adult ballerina, and something she said then struck me: 'My mam always says that I only want the nice parts of being a woman, but not the bad parts: not the chores or the standing over the kitchen sink, just the pretty clothes and the glamour.'

I want to ask Adrianne if she agreed with her mother's analysis, so I visit her and Michael at their Belfast home. They've just moved into a new apartment in the city centre, and the walls are bare apart from *Harry Potter* posters and a collection of vintage pub beer mats. A few boxes are still unpacked, arrayed around the foot of a black leather sofa – and this, Adrianne told me, was the point.

'Michael and I always joke that our home is like a thirteen-year-old has been given the keys to the flat,' she laughs.

Adrianne's theory is that certain categories of feminized domestic labour — interior decoration, good housekeeping — simply don't apply for LGBT* couples.

'It's that thing about compliance, isn't it,' Adrianne muses. 'Heterosexual cisgender** nuclear families have been the norm for so long that expectations are set that houses look a certain way and there's this "woman's touch". In Belfast we call them the "cornflake" families. They have these big mortgages and nice-looking houses and have to live on cornflakes to pay for it all. But as LGBT people, we get to escape those expectations.'

She takes a glug of milkless builder's tea from a mug featuring a picture of a railway signal box. Adrianne later tells me she has railway-themed 'work day' mugs and separate 'day off' mugs, the latter bearing pictures of Harry Potter, the Liverpool-to-Belfast ferry or the Queen and Prince Philip.

Was your mum right? I ask. Do you just want the 'glamour' of womanhood's lipstick and heels, and not the stale doom of Brillo-padding a greasy pan?

Adrianne shakes a jar of nail polish and smiles.

'Maybe,' she says.

---

* The current inclusive term LGBTQI, which includes queer and intersex identity categories, does not wash with Adrianne. 'I think people are just getting their heads around the "T", to be honest.'
** 'Cisgender' = individuals who identify with the biological sex and/or gender they were assigned at birth.

4

The Mother of All Reality Checks (aka the Parent Labour Trap)

Maternity is the key by which women's total adhesion to the system is obtained.

— Italian Wages for Housework pamphlet, 1972[45]

In motherhood everything collides. The public and private sphere... suddenly merge. She cannot leave her pregnant belly at home with the rest of her private self.

— Katrine Marçal, *Who Cooked Adam Smith's Dinner?*

Is division of labour in your household as you expected it to be when you were growing up?

'I was a fierce feminist. Now I would call myself a realistic/ surrendered/exhausted feminist. I wanted it to be 50/50 as a young woman. I even hated seeing men being the driver all the time — now I hate driving and love it when hubby drives and I can sit there and look out the window and scroll away on my phone and relax.

'Adult reality is different than a teenager's expectations, especially when kids come along, and fighting for "equality" is exhausting. Find someone kind and giving and open to negotiation and fairness, that's your only play,

ladies, IMO!' White woman in different-sex married relationship, aged 33–45, Australia

'I didn't think about it much but I never thought I'd get a degree and then end up cleaning hair out of plugholes every week…' Mixed-race woman aged 22–34, UK

'I think I need an extra 60 per cent of a person,' says a friend of mine, Christine, one day. We're having one of those distracted catch-ups common to young parents: chatting while looking in the opposite direction at small children trying to tug the plastic tablecloths off a café table like they're trainee magicians.

'As I figure it, having kids – what – quadruples your workload at home? A load of washing a day rather than one a week, plus that thing of being constantly stooped over picking shit up from the floor.'

I *hmmm* in agreement as Leo grabs at my coffee with a hand sheened with dried snot. Christine continues:

'So I'm back at work on a four-day "mum shift" – which is actually five days' work in four days, as you know 'cause I'm always whingeing on about it – and my husband's working even longer hours; he got that promotion he couldn't turn down because we needed the cash to feed the mortgage.' Here Christine shakes her head bleakly. 'So the way I figure it, we're missing 60 per cent of a person at home, or the four days a woman needs to be at home doing all of the shit to keep the show on the road.'

'Shitwork?'

'Jay, stop kicking the table leg – do you need a pee? Yes, house shit. Shitwork. Exactly.'

I fill Christine in on Judy Brady's yearning for a mythical wife (from 1971's 'I Want a Wife'): a cosy, self-denying figure who'll take care of the children when they're sick, keep track of appointments and social arrangements, and have one eye on your exasperation levels as well as her own. ('*I want a wife who knows that sometimes I need a night out by myself.*')

'Yes, that's it!!!' Christine snorts. 'I want a wife — a nice doormat of a wife. Where do I get one? And, I don't know, shall we sod it and order a bottle of wine?'

A few weeks later, I'm having lunch with a 20-something feminist, Laura. Like many childless feminists, Laura is hopeful about her prospects when it comes to the gendered division of domestic labour. She's straight, cis and lives in a sprawling houseshare in Battersea with five other professionals: a straight couple, one 'queer girl', and two single straight men nicknamed Saint Nick and Dick Nick, for their comparative social charms. They rub along pretty smoothly on the domestic front.

'You know, we're lefties; you just can't get away with leaving clearing up the kitchen to the women. It would be social death. If it's too messy, we just order a Deliveroo and feel conflicted about the driver's wages so we tip him a fiver. The couple can be a pain, you know, kicking around the sitting room and spreading their stuff everywhere and making it their own, but that's pretty standard-issue.

'So, how is it when you have kids?' Laura then asks, lightly, frowning as a slab of Massaman tofu skids away from her fork (we're at one of those hip vegan joints that are full of glowy-skinned millennials hammering away on dating apps as they absently thrust food into their mouths).

Fish-belly white. That's the colour Laura turns when I tell her about the heterosexual Parent Labour Trap. That, however egalitarian a couple's outlook before kids arrive on the scene, it's tough to keep it up. Tough to keep up a fair division of labour when one of you gets a rushed two weeks' parenting leave, although he'd like more (the boss having made it clear that his 'organizational commitment' will be in doubt if he asks for the shared parental leave that's his legal right). It's tough when one of you has mammaries and has to breastfeed – and God how you're pressured to breastfeed, it's never-bloody-ending with the fucking Breast is Best cult – and so of course you're the one at home and you need to eat and not live in a pigsty and you hobble around picking things up with your baby in a sling screaming like a livid prawn as your C-section stitches prang like guitar strings. And when your other half comes home after his first day back at work with a bag of deli stuff from M&S and says he'll cook, you've spent the past 12 hours with a bellowing newborn – and don't let anyone tell you it's all cute, it's like caring for an angry leaking alien until they're six months old and can do more than scream or spew – you'd rather hand the being over, shut the kitchen door and make a spag bol.

Then a year down the line and your kid's at nursery, but someone needs the flexibility to run off and collect her when she has hand, foot and mouth, or slapped cheek, or molluscum contagiosum, or anything else in that portfolio of medieval-sounding early-years viruses you'd never heard of before you were daft enough to reproduce. So you go down to four days a week and you're still playing catch-up at home; meanwhile your partner is working the 'dad shift', picking up more hours of overtime to plug your income gap, and there's less and less time and energy to *live* your feminist ideals. And, of course, just as you're coming to terms with the Fatherhood Bonus – your other half's rising wages and blossoming career – the Motherhood Penalty[46] hits you in the face like a wet nappy as your career and income stall.

> *'I thought it would be totally equal, which it was until I started having babies and then resented being the one left at home breastfeeding babies and having to press pause on my career.'* Woman aged 33-45, UK

I wonder whether delayed fertility is one of the reasons Fourth Wave feminism – making such strides with the public exposure of sexual and power abuses through #metoo – suffers a domestic labour blind spot. Young feminists forging this new wave are not only twice as likely as their 40-something counterparts to pay a cleaner to perform their domestic dirty work,[47] they're also more likely than (even the late-breeding) Gen Xers to delay childbearing into their late thirties and beyond. More likely, too, to live with their parents past the age at which, a few decades before, they'd have had their own teenaged offspring.

As a young Fourth Wave feminist, it is easy, perhaps, to be hopeful about how things will pan out when our lived experience is of a no-problem problem: one of heterosexist male jerks with Neanderthal attitudes and Gen X women who aren't truly 'living' their feminism. But then – in the spirit of airing our dirty laundry – where have we late Gen Xers been when we could have been reinvigorating the domestic labour debate? Sharing feminist aphorisms on social media and drowning our feminist disappointments in cheeky bottles of Pinot?

Friends have stories about how it happened to them. How motherhood took their long-nurtured feminist ideals and put them through the 1000hp spin cycle of a new domestic reality. Some comfort themselves with the hope that their household will return to a more symmetrical division of labour when their kids start school ('The way I see it, it's not ideal but just temporary'); others commute their feminist disappointment into tough-broad-who-gets-it-all-done mode ('I nailed it at work and now I have to nail this mum thing'). Many seem, frankly, dazed at how they've gone from having a partner who was a whizz in the kitchen in their courting years to being the one who now serves up a balanced meal, nightly, at 7 p.m. on the dot. ('And he used to bring ingredients round to my flat to make me Delia's chicken jalfrezi. From scratch. Although I'm beginning to wonder if I hallucinated it.')

The Parent Labour Trap is not a figment of these overworked women's imaginations. Using longitudinal data gathered from dual-earner heterosexual couples before and after they became parents, US sociologists Jill Yavorsky and Claire Kamp Dush examined the change in divisions of paid and unpaid work across the crucial life transition to parenthood. In their 2015 study, they found that the birth of a child increases the unpaid work demanded of the couple by several hours a day, and that these extra work hours – the relentless laundry and the picking up of strewn toys – were disproportionately shouldered by women (more than two hours of additional work per day fell to women compared to an additional 40 minutes for men, an effort gap the length of the average movie). But we've been socialized not to see the enormity of the labour that parenthood – and in particular motherhood – entails.

All would be well, of course, if women were sanguine about the Parent Labour Trap; resigned to the second shift that seems to be a condition, in particular, of heterosexual motherhood. Qualitative data gathered for this book – in Europe, the US, Australia and New Zealand, and South and East Asia – finds that this is not the case. The satisfaction gap is most stark between women and men in different-sex relationships, with 75 per cent of men in these relationships citing themselves as happy with the division of labour in their home, compared to 53 per cent of their female counterparts. The disquiet is most stark in English-speaking countries: 47 per cent of women in different-sex relationships in the UK declare themselves happy with the current division of labour in their household to 83 per cent of men; and 42 per cent and 75 per cent respectively in Australia and New Zealand. Curiously, this gender dissatisfaction trend extends to women in same-sex couples in these nations, who are more likely to cite high levels of dissatisfaction if the division of household chores is unequal in their home, as compared to men in same-sex relationships.

Could it be that the paid-working patterns that arise with parenting have something to do with the yawning gap in effort that opens up when heterosexual couples reproduce? That many heterosexual mothers go part-time in children's early years out of preference, and that this might naturally result in a temporary 'traditionalizing' of labour division roles: the body at home wielding the bog brush, so to speak? It's a commonly held belief, but it's not one borne out by facts. Yavorsky and Kamp Dush's survey did not find that women in the US with small children decreased their hours in paid work; rather they saw the opposite, with these women putting in an average of 45 hours per week of paid labour to childless women's 41. Since 2010 in the UK, the employment rate for women with children is higher than for women without dependent children, with 5 in 10 (50.5 per cent) mothers working 30 or more hours in their usual working week (excluding overtime). Dual-earner families have become the norm in the West, with the Double Day as prompt in its arrival, postnatally, as sleeplessness and stretch marks. Many of us are missing 60 per cent of a person. Many of us want a wife.

So if women's presence at home can't account for the Parent Labour Trap, does parenthood in some way catalyse traditional gender norms? Well, there's something peculiar going on when it comes to social attitudes to mothers, fathers and work. A 2012 Pew Social and Demographic Trends report in the US found that working fathers were as likely as working mothers (48 per cent of dads to 52 per cent of mums) to say they would 'rather be at home with their children than in the paid workforce', but that they needed to work because they needed the income. As one of our survey respondents resignedly put it:

'I'd love to be a stay-at-home dad and I don't give a shit about what anyone thinks, but financially we can't do it.'
Man aged 33–45, Australia

When, however, many Westerners are asked abstract questions about the ideal division of paid and unpaid labour in families with children, traditional attitudes quickly emerge. Breadwinning is still more often viewed as the father's role, with 4 in 10 Americans in a 2013 Pew survey saying it was 'extremely important' for a father to provide income for his children, compared to 25 per cent who said the same of mothers. In the 2018 British Social Attitudes survey, a third of respondents (33 per cent) said mothers of pre-school children should stay at home; 38 per cent that they should work part-time; and 7 per cent full-time. Similarly, 57 per cent of survey respondents believed women with small children should not work at all or only work part-time, with only 9 per cent supporting an equal split of parental leave between men and women.*

We also seem, as a sad corollary, to distrust men's competence on the domestic front, with 53 per cent of Americans in a 2016 study agreeing that, breastfeeding aside, women do a better job caring for children than men; and only 1 per cent of American men feeling that fathers do a better job than mothers.

Barbara Risman speculates that the hidden force between these statistics are a group we might call the 'resistant traditionals': a cohort of older (and often power-wielding) white males who support traditional gender roles at home, irrespective of the existence or age of children (28 per cent of Americans in a 2018 study stated that they believed gendered roles of labour division should hold in all households). It seems that our attitudes towards stay-at-home parenting in the abstract are oddly out of sync with both parents' dual-earning reality and many individuals' personal preferences.

Could it be that the act of becoming a parent has a traditionalizing effect on heterosexual women and men's attitudes? In a 2018 Gallup poll, Americans were asked – if they were free to

---

* Middle-class professionals were over-represented in this 9 per cent.

choose between these two options — whether they preferred to work outside the home or solely take care of their home and family. Fifty-three per cent of women overall responded that they would rather work in full-time paid labour compared to 73 per cent of men. Amongst women and men with children under 18, however, attitudes tended more to the traditional, with 39 per cent of mothers preferring the idea of working outside the home compared to 72 per cent of fathers. Meanwhile, a 2015 University of Queensland study found that, after the birth of their first child, men are less likely to subscribe to the idea that household chores should be shared equally and more likely to say that women should only work if they need the money.

The grass isn't necessarily greener for men, of course, when it comes to gendered expectations and the transition to parenthood. For fathers in heterosexual relationships, the breadwinner expectation can feel like a sanction, foreclosing their life and career options as their partner gets the right to choose which gender strategy she'll subscribe to.

'When my daughter was born, I felt like I was waiting for my life sentence. Did my wife want to continue her job as a teacher? Or would she decide to give up work or go part-time, meaning I'd have to look for a higher-paying job? I've always wanted to retrain and do something less tedious than accounting, but as I see it, my career is no longer my own. Whatever my wife wants, I have to fall into line.' Male professional aged 33–45, UK

I have to fall into line. Tim corroborates this general mood amongst his heterosexual, middle-class male friends. When Tim began his primary-carer leave when Leo was one, his 'more liberal-minded friends' reacted with a mixture of jealousy and awe.

'Most of my male friends said that it's something they would love to do, but only one of them has. But then he did it for a few months and went back to work early, saying he couldn't handle being at home with a kid five days a week.'

Saddest, he reports, are couple friends where the woman loves her job and is well paid, but ends up going part-time and slipping off the career track due to her husband's inability to cope with the stigma of not being Breadwinner Man.

'A very common story with lawyers. Frankly, I find it a bit mad.'

Barbara Risman believes that heterosexual millennial men are uncomfortable with this new reality of 'falling into line'. With their life trajectory, these men feel, depending upon their female partner's decision whether to be a full-time stay-at-home parent or to work. Which pink-collared outfit to try on for size.

'It can weigh really heavily on young men,' she says. 'This expectation of slipping into the shoes of the paterfamilias: their father's shoes.'

Marriage – often the preamble to parenthood – could be an additional factor in 'operationalizing' these traditional gender norms, with a 2014 study finding that married men contribute three fewer hours of domestic labour a week than males in a heterosexual cohabiting relationship, even correcting for factors such as class and political leaning.

The work of Shelly Lundberg, who we'll meet in Chapter Six, has found that child-related reallocations of time are, in fact, one of the surest boosts for American males' income. In households where the female partner experiences an interruption in her employment, her male partner's hours and wages increase.[48] Notably, the greatest increase in a father's wages and hours worked comes with the birth of a son.[49]

Partnered heterosexual women with children seem to have the rawest deal, shouldering the sex-role expectations of being a stay-at-home mother whilst in most cases working for a wage 30 hours or more a week. If women can't manage in this soul- and energy-sapping situation, we are at once made to understand that it is a personal problem we must solve for ourselves: by passing our work to another, underpaid, woman; by being 'tougher' in demanding flexitime from a recalcitrant boss; by putting ourselves on antidepressants,[50] or seeking restorative 'me time' in that ever-expanding list of spa-spiritual-yogic sops for late capitalism, from women-only retreats to online therapy. A 2014 US study in the *Journal of Science and Medicine* tracked levels of the stress hormone cortisol in a variety of workers throughout the day. The data clearly showed that men and women with children are both significantly less stressed out at work than they are at home, but that juggling both roles is the most stressful. Similarly, mothers who work full-time throughout their twenties and thirties report better mental and physical health at age 45 than mothers who work part-time or stay at home with children.

The past four decades represent a squandered opportunity for men and women to come together, in allyship, and change the experience of parenthood. It was key to the Second Wave feminist project that feminists should demand 'child-rearing' leave for fathers – and not simply to lighten their female part-ners' domestic load. It was also central to this great expansion of ideas that something had to be done about the ever-length-ening days the working world demanded of men. When, in 1973, former National Organization for Women (NOW) president Aileen Hernandez testified to the Joint Economic Committee of Congress about women's status, her 10-point proposal included a Humane Labor Standards Act that would extend to all workers, male and female, and include 'adequate wages, flexible hours of work, shorter work days and weeks, [and] child care facilities' alongside insurance and pension protection programmes, to mitigate income penalties paid by women and men who took caring leave.

In 2020, men are too often sidelined from the project of quality, non-sexist, hands-on parenting, because some women – frankly too fucked off with being white heterosexual men's meal ticket – fail to give up ground. Too many women respond to the disappointments of the Parent Labour Trap by going into tough-broad-who-gets-it-all-done mode, clinging on to the few privileges of that condition.

There are many uncomfortable feminist conversations we need to have, and here's one. If you're a woman in a hetero-sexual relationship, maybe six months pregnant with your first, flatulent and a bit waddly, turn to your male partner (and try not to let one rip while you do so) and ask him: would he like to take six months – a year, even – off with your kid? And ask yourself: *Would I relinquish six months of maternity leave to give my other half the opportunity to become a capable, non-sexist dad?*

If you're a father who'd thrive as a 'latte pappa':* set out your stall. Cast a scrutinizing light on those shadowy Breadwinners and Housewives that stalk us all. There might be a model of parenting that leaves everyone in your family happier, if a little less financially well off.

In Search of 'Crap Dad'

One of Tim's chagrins about being out and about with a young child is the unsolicited parenting advice he receives from women. He's been told that the food he's giving his son is 'too hot', or that Leo is being 'smothered' by his hat. On one recent outing to a children's event at a museum, Tim was repeatedly asked by women strangers whether our rosy-cheeked son had slapped cheek syndrome or was teething; 'As if I was too thick to know what colour a small, Caucasian kid should be,' he said. Male friends of mine echo his experience, sharing stories – from the UK, China, India – of being repeatedly buttonholed by women with admonishments that the dad's child is too warm, not warm enough, 'not playing right', teething, or in vari-ous specific forms of distress.

* The Swedish fathers on paternity leave that you're about to meet.

A Londoner I chat to in a coffee shop one day bridles about being congratulated for 'babysitting' his three-year-old daughter. And, in an article for the BBC's website titled 'The everyday sexism I face as a stay-at-home dad', one gay father of a toddler similarly complains: 'Instead of support, I was offered pity and condescension. "Have you thought about changing her nappy?" suggested one mother. "Do you think she's hungry?" And worst of all: "Perhaps I should hold the baby for you?"'

In her 1998 book *Gender Vertigo*, Barbara Risman asks, 'Can men mother?' Her answer: yes, but only if they don't have a woman on hand to do it for them.

'There's something about the proximity of women and gender structures that means that women will always step in,' Risman told me when we talked over Skype. 'With no mother present, men adequately perform all of the features that we'd class as mothering: attending to nappies in a timely fashion, keeping babies warm and well fed.'

Tim thinks the popular representation of fathers is to blame for this patronizing − if well-intentioned − advisory assault. 'There's this figure, Crap Dad, and you see him everywhere in adverts and on TV,' he says. 'That Boots ad, for example, when the man's at home being pathetic with a cold and his wife's holding it all together even though her arm's falling off or something.'

Crap Dad is a repeat theme in our household. Tim invokes it when I 'mumsplain' Leo's clothing and dietary requirements before a day when Tim's in sole charge of our son: 'Yes, yes, I know not to put him in soiled clothing. Am I wearing my Crap Dad T-shirt or something?'

The mention of the term, for me, always calls to mind a story that did the rounds a few years ago about a man who mistook a heated iron for a landline and suffered third-degree burns to his ear and right cheek. That's Crap Dad: staring out the window distractedly as his earlobe sizzles.

Crap Dad has a long and hapless heritage. First appearing in the 1960s, the comic trope of a man ineptly performing domestic tasks became a staple of TV sitcoms. *The Andy Griffith Show*, which aired on CBS in the US from 1960 to 1968, sees widowed husband Andy and his bemused son Opie regularly rescued from the brink of domestic disaster by spinster 'Aunt Bee' Taylor. In one episode, Opie's attempts to prepare breakfast see him dropping grapefruit, cleaning the kitchen floor using a toothbrush, burning toast and leaving eggs boiling on the stove for 45 minutes.

Matters hadn't much improved by the time of *My Two Dads*, which aired in the US from 1987–90 and the UK from 1990–2. The sitcom follows odd-couple co-parenting 'dads' Michael and Joey, who have been awarded joint custody of 12-year-old Nicole after the death of her mother Marcy (in an unlikely plot device that hinges on the uncertainty around Nicole's biological father). Michael and Joey's domestic ineptitude is routinely milked for laughs. One episode had Nicole looking in the freezer for something to eat for dinner and finding only toys; she orders pizza, gathers plates and napkins when the pizza arrives, and tells her dads to eat their vegetables.

Crap Dads are rife, too, in children's TV, with Peppa Pig's dad a porcine dolt who, in two episodes picked at random, a) gets confused about the day of the week and b) tries to put up a picture and instead hammers a massive hole into the wall. And Crap Dad's apotheosis is, of course, Homer Simpson, a man whose baby daughter is found asleep on the roof of an ice cream parlour after a day in his charge.

But it's in the world of advertising that Crap Dad put his slippered feet up, set fire to his supper and found his spiritual home. In a typical example, from a washing powder advertisement that aired in the 1990s, dad is left at home to fend for the family while his wife languishes in hospital with an unspecified illness. Rather – *doh!* – than washing his children's clothes with common-or-garden washing powder, the loveable doofus instead fills the washing machine drawer with baking soda, which foams across the floor in a seething mass. Reserve pity, too, for the infantile buffoons in nappy brand Huggies' 2012 'Dad Test' campaign, who forget to change nappies and seem incapable of holding a newborn the right way up; the dozy dads who accidentally leave a baby on a conveyor belt in the 2019 advert for Philadelphia cream cheese; or the husband in a 2010 advert for the Libman Wonder Mop, who's shown trying to clean a kitchen floor with an outdoor pressure washer. Or, indeed, the bumbling dad in AT&T's 2015 commercial 'Piece of Cake', whose wife's departure on a business trip prompts a litany of bemused screw-ups, from forgetting how to get the kids to school, to leaving the dog walker stranded outside the house and the garage door gaping open after driving away.

In 2017, the British Advertising Standards Authority (ASA) published a report, *Depictions, Perceptions and Harm*, in response to a rise in complaints to the body regarding the depiction of women and men in adverts. (Between 2015 and 2016, the ASA considered 913 cases relating to the depiction of women, and 465 relating to men.) Amongst the adverts the ASA considered harmful were those featuring 'a man trying and failing to undertake simple parental and household tasks', and those that suggested 'a specific activity is inappropriate for boys because it is stereotypically associated with girls, or vice-versa'. Proposing stronger regulations, the ASA argued that such adverts reinforce assumptions 'limiting how people see themselves and how others see them'.

A 2016 report by the consumer goods company Unilever bolsters these findings, noting that women are 'disproportionately' represented in domestic roles in TV and print advertisements globally, with just 3 per cent of advertising featuring women in managerial, leadership or professional roles. Forty per cent of the women surveyed by the multinational said that they did not identify at all with the women they saw in advertising.

'Would you like a green juice, or a coffee? They're foul, to be honest, but they're free.'

I meet Jemima in one of the branded co-working spaces that have proliferated in recent years, full of creatives scrabbling around for hot desks like kids playing a game of musical chairs. We sit on a feature settee that's as lumpy as a moonscape, and chat over the *thwack-thwack-thwack* of middle-aged white men playing ping-pong in an adjacent breakout zone. Jemima works for an advertising agency, but is about to jump ship for an extended sojourn in South America, where she intends to drown her neoliberal capitalist woes in 'an ocean of dirty Mai Tais'.

Perhaps for this reason, she's candid about the industry that's been keeping her in millennial consumables. Pale and slight and dressed top-to-toe in black, Jemima's in aesthetic – if not spiritual – harmony with her hip, late-capitalist setting. She joined the industry, she tells me, as a feminist cultural studies graduate, with some trepidation.

'I just assumed that it was full of arseholes and horrible greedy capitalists,' she says, wincing as she sips the sour black brew in her co-working branded 'hug mug'. 'It kind of is. The creative side of the advertising agency is run by white privileged males, but these are white privileged males who think that they're nice guys and that they're listening because they've done their focus groups and research...

'But, of course, consumers being paid a few quid tell you what you want them to...'

In *The Feminine Mystique*, Betty Friedan describes a visit to the head of a *Mad Men*-era American ad agency's mansion in upstate New York. The adman's ballroom has been repurposed as an office, its two-storey-high walls crammed with folders of 'depth interviews' with American housewives, the raw material for this business of 'hidden persuaders' that, by the year of the book's publication, 1963, had catalysed the greatest consumer boom in human history.

The adman's research, to Friedan, displays 'a shrewd cheerful awareness of the empty, purposeless, uncreative, even sexually joyless lives that most American housewives lead' – a lacuna of meaning he is unabashed about manipulating into dollar spend.

'I suddenly saw American women as victims of that ghastly gift,' Friedan muses, 'that power at the point of purchase.'

In 1963, American women wielded 75 per cent of the purchasing power in a rapidly growing economy. A housing boom was underway, and hundreds of thousands of ranch-style homes spidered across newly built city suburbs. These new households were ready markets for consumer goods – the cars being disgorged from Detroit's production lines at the rate of 20,000 a day, but also new householder technologies: kitchen appliances, labour-saving devices, and cleaning products formulated with the petrochemical breakthroughs of the Second World War. Indeed, many corporations explicitly shifted their focus – at the war's close – from military contracts to the American housewife.

Enter the adman, the oleaginous figure of fable who elevates the hard sell to a science. And it was, from the outset, a sexed sell.

In the adman's files, Friedan finds a 1945 study on American women's attitude towards electrical appliances. In it, American women are organized into three 'psychological' types: the True Housewife, the Career Woman and the Balanced Homemaker. The Career Woman, the report warned, was an 'unhealthy' phenomenon and 'not the ideal type of customer... too critical'; with the study advising it would be in advertisers' best interests if this social grouping did not grow any larger. It was the Balanced Homemaker

— a woman more alive to the inventions of modern science than the True Housewife (who preferred the old-fashioned elbow-grease methods) — who held promise for advertisers of appliances, a woman whose *raison d'être* was 'modern' household management (but who had helpfully low expectations). 'She "readily accepts" the help mechanical appliances can give — but does not "expect them to do the impossible" because she needs to use her own executive ability "in managing a well-run household".'

'It's nice to be modern,' the study quoted one young housewife as saying. 'It's like running a factory in which you have all the latest machinery.'

Tellingly, the appliance manufacturer's job was not to target these pliant, uncomplaining consumers, but to bring them into being: 'It would be to the advantage of the appliance manufacturer to make more and more women aware of the desirability of belonging to this group. Educate them through advertising that it is possible to have outside interests... (without becoming a Career Woman). The art of good homemaking should be the goal of every normal woman.'

Elsewhere in Friedan's account of the ad scene, we witness a more sinister manipulation of American women's desire for meaning. The housewife may buy canned food to save time and effort, but in those canned peas she'll find an opportunity to express her thwarted creativity, by 'doctoring [them] up' with her culinary skills: maybe she's a dab hand with the paprika, or — I don't know — able to render the atom bomb in raw mushroom.

'Creativeness is the modern woman's dialectical answer to the problem of her changed position in the household,' says another study Friedan quotes from. 'Thesis: I'm a housewife. Antithesis: I hate drudgery. Synthesis: I'm creative!'

Encourage women, a 'depth test' of 250 housewives concluded, to seek a 'sense of completeness' by ripping their homes apart in a 'deep cleaning' operation against that foe: 'hidden dirt'.

The adman in Friedan's report imagines this moment of putative completeness as something weirdly transcendental: 'She seizes the moment of completion of a task as a moment of pleasure so pure as if she had just finished a masterpiece of art which would stand as a monument to her credit forever.'

Sitting on the lunar landscape sofa, I ask Jemima if she thinks contemporary advertising manipulation is as rank and unapologetic as the industry, as depicted by Friedan, at its post-war height.

She pauses for a moment.

Thwack-thwack… 'Oi! Oi! Bro…' A ping-pong-playing We Worker pirouettes like a pudgy ballet dancer as he hits a clean winner over the net.

'Yes and no,' she says. 'Consumers are still segmented and narratives are developed to appeal to them, so women get squashed into these weird shapes. Advertisers decide they want to appeal to the segment they call Casual Nature Superwoman, say, so they decide they'll depict whatever scented goo they're selling as being somehow both natural and "empowering".

'But you won't find anyone in advertising using the word "manipulation"; we're all too sincere for that. Manipulation is a meta-conversation that's happening on a whole other level, as we talk about segments and how we can enhance women's lifestyles through whatever goo it is we're trying to sell.'

Jemima has agreed to show me a crop of the latest ads for detergents and appliances, to get a sense of the advertising industry's recent approach to domestic labour. First up is a 2018 advert for a fabric conditioner by market-leader Lenor – 'Parfum de Secrets Mystery'. This is a reimagining of Red Riding Hood, in which a heavily made-up young woman in a red ball gown and hood prances around a misty forest scene with a wolf in pursuit. After a bit more breathy prancing, Red Riding Hood stops at the edge of a lake, pulls her hood off and throws it over the wolf, who transforms into a dishy naked man with a carefully groomed beard.

'The product's name kind of gives the game away,' says Jemima. '*Parfum de Secret*, like a tacky French perfume. The message is: "Don't worry, love, we know you're only doing the laundry but really it's erotic and exotic and sensual."' She shakes her head and shrugs. 'I don't know... it's worse in a way, isn't it, than the mother's-love narratives that are fabric conditioner ads' stock-in-trade – you know, the soft swaddled babies and purity and all that – because whether or not the product does its job is irrelevant. What they're offering is sexual emancipation via this chore; not that you're going to get the job done quicker. Or even get it done at all.'

Despite such efforts, Jemima thinks the attachment of fabric conditioner to narratives of soft and cuddly mothering will be tough to break. Her ad agency was recently commissioned to explore the appeal of laundry products in South Asia, a market many Western peddlers of soaps and fabric softeners are trying to crack.

'We found that women who launder clothing in public prefer products that produce visible suds; almost as a way of performing their mothering in public,' Jemima says. When it came up in research workshops that her own mother had never used fabric conditioner, her fellow ad folk were aghast. 'It was bloody weird – as if I'd never been mothered, somehow.'

We move on to a category I'd had some hope for: domestic appliances. Surely the smiling, hoovering woman demonstrating the vac in heels and lippy has gone the way of the twin tub and Baby Belling?

We scroll through Samsung's recent campaign, 'Modern Masterpieces', which features renderings of Michelangelo's *David* in a pair of underpants on top of a washer-dryer and Rodin's *Thinker* staring at a spin cycle.

Samsung's 'Modern Masterpieces' advertising campaign,
Taylor Herring, 2018

'This one's interesting,' Jemima muses. 'They're clearly trying to make a statement about men's involvement in domestic chores. Yet it's still the very macho, man-and-machine image that you tend to get when men are pictured using domestic products and appliances: think of Cillit Bang or Dyson, where the images are encoded with militarism: dirt-killing machines, that kind of thing.'*

I ask Jemima if she sees glimmers of change in the industry in response to the ASA's criticism in the UK, Unilever's report, or consumer demand for something a bit less, well, 1950s. The ball hits the ping-pong table metronomically. Jemima shrugs.

'You get a few attempts to do radical things in the personal care sector: the Billie razor advert showing hairy women, for example, or the recent Bodyform sanitary towel ad showing period blood. But ads for domestic goods are still kind of conservative.'

The ASA disagrees with this gloomy prognosis. In June 2019, following their review, the agency took a stand: banning 'harmful' gender stereotypes in advertisements, including portrayals of men struggling with household chores and girls being less academic than boys.[51]

In a way, Jemima says as she drains her foul brew, the rise of identity politics such as feminism has led to a gold rush of identity and diversity issues for advertisers to mine that leaves deeper narratives intact.

'What you end up with is an exercise in box-ticking. "Hey, we've done a mixed-race family, now let's do a divorced dad with an ex-wife rolling her eyes as she loads the dishwasher."'

The same old sexed sell.

In Search of Latte Pappa

Thirty-nine-year-old Swedish computer games animator Anders whistles as he pushes his infant son Ingo through the crackling leaf-fall of Stockholm in autumn. Tim, Leo and

---

* Cillit Bang is a repeat offender. In 2015, an advertising watchdog in Spain banned a series of adverts for Cillit Bang cleaning products because they showed only women doing housework.

I have joined him on his late-morning stroll along the archipelago promenade of Reimersholme, a small island in central Stockholm that's earned the nickname 'Pappaland' for its preponderance of stay-at-home dads. Buggies abreast, we pass a playground full of bearded fathers pushing fat-cheeked children on tyre swings. Ingo lets out a wet snort.

'He's adapting to formula,' Anders explains. 'He's used to teats because when my wife was on leave, her flow was so quick he'd end up drenched. It was like we were waterboarding him, so we switched to bottles. The formula is making him gassy, though.'

Anders is amongst the 90 per cent of Swedish fathers who exercise their right to parental leave. Of these he's in a minority (14 per cent) who evenly split Sweden's generous state-funded leave – 480 days – 50/50 with their child's mother. Fourteen per cent sounds like a paltry figure, but by global standards it's remarkable. In only two other countries – Norway and Iceland, both of which have 'daddy quotas' of leave earmarked for men – do fathers take on average more than a month of fathering leave[*] (Norwegian dads average 60 days, to Swedish fathers' average of 91 days). Contrast that with the picture in much of the rest of the rich world, where fathers have the right to – at most – two weeks of paid leave, and up to 30 per cent of the men who qualify take nothing. In that other Nordic social democrat bastion, Denmark, men take a comparatively stingy 30 days of leave from a potential 32 weeks of shared leave; but that nation, tellingly, has yet to introduce an earmarked 'daddy quota'.

For all of our injunctions for women to loosen their grip on the buggy handles, state policies do little to help. In 2019, UNICEF, the United Nation's children's agency, ranked Sweden as the best place to raise a family out of 31 wealthy countries.

---

[*] Fifteen weeks are earmarked as male leave for Norway; three months for Iceland.

The UK was amongst the five lowest-ranked[52] in the report, which took into account national policies on paid parental leave for mothers and fathers, accessibility of childcare services offered up until school age (six years old), and breastfeeding rates.

In the US, famously, there's no right to paid maternity or paternity leave, with Australia only introducing a right to paid leave in 2011 (18 weeks).[53] Commensurately, men's take-up of parenting leave in these countries is low: only one in three fathers takes any time off in the US,[54] and in Australia only one in four men take the two government-funded weeks of leave available to them on becoming a parent,[55] and fewer than one in twenty exercises their rights to a period of primary parenting leave.[56] In the UK, Shared Parental Leave, introduced in 2015, allows for the transfer of up to 50 weeks of leave – 27 of them paid – from a child's mother to the father.[57] Despite the UK government heralding this policy as a 'new era', only 2 per cent of the approximate 285,000 couples a year who qualified were taking up the option by 2017–18. In fact, in the same year there was a 3.3 per cent drop in the total number of fathers who took any paternity leave, despite an increase in live births.[58]

Yet if there's a metric we should pay attention to, when it comes to the division of the drudgery and joy of new parenthood, it's parental leave. The choices we make around who will be at home with baby in those early months of parenting write the blueprint for what comes next: knowing what to do when the kid's running a temperature; knowing where the playgroups are; being able to cook supper with a child balanced on one hip.

So Leo, Tim and I had packed up the Rubik's Cube–like travel cot, 15 barely ripe pears (slow-eaters being a godsend for occupying toddler hands and gob) and a selection of mind-bendingly irritating toddler music books, and boarded a flight to Sweden.

Prosperous, tolerant and liberal, this small Scandinavian nation is the lodestar of many feminists' hopes. It has the world's highest proportion of women in paid work (72 per cent, to the US's 66 per cent) and in parliament without a quota (44 per cent of its parliamentary seats are held by women). It was the first country to declare its government and foreign policy 'feminist', and to make a feminist intervention in language (through the Swedish Academy's official adoption of the gender-neutral pronoun *hen*). But it's Sweden's latte pappas – men on paternity leave – that many disillusioned Western feminists thrill for. Amongst London women of my early-middle-aged demographic, it borders on a fetish: the fantasy of a man who melds competent fathering with effort-less masculinity and model looks.

'My dream latte pappa would be wearing ripped jeans and a tight white T-shirt like Morten Harket,' my fellow jour-nalist and disgruntled second-shifter, Maria, said on the subject. 'Hang on, no, he's Danish. Who's a dishy Swedish one?'*

'Dolph Lundgren?' I ventured.

'No – too lantern-jawed,' Maria replied. 'Alexander Skarsgård, he'd do... He could bend over and pick my socks up any day.'**

Many of us first came across the latte papas in 2017, when Swedish photographer (and latte pappa) Johan Bävman pub-lished a photography book called *Swedish Dads*. It lovingly documents Swedish dads on paternity leave in their natural habitats: vacuuming with babies on their back; washing tod-dlers in kitchen sinks and looking a bit knackered as they blow up balloons for a kid's party. The first run of *Swedish Dads* sold out within months, and its images have been exhibited, to date, in 65 countries. I interviewed Bävman about the fact

---

* I've since learned that Morten Harket is, in fact, Norwegian.
** Note from a feminist killjoy: sexy sock-pairing males are no excuse for idle objectification.

his project had become a surprise sensation and he was a little bemused. 'These intimate images of dads and their children must seem exotic to many people,' he speculated. 'If so, that is a little tragedy.'

When you consider the routine portrayals of his Anglo-Saxon counterpart – the stay-at-home dad (or SAHD) – there's little wonder that the hale and healthy latte pappa holds such a cultural cachet. Kevin, the damp stay-at-home dad in BBC's *Motherland*, is a classic example of this breed (SAHD with a silent 'h'): drippy, accident-prone, and struggling to interest his wife in sex. In a typical moment, Kevin's quivering inferiority complex leads to him almost drowning after he tries to become a 'human wave machine' at the local swimming baths in an effort to upstage charismatic dad James in front of the stay-at-home mums.

Anders and I were introduced online by a shared friend. 'You should speak to Anders – he has a *lot* to say about being a stay-at-home Swedish dad,' our friend-in-common had enigmatically promised. Anders was in the first month of a six-month stint of paternity leave for his now seven-month-old son Ingo, his wife Erin having recently returned to her job as a graphic designer.

'When I was back at work I thought Ingo's eyes were avoiding me,' Anders explains. 'So it is nice to be at home and enjoying him, although trying to keep the apartment tidy now he's crawling… phew!'

Erin and Anders have agreed that Anders will do the lion's share of the domestic chores while he's on pappa leave. Happily, Ingo enjoys bouncing on Anders's back while he does the hoovering because 'he loves the noise'. Anders enjoys cooking and gets a 'secret kick' from sorting and folding tiny socks fresh from the wash, but says Swedish minimalism can be a bind for the house-proud housespouse: 'It just shows up the dirty fingerprints more.' When not out strolling or with other dads at the latte pappa meetups staged locally (which are arranged through online dad boards that read like apologetic dating profiles), Anders and Ingo play with gender-neutral toys.

It's important to Anders that he interrogates the gendered behaviour he projects in front of Ingo: 'As I see it, even if you personally like trucks you cannot say to your son "I like trucks". There's such a weight of assumption behind that idea of men liking trucks and cars that it's just not cool, you know? You have to be vigilant and to self-correct.'

Many of the couple's liberal friends have eased the parenting labour load by contracting an Eastern European cleaner to vacuum around their minimalist mid-century modern furniture. Anders confides that he was surprised, and a little disappointed, by this. As feminists, Anders and Erin consider it unconscionable to pay an immigrant woman a subsistence wage to do their dirty work.

'How can you show off about using washable nappies when you're not washing them yourself?' Anders says. 'That's not ecological, that's unethical.'

The district we're walking through is represented in the EU by Gudrun Schyman of the radical feminist party Feminist Initiative (FI), who flamboyantly stood for a seat in the 2010 and 2014 Swedish general elections. Set up in 2005 and supported, somewhat improbably, by Jane Fonda, Pharrell Williams and the bearded man from ABBA, FI won 13 seats in the municipalities (and 3.1 per cent of the vote) in the 2014 election, running on manifesto pledges to replace 'patriarchal' marriage with a new Cohabitation Act and fund initiatives against gendered violence. In 2010, the party memorably set fire to 100,000 Swedish kronor in protest against unequal pay. Feminist Initiative campaigning was behind the parenting leave Anders is currently making the most of: three months' leave that's reserved for each parent in Sweden's government-funded 480-day shared parental leave.

We stop next to a waterfront jumble sale whose stalls are

peopled by earnest-looking dads. Booties are on sale, alongside second-hand hemp shorts and handmade kites.

Anders leans on a railing to burp Ingo and shakes his head. The portrayal of Sweden as a family-friendly feminist idyll is, frankly, a bit irritating to Swedes, he admits.

'Women only earn 85 per cent of what men earn in this "feminist country",' he says. 'Men are still five times more likely to commit suicide, and right-wing ideas are coming back. The far right, for example, are running on "family values" manifestos that want to put the father back in the office and the mother back in the home. And men are voting for these messages in their thousands. These are the men we call the *Vita kränkta män*, or "White Offended Men". They blame feminism and social democracy for all of their problems. So even in Sweden we are not living, as you suppose, this feminist dream.'

It's time to purée some butternut squash for lunch, so we leave Anders and Ingo at their apartment door. As we part, I ask Anders if he's optimistic, despite this growing assault on feminism's gains?

'Well, we now know we still have work to do,' he says, bouncing a still windy Ingo, who's looking every inch the angry white male in his buggy.

'As I see it, out-of-date masculinity – that's our next frontier. The man who thinks his self-worth is in money and that housework is effeminate. The man who denies himself time with his children out of misplaced male pride. He's the straw man we need to burn...' He smiles. 'Maybe, you know, we could mop him away?'

The next day, I leave Leo and Tim at the playground and take a train to Stockholm's suburban outskirts to meet Jens Karberg. Lanky and bearded and dressed in the sort of tight knitwear last seen on 1970s children's TV presenters, Jens is business developer at MÄN, a non-profit, feminist organization founded in 1993 to help men navigate toxic masculinities. Since the late 1990s, MÄN has run *pappagrupper* ('daddy groups') for new fathers, to help them with the emotional and familial fallout after the arrival of their first child.

We meet in the therapy room at MÄN's headquarters: a tall glass office on a strip of vegan juice bars and hi-tech buggy stores. I'm here to get Jens's take on Sweden's parenting policies, and their intimate effects. MÄN's first few years coincided with the first use-it-or-lose-it father's leave, in 1995: a month's allocation, funded by the state, that only the father could use. The second father-only tranche was introduced in 2014. I tell him that the UK, like much of the rich world, leaves the decision about who should use leave allocation to the family.

Jens knits his fingers together. 'You can say that it should be up to the family as much as you like, but the Swedish model shows that this doesn't work. We had these policies. from 1970 to 1990, and they didn't bring about change. To cut through the structural sexism – gender norms, the resistance of workplaces – leave has to be obligatory and has to be lost if men don't take it. All other examples don't work, and didn't work in Sweden.'

The Swedish example shows that, without the messaging of radical policy change, shared parental leave policies will fall flat, putting the lie to the light-touch policy solutions favoured by governments such as Britain's. At the very least, finances will dictate that, for many couples, it's heterosexist business as usual.

Jens has seen a big change in attitudes to at-home fathering since the introduction of use-it-or-lose-it leave. In the *pappagrupper* of the mid-1990s he'd ask men how they were coping with new fatherhood, and some of them would admit to stopping in a car park on the way home, pretending they were still at work to carve out time away from their families.

Now most fathers want to be hands-on dads. 'The issue now is: *How can I get more time with my kids?*'

The first studies into this cultural shift around Swedish parenting were published in 2017 and 2019. They show that parents who equally split parental leave form much stronger family units: they're more likely to stay together; if they do split it's less acrimonious; and their children are more emotionally stable. 'Equal families produce emotionally healthy children. It's pretty simple,' Jens says with a smile.[59]

Tim and I take a seat in a café in the hipster neighbourhood of Hornstull and park Leo next to a sea of other strollers. Handwritten signs advertise vegan smorgasbord and open sandwiches, the loo is covered in feminist slogans, and a sign on our café table reads: 'No we don't have Wi-Fi: we TALK to each other.'

Tim has always aspired to be a Scandinavian man, but these aspirations centre, I suspect, around an abstract yearning for chunky cable-knit jumpers and salt-and-pepper hair. How does he feel about Anders' complaint about liberals' celebration of Sweden as a star in social democratic family policy?

'I get it, but I'd still be Swedish in a heartbeat,' says Tim. 'It would be nice to have the right to decent paternity leave without being made to feel like a beta male when you ask for it. That, and I like the jumpers and bobble hats.'

We're at a moment in time when changing lives are colliding with resistant institutions.

Throughout the world, public sectors and workplaces aren't

fit for feminist purpose; they were designed for an era in which there was a presumption that workers had wives and no caring and reproduction responsibilities, even for themselves. We need a new feminist project that emphasizes a human work-life balance that takes all of our caring responsibilities and human vulnerabilities into account.

As well as taking on the structures that tame, restrain and discipline us into old modes of heterosexist parenting, women need to give ground to let men 'mother'. At a toddler music class in early 2019, I met three British dads on paternity leave who shared their principal gripes: this included the lack of men's loos with baby-changing facilities and the height of baby changing mats, but also their female partner's tendency to co-parent from the wings. Keith, who was banging a tambourine with his one-year-old daughter Silvia, was struggling with his wife's distance parenting.

'We're on reusables [nappies] and I keep finding that they've already been washed when I go to the machine in the morning. I tell Tina that it's my job to do it now, but she's just weirdly pre-programmed to do it. It drives me mad as it mucks up my laundry cycle.'

Two months after our visit to Sweden, and partly inspired by our interviews with the latte pappas, Tim and I transitioned to three months of 'pappa leave'. Soon, Tim had similar complaints to Keith's. He made it clear that my disapproval of the eccentric outfits he dressed Leo in — turned-up posh-boy collars and Christmas socks in February! — were not an excuse to micromanage our son's daily dress; and he also pointed out that I have no say, in absentia, over what the family lunch consists of, even if Leo was becoming constipated on a 'daddy diet' of pizzas and pasta carbonara.

Three weeks into Tim's stint as a SAHD, and with the early euphoria of escaping the nine-to-five having receded, Tim was looking a bit frayed. His hair, always a high-maintenance proposition requiring a specific brand of wax and ten minutes of bathroom teasing, was about as erect as a late-season dandelion, and he answered any questions more penetrating than 'What's for dinner tonight?' with near hysteria. 'I can't think about that right now, I've got too much to do! I can't think about ANYTHING!'

True, he'd made two stay-at-home dad friends, with a potential third subject to a long audition process due to the infraction of wearing cut-off jogging bottoms in the depths of winter ('I suspect he's hanging on by a thread: to parenting as well as his shorts,' Tim speculated).* But Tim was feeling isolated and, with the arrival of Leo's secondary molars waking us up seven times a night, on the edge.

One Tuesday morning, things came to a head. I was at work, having crept out of the house in near-darkness with all of the household's phone chargers in tow. Phone chargers had become a lightning rod in our home after I'd left Tim's on a train a few months before. We were now down to a tangled nest of leads that variously sparked, refused to charge or required a leaning tower of international adapters to work.

I'd screened two calls in succession from our home landline when I picked up the third. Leo's the only one who uses the landline phone – usually as a rudimentary keyboard-cum-wall club. Within a second of picking up, Tim was bellowing in my ear:

Tim: WHERE ARE ALL OF THE BLOODY PHONE CHARGERS? YOU'VE LEFT ME WITH A TODDLER AND NO PHONE!!!!

Me: Arggghh, sorry! Why don't you walk round the corner to the guy with the shop and buy one and I'll give you the money when I get back?

---

* It has since transpired that Shorts Man was airing his testicles as he has a low sperm count and his wife was keen to conceive a second child.

Tim: NO, I'M NOT GOING TO DO THAT. NO! [*I was tempted to put this last 'no' in 36-point type. It was a very shouty 'no'.*] I WANT A PROPER APPLE ONE LIKE THE ONE OF MINE THAT YOU LEFT ON THE BLOODY TRAIN. I WANT YOU TO GO TO THE APPLE STORE ON THE WAY HOME AND GET ME ONE. I'M NOT GOING TO LEAVE THE HOUSE AND GO ROUND THE CORNER AND GET A CRAPPY—

Here, I hung up. Then Tim called me back, shouted, 'HOW DARE YOU HANG UP ON ME??????' and then *he* hung up.

That night, we had it out. He wasn't finding the SAHD's lot as easy as he had hoped. Leo was unrelenting, home life was lonely, mums were unfriendly, and those hours before I walked through the door matched the old 6 p.m. witching hour that haunted the first six months of wrangling an ululating newborn — in all its nerve-fraying horror.

'I can handle it if I know he's going to nap, but when I don't get those two hours off it can be brutal,' he confided, blinking back tears. 'I think the problem is that I have no male friends around from my former life who are doing the same thing. Not one; they're all at work. And the standoffishness of mums — well, it gets you down after a bit.'

For optimistic feminists, parenthood is the mother of all reality checks. Even couples who, like Tim and me, approach parenthood with egalitarian ideals, are squeezed into traditional patterns when kids arrive on the scene. Becoming a parent should bring joy. Too often, however, this life transition congeals into misery and disappointment: wrecking parental relationships and impoverishing family life. In her 2001 book *Misconceptions*, Naomi Wolf describes babies as 'enemies to equality'. But it's not the pink-squealing tiny bipeds we have to worry about — it's the sexist social and economic practices of mothering and fathering that we all participate in, as they mitigate against us. Against the interests of women who might want to reduce their household work; against men who'd be happier carers than compulsory breadwinners; and against anyone with ambitions of establishing a fair family.

5

The Domestic Backlash

'I think, despite the emergent movement towards equality, there is also a resurgence in this Stepford Wife/ home baker/homemaker ideal which is in conflict with equality. And it leads to pressure and confusion.' Man aged 33–45, UK

*I*A concern of mine in society is that the masculine man is falling,' says a 40-something with laboriously curled hair. The woman's white floral dress echoes the motif on the tablecloth in front of her, where a three-tiered silver cake-stand is populated by pink-frosted cupcakes.

A 50-something woman wearing a white rose corsage nods vigorously, clasping a tea saucer in a hand tipped with pink-frosted nails. 'Men's pants are no longer *men's pants* anymore,' she says. 'It's like they're *skinny jeans*. They're *very...* feminine.'

The women gathered for afternoon tea in this Illinois ranch house are disciples of a movement that many believed was lost to the 1970s. In 1963, Betty Friedan's *Feminine Mystique* – the book credited with kick-starting popular Second Wave feminism – was published. That same year saw the release of a book called *Fascinating Womanhood*, and it quickly came to be seen as the anti-feminist companion to Friedan's sub-urban feminist *cri de cœur*. The author, Helen Andelin, was a middle-aged married mother of five who'd majored in Home Economics and was an observant member of the Church of the Latter-day Saints. Subtitled *How the Ideal Woman Awakens a Man's Deepest Love and Tenderness, Fascinating Womanhood* interweaves examples of ideal womanhood from history, literature and myth – the domestically minded Amelia of William Makepeace Thackeray's *Vanity Fair*; the 'angelic' Mumtaz Mahal, who inspired her mourning husband to build the Taj Mahal – with advisories on 'ideal' feminine behaviour. In a 1975 interview, Andelin told *Time* magazine that she wrote the book, and launched the Fascinating Womanhood movement that accompanied it, after realizing her marriage 'wasn't the romantic love affair she had dreamed of'. Fascinating Womanhood, Andelin added, offered a diet of spiritual self-help to 'traditionally minded women' who likewise wanted their marriages to be 'a lifelong love affair'.

Second Wave feminists soon smelled a rat in the connubial kitchen. In addition to injunctions to maintain, at all times, 'a feminine appearance', the Fascinating Womanhood movement schooled women to embrace, at all times, feminine mannerisms – 'a feminine woman is the divine adornment of humanity' – and practise obedience to their husbands, pursuivant to what Andelin biblically termed the 'Divine Order of the Family'. The book, which sold 2 million copies at the height of Second Wave feminism, quickly became known as 'the book feminists love to hate'.[60]

In 1969, Andelin followed her bestseller with *The Fascinating Girl*, which was aimed at single women; and in 1980 she published *The Domestic Goddess Planning Notebook*, designed to help aspirant ideal women to 'organize their busy lives'. In 1972, Andelin's husband Aubrey published a book on ideal 'masculine development', *Man of Steel and Velvet*.

In the mid-1980s, with sales dwindling, the movement was mothballed, along with the frowsy ruffled blouses favoured by Andelin's devotees. But with the arrival of the new millennium, something curious happened. Her worldview suddenly, unexpectedly, returned to the mainstream, as a brace of new publications – including Laura Doyle's bestselling *The Surrendered Wife* (2001) and Dr Laura Schlessinger's *The Proper Care and Feeding of Husbands* (2004) - recycled the argument for wifely obedience in pursuit of the ideal marriage. Almost 20 years later and we're in the throes of what can only be described as a Fascinating Womanhood revival. Helen Andelin's daughter Dixie Andelin Forsyth and her husband Robert D. Forsyth now run the on- and offline Fascinating Womanhood business (rebranded 'FW') from their ornament-littered family home in Springfield, Missouri. This new incarnation of the movement revolves around tea parties, femininity coaching and online femininity webinars, with over a quarter of a million followers signed up to these online tutorials in countries as scattered as the US, UK, Japan, Australia, Mexico and South Africa. In 2018, Forsyth published a sequel to her mother's book titled *Fascinating Womanhood for the Timeless Woman*, which urges women to look to Queen Elizabeth II for a model in 'poised' feminine dignity and advises them to perfect a 'girlish handshake' and create 'curves as you walk' (these efforts presumably being two differ-ent things – unless Missouri's cable TV is piping in some weird footage from the palace).

A youthful strand of the movement, #tradwives, reworks Fascinating Womanhood's fare for the confused millennial. Jalisa Cater, a 20-year-old African-American single mother from Maryland who describes herself as a 'certified and trained Fascinating Womanhood teacher' writes the blog 'The Millennial's Guide to Fascinating Womanhood'. Cater first came across Fascinating Womanhood as a teenager, when she watched an episode of the reality TV programme *Wife Swap* in which one of the contestants modelled herself on a 1960s housewife and was filmed reading a vintage copy of *Fascinating Womanhood*. She wholeheartedly embraced the FW movement at the age of 19, after her relationship with her son's father fell apart in the later stages of her pregnancy. She sees FW, she tells me via Instagram direct message, as speaking directly to our moment.

'I feel that women in my age group have been taught to hide their femininity. We don't know how to have lasting relationships, and we have been told to adapt to our Tinder culture and that Netflix and chill is the best we can get. It's difficult to be a feminine lady in a swipe right society. But that's the power, the feminine power, we need to find again.'

The broader #tradwives movement includes Make Traditional Housewives Great Again, a US group that shares a mixture of vintage recipe tips and Christian aphorisms on their social media accounts and who claim 'feminism… is based on an attempt to repeal and restructure human nature', and Women in Submission, who school women 'not to be slanderers or slaves to much wine'. They are in the company of the tens of thousands of 'vintage', 'merry/happy' and 'surrendered' homemakers who populate social media and whose profiles are awash with cake recipes and images of dewy-eyed 1950s brides.

After the Illinois tea party, host and Fascinating Womanhood femininity coach Jenny Cross loads her mother's tea service into the dishwasher and stares out of the kitchen window.

'For some reason you lose friends when you make a passion like this your life,' she says. 'I don't know what happened but I don't get as many invites from old friends.' Her voice falters, then she gathers herself, adding, brightly: 'But it's OK, because I've made lots of new friends.'

In 1991's *Backlash: The Undeclared War on American Women*, Susan Faludi charts what she describes as a popular media backlash against the gains of Second Wave feminism. Reports of such phenomena as 'the man shortage', career-woman 'burnout', 'the infertility epidemic' and 'toxic day care' were rife in the 1980s – and, as Faludi argues, erroneous. Rather than these dire predictions being true, men were in fact disadvantaged on the marriage market; housewives were more likely to suffer mental illness than working women; the fertility crisis was down to the US government's ineffectual response to a chlamydia epidemic; and day care, albeit in short supply, was showing no signs of damaging children, with the vast majority of child abuse happening in the home. And Faludi goes further, excavating a trend of alarmist reactions to women's movements – from the demobilization of Second World War workers to the depiction of suffragists as sterile – that have tracked every great feminist leap forward, from the 1840s to the 1940s, and beyond.

In 2017, US sociologists Joanna Pepin and David Cotter published the results of a study that tracked gendered social attitudes through four decades of surveys of American high school seniors. What they found surprised them. In 1994, 42 per cent of seniors (aged 18) agreed that the 'best kind of family' was one in which the man was the provider and the woman took care of the home. In 2014, however, 58 per cent of surveyed 18-year-olds believed this was true, a 38 per cent increase in preference for the Breadwinner/Housewife model.

Curiously, this reversal of attitudes towards the domestic did not hold when it came to attitudes to gender in the public sphere. More than 90 per cent of 2014 respondents, a similar figure to 1994, believed women should have 'exactly' the same opportunities as men in business and politics, indicating that millennials' traditionalizing mood extended only as far as the home. The authors dubbed this confusing phenomenon 'egalitarian essentialism', which historian Stephanie Coontz went on to define as combining 'a commitment to equality of opportunity with the belief that men and women typically choose different opportunities because men are "inherently" better suited to some roles and women to others'.

Essentialism in its original Platonic definition is the belief that all things have a set of characteristics that make them what they are; or their 'essence'. In the 1960s, Second Wave feminists repurposed the term to account for the mechanism of their oppression, by which tasks and behaviours expected of women as a group were presented as 'natural' and intrinsic to their very being. Women, so the sleight of patriarchal logic went, are natural carers, nurturers, bakers and pretty things ('*You make me feel like a nat-ur-al woman*', as Aretha memorably sang in 1967). 'Essentialism', of course, also captures the pernicious naturalized depictions of other, multiply oppressed categories of people: East Asian women being depicted as self-effacingly eager to please; Afro-Caribbean men as God-born entertainers and Afro-Caribbean 'mammies' as natural-born, generous cooks.

So why would this 'natural aptitude' argument – adroitly dismantled by 1960s and '70s feminists – be resurgent amongst a generation portrayed as socially liberal to a fault? It would be one thing if egalitarian essentialism were just a story we told ourselves in order to make sense of things; in order to live. But backsliding is evident, too, in 20- and 30-somethings' lived experiences. Despite those abiding clichés of the gender labour gap – the self-negating boomer housewife and overwrought Gen X mum – it is, in fact, younger women, aged 26 to 36, who put in the greatest number of hours of unpaid work: 22 hours a week in a 2015 Office for National Statistics survey; and 17 in the US. In the UK, the number of men opting to be stay-at-home dads, which had been steadily rising since 1993, went into a pronounced decline in 2017.[61]

So what's going on? Pepin and Cotter suggest that a 'cultural panic' about women with higher earnings, and their threat to the gender order, might be to blame for this backlash, but with women only out-earning men in 25 per cent of US families based on a heterosexual union – and in 31 per cent of their

UK equivalents — the argument seems somewhat weak. Dan Carlson, assistant professor of Family and Consumer Studies at the University of Utah, has another explanation. Carlson sees the rise of egalitarian essentialism — which is far from egalitarian, as we've seen, in its effects on gendered workload — less as a product of 'gender threat' than as a pragmatic response to the absence of work/family policies that make domestic equality possible. Carlson argues that support for domestic equality persists among children of dual-earners whose parents had access to family-friendly work policies, but that children who have seen their working parents 'overwhelmed by economic and time pressures' may have become discouraged. Harking back to natural roles can, in this view, be read as a case of nostalgic reimagining: egalitarian families don't work out, but hey, that's OK, we can cosy up with the eiderdown of natural-born maternal love.

I meet Toya, Kate, Tony and Loll in a chain café in South London, where they order sugary drinks piled high with marshmallows and drink them with their heads bent over their smartphones. 'Sugar is our drug. Probably because we can't afford alcohol,' Toya jokes, before adding: 'Guys, let's pile our phones.'

Toya, a Nigerian-British film studies graduate who babysits Leo at weekends, has helped me to convene an informal group of Britons in their teens and early twenties to chat about young Britons' attitudes to housework. Phone-piling, she tells me, is her social group's signal that it's time to put away the devices for a heart-to-heart. The first of the group who reaches into the Jenga pile of black boxes — to check an Instagram feed or message a potential date — gets the forfeit of paying for the next round of sugar-laden pick-me-ups.

'Kate's dating, so it's usually Kate,' Toya says, with a conspiratorial wink at her friend.

I ask the assembled young people if they ever consider the prospective division of chores in their adult homes.

I'm greeted with silence and a few slurps. Then Loll, who's 19 and non-binary, answers.

'The way I see it, for our mums there used to be two, I guess you'd call them, life options. Either you'd become this, like, hotshot career woman, or you'd do the whole stay-at-home-mum thing. But for us there are different options. Girls who don't want to go to uni usually say they want to get famous, or marry someone famous.'

'Yeah, it would not be, like, cool to say you wanted to stay at home and change nappies, you know?' Kate adds.

I report the US findings to the group: that today's teens in that context have become more traditional, or perhaps more cynical, in their attitudes to division of labour in the home. I notice Tony, a young man with a very pale face, pulling at his tawny-blond fringe. It's the only hair on his shaved head apart from a narrow ponytail-style tuft at the back. A phone beeps and eight eyes dart to the pile. 'What do you think?' I ask him.

'Well, my mum just does it all in our house,' he says. 'She nags me to do it and I do a bit, but I just see it that having my clothes washed and food in the fridge is the only plus side.'

I raise an eyebrow in enquiry.

'Yeah, because I won't get to leave home until, like, 2032, because I won't be able to afford it.'

Toya cuts in.

'I was raised by a single mum and so me and my sisters do loads,' she says. On balance though, she adds, she understands where the US respondents are coming from. 'I don't think they're – you know, conservative,' she says. 'I just think they're being realistic. There's a lot of boring bollocks to do in life, and some people, usually women, just have to get on with it. Maybe we're just realistic.'

For some US cultural commentators, the portrait of disillusioned millennials turning to the comfort of essentialized sex roles lacks nuance. Barbara Risman talks[62] of a fragmentation of millennials' attitudes to gender. As Risman sees it, American 1980s- and 1990s-born cohorts include a number of extremes: 'true believers', who subscribe to the notion of binarized gender attributes and roles, and often come from literalist religious backgrounds; 'innovators', who experiment with 'masculine' and 'feminine' behavioural traits (and are often 'gender policed' by contemporaries when they do so); and 'rebels', who totally reject the gender binary and are opposed to social organization based on sexual roles. Toya and her group – the non-binary pessimist, the trad punk, the pragmatic daughter of a single mum – have characteristics of each of these groupings. This echoes Risman's contention that the largest cohort are in fact 'straddlers': proud to combine masculine and feminine traditions, but on some level believing in intrinsic male and female characteristics ('that women are soft, say, and men rough,' as Risman put it in our interview).

Diversity notwithstanding, it's clear that we are seeing a hardening of some young women's attitudes to their future prospects – at least in the US, and at least amongst heterosexual women. Millennial women in early adulthood are already making the choices that will allow them to balance work and motherhood – or opt out of motherhood – in the future, with 40 per cent of the female undergraduates who spoke to Risman stating that their choice of degree, and career, was made with a clear view to the demands of future parenthood's Double Day.

Could it be that the cohort unfairly derided as 'Generation Me' has given up on structural change, privatizing material and sex-role pressures with their own 'workarounds' to the stalled revolution? It's a depressing outcome if so. Yet it fits with something my 23-year-old house-sharing friend from Chapter Four, Laura, told me at the end of our vegan rendezvous:

'My generation want our social lives tailored to our uniqueness: to our identities and political affiliations, so we curate our social lives to people we have common beliefs with. There are good reasons for this: I self-select because I find it exhausting and undesirable to have to explain things like intersectional feminism. The problem being, of course, that we disappear into our individual identities. How do we come together to create any sort of social change when we're so atomized?'

The generation who grew up in the shadow of 9/11 will spend most of their young adult lives battling housing and job insecurity, which will naturally affect fertility rates and the setting up of stable homes. And what will they be greeted with when, in middle adulthood, they step, keys clinking, over the threshold of their first, settled home? If they're female, heterosexual and cisgender – and often even if they're not – they'll find a broken feminist promise festering like a forgotten chip pan in the sink.

Fireside Nationalisms

If the cohort we might dub the 'resistant traditionalists' are small in number, their attitudes are gaining political influence. From Sweden's Democrats to Trump's Republicans, right-wing nationalists are thundering, cocks aloft, through the halls of power. The US, India, Brazil, Austria, Italy, Hungary and Poland all have radical right-wing politicians as leaders or in government. Far-right parties have also notched up electoral triumphs in France and Germany, and the UK's vote to leave the EU was a decision encouraged, in part, by populist nationalist rhetoric.

Central to this wave of nationalist narratives, alongside much-documented immigrant scares, is social conservatism: appeals to traditional 'family values', in which mother and home are sanctified as antidotes to globalization and 'multiculturalism'. These administrations share two broad features: hostility to liberal democracy and a desire to subordinate 'uppity' women. Propping up male authority and promoting a nuclear family that sticks to the gender binary are central tenets of the broader nationalist project.* Part of a politically expedient program that pits a certain and immutable 'us' of the nation-state against a slippery and alien 'them'.

Donald Trump has long made his attitudes to domestic responsibilities clear. When asked if he changed nappies on the *Opie and Anthony* radio show in 2005, he said: 'There's a lot of women out there that demand that the husband act like the wife, and you know, there's a lot of husbands that listen to that… I'm really, like, a great father, but certain things you do and certain things you don't. It's just not for me.'

That same year, in an interview with shock jock Howard Stern, he continued in a similar macho vein: 'Marla used to say, "I can't believe you're not walking Tiffany down the street," you know, in a carriage. Right, I'm gonna be walking down Fifth Avenue with a baby in a carriage! It just didn't work.'

Brazil's far-right populist president, Jair Bolsonaro, is the epitome of the new-model heterosexist lug. In 2016, as the then Federal Deputy for Rio de Janeiro, he called the birth of his daughter 'a moment of weakness' (coming, as she did, after Bolsonaro had sired four sons). In 2003, he was caught on camera telling a Brazilian congresswoman, 'I would never rape you because you don't deserve it'; and in 2000, when questioned about his ex-wife's domestic abuse allegations: 'I never hit my ex-wife. But many times I wanted to shoot her.'

Bolsonaro's voting record is unambiguous. In 2013, he voted against the introduction of a bill of labour rights for Brazilian domestic workers, later going on record with his

---

* As are explicit attacks on ideology that proposes gender as something fluid or unfixed, as seen in the assault on the Gender Studies academies in Turkey, Brazil and Hungary.

opinion that women should earn less 'because they continue to draw a salary when on maternity leave', and shortly after attaining office as president, Bolsonaro pledged to remove references to feminism, homosexuality and violence against women from school textbooks.

Trump, Bolsonaro, and strongmen Rodrigo Duterte in the Philippines and Viktor Orbán in Hungary, use the notion of an upside-down gender order as a device to both validate their political order and discredit preceding regimes. The majority of Trump voters agreed with the statement that America, under foregoing administrations, had grown 'too soft and feminine' in a 2016 poll. 'We want a Brazil that is similar to the one we had forty, fifty years ago,' Bolsonaro declared, in linking his 'counter-revolution' to a revolution against uppity women; eliding the fact that the Brazil of this supposedly halcyon period was a military dictatorship.

In Britain, nationalist politician and father of six Jacob Rees-Mogg boasts of never having changed a nappy: 'No, I haven't. I don't think nanny would approve because I'm sure she'd think I wouldn't do it properly.' Rees-Mogg often whimsically invokes his traditional household, where women retire from the table after dinner and 'we still have Lux soap flakes in our pantry that my grandmama stockpiled for the Second World War' (you may recall that soap flakes left post-war women's hands red-raw). And don't look to our current prime minister (a man who once promised that voting Tory would 'cause your wife to have bigger breasts') for a progressive view on domestic labour. In 2017, the Foreign Office – under the then Foreign Secretary Boris Johnson – was found to be paying its cleaners £7.20 an hour, which was less than the London Living Wage.*

Narratives such as Rees-Moggs', in which pre-feminist domestic arrangements are presented as both playful and natural, might seem little more than daft. But they are, in

---

* An average of £2 less, per hour, than other government departments.

fact, odd and dangerous. Odd in the fact that they're an abrupt reversal of the political discourses that have held sway for decades, in which centre-right economic policies have combined with liberal attitudes to social issues such as gay marriage and (outside the US, at least) women's reproductive rights, to create the new liberalism. Today, the social liberalism/economic conservatism compact is out, as this new wave of right-wing nationalist politicians posit liberal social policies as the bogeywoman, conflating feminism with the failures of global free-market capitalism and stoking unease felt by many voters about rising inequality and the pace of social change. In the 2016 US election, Hillary Clinton became the focus of these collapsed-together hatreds. 'Iron My Shirt, Nasty Woman' — a 2016 presidential race poster, carried by a corpulent white man and designed to taunt Hillary supporters, summed up the mood.

In *The Hillary Doctrine*, US political science academic Valerie M. Hudson and co-author Patricia Leidl chart Trump's manipulation of Clinton's 'debased femaleness' to undermine her political plausibility. Populists' narratives of righting an upside-down and feminized gender order, she says, play upon naturalized power asymmetries within the domestic sphere. 'The first [gender] difference that individuals notice is the difference between sexes in one's own home,' Hudson told *The Atlantic*. 'That establishes the first political order, the nature of how things should be in the country.' Right-wing conservatives, it follows, wield a powerful tool in countries where men reign in the private, domestic sphere and women — especially feminist women — threaten male dominance in the public arena. In the words of US journalist Zoe Chace, 'for a lot of people, Make America Great Again was about "Mak[ing] Men Great Again".'

Parallels can be seen in Italy, where Deputy Prime Minister Matteo Salvini compared the female president of the lower house of parliament to an 'inflated sex doll'. Italy's populist coalition government, which assumed power in 2018, is promoting legislation that critics say would eliminate child support and prosecute women who accuse their husbands of domestic violence if their husbands are not convicted. In Hungary, Prime Minister Viktor Orbán has spoken of a 'comprehensive agreement' with Hungarian women to bear more children – promoting debt relief for these women if they give birth to at least three children, and a lifetime income-tax exemption if they produce four or more offspring. This state-promoted fertility drive, under the rubric of 'traditional family values', is an explicit attempt to 'restore Hungarian identity', which Orbán depicts as under threat from immigrants and the nation's Roma population. (Hungary's 'migration problem', the Organisation for Economic Co-operation and Development notes, is in fact an emigration problem rather than an immigration problem, with over a million Hungarians having left for Europe's more prosperous northern and western regions since 2006, a demographic trend that's increased since Orbán came to power.)

Predictably, religious conservatives have seen their moment to weigh in on the debate that's taking shape around that old conceit: traditional family values. In a 2019 piece for the *New Statesman*, postmodernist gender theorist Judith Butler discussed a new mood of anti-feminist rhetoric within the Catholic Church. Butler tracks the trend back to a 2004 letter written by the Pontifical Council on the Family to the Bishops of the Catholic Church. The letter, invoking Mary and her 'dispositions of listening… humility… waiting' as a model of feminine passivity, warned that 'gender' (aka feminist theory) threatened to destroy feminine values important to the Church, foster conflict between the sexes, and contest the 'natural' hierarchical distinction between male and female upon which family values and social life are based.[63]

The positioning of feminist theory as the enemy of family values is gaining traction and saliency across the far right. Alternative for Germany (AfD), the first far-right party to enter the German parliament since the Second World War, has pledged to discontinue all Gender Studies funding, university appointments and research, and in 2018 Viktor Orbán banned Gender Studies courses at Hungarian universities. In Turkey, Recep Erdoğan's populist Sunni-Turkish nationalist Adalet ve Kalkınma Partisi (which, surreally, translates as the 'Justice and Development Party') has waged a campaign of intimidating feminist academics and purging them from their posts. Erdoğan unambivalently dismisses childless Turkish women as 'deficient' and 'incomplete'.

Graffiti in Istanbul responding to Erdoğan's depiction of childless women as 'deficient... incomplete'. It reads: 'Half a woman (multiplied) by (square root) of trans (plus) 3 lesbians (divided by) 5 bisexuals = how much?'

These tendencies are nothing new. In times of economic and political uncertainty there's often recourse to ideologies that glorify the family as a private world and frontier that keeps the souls of men, women and children alive. In 2009, in the throes of the subprime mortgage crisis, a mainstream US newspaper, remarkably, ran a story invoking such rosy ideologies. 'Love kept us warm in the depression,' it read, 'and we'd better look to love in our contemporary excursion into hard times.'

It's this appeal to women's labours of love as solution and succour that saw women bearing the brunt, in crisis-hit Greece, of the collapse of the state childcare, adult social care and healthcare systems, even as they were the first to be laid off from their waged jobs. It's also the mechanism that sees females who've fought for their nations and revolutionary causes – from the Second World War to the Arab Spring – being disciplined back into the home as an act of emergency nation-state building in the aftermath of uprisings and revolution. When the Muslim Brotherhood's Mohamed Morsi replaced long-time dictator Hosni Mubarak as President of Egypt in 2012, Morsi overturned a ban on female circumcision, abolished a quota guaranteeing women's seats in parliament, and brought in legislation that made it trickier for a woman to divorce an abusive husband – despite the fact that the 2011 revolution had seen tens of thousands of women taking to the streets. Similarly, after the ousting of Muammar Gaddafi in Libya, one of the new government's first acts was to repeal a Gaddafi-era law that effectively banned polygamy.[64] Time and again women activists have been failed by promises of a post-revolutionary feminist utopia.

In times of crisis and rapid change, it's a human tendency to resort to cosy ideologies of hearth and home – and as it was after the two world wars and after revolutions, so it is now in our moment of existential crisis, and so it will be again. Populations voting for these right-wing strongmen (not to mention right-wing beta males such Trump and Boris) have grievances that we can't simply discount as ill-founded or fictitious. Jobs have disappeared, and as automation continues its march they will continue to do so. In the wake of the 2008 Great Recession, inequality has risen across the rich world as the social security net has, in many nations, been worn threadbare. Little wonder that the field has been left wide open for political parties that the LSE's Dr Jonathan Hopkin refers to as 'anti-system' rather than populist[65] – right-wing parties such as Alternative for Germany and the Swedish Democrats, but also the anti-system left such as Podemos in Spain and Jeremy Corbyn's Labour Party. These political disruptors all seek, from their differing political stances, to undermine the legitimacy of the global order they oppose.

For all this, the narratives employed by the nationalist right need to be countered. And their tactics present a dilemma for feminists in the public arena in countries where these discourses become normalized – for the more we resist these stories of hearth and home, the more we fall into the 'Clinton' trap of being uppity, unnatural women. Resist, however, we must: there's simply too much at stake. A February 2019 piece, by *The Atlantic*'s contributing editor Peter Beinart, drew a parallel between the average hours of unpaid labour a woman performs in the home and the success of narratives attacking women's power in the public sphere. Looking at 2019 OECD figures for unpaid household chore allocation, it concluded:

> There is a striking correlation between countries where women and men behave more equally in the home and countries where women are more equally represented in government. Take Sweden [it's always Sweden], 44 percent of whose parliamentarians are women. There, the gap between the amount of housework done by men and that done by women is less than an hour a day… In Hungary, where women account for 10 percent of parliament, it is well over two hours.

The new authoritarian nationalism reminds us of the ongoing relevance of the Second Wave feminist mantra 'the personal is political'.

I f the old battles have to be fought with fresh impetus in politics, do we have to fight the same fight in the field of pop culture, too?

Superficially, cultural representations of the proper division of labour in the domestic sphere are more nuanced than in the early 1990s, when Susan Faludi chronicled the backlash to Second Wave feminism. An archive search of major newspapers yields, from the past decade, stories celebrating egalitarian householding ('Housework "makes British men more attractive"', *Telegraph*, 2009; 'Fathers are happier when doing more of the housework, says study', *Guardian*, 2010; '"What century are you living in?" Facebook post urging women to "live unselfishly towards their husbands" and "do their housework joyfully" is slammed by working mothers', *Daily Mail*, 2018). However, for each of these there are multiple alarm-sounding reports about the payoffs and penalties of egalitarian domestic arrangements ('Couples who share housework are more likely to divorce, study finds', *Telegraph*, 2012; 'What they DON'T tell you about being a stay at home dad: No one will give you a job afterwards', *Daily Mail*, 2018). In a new twist on Faludi's theme, these warnings are often couched as concern for women's well-being ('Not doing enough housework is "making women fat", study claims', *Daily Mail*, 2015; 'Housework adds 3 years to your life (if you're a woman)… but cleaning, hoovering and doing the laundry is of little benefit to men's health', *Daily Mail*, 2016; 'Can daily housework help you lose weight? Chores like vacuuming, ironing and dusting can help you drop more than ONE KILOGRAM per month', *Daily Mail Australia*, 2016; 'Housework could reduce the risk of breast cancer by 13%', *Daily Mail*, 2012).

Then there's the novel strand in which alarmist declamations are made about the effect of domestic labour arrangements on couples' sex lives. In 2014, a *New York Times Magazine* cover story by Lori Gottlieb entitled 'Does a More Equal Marriage Mean Less Sex?' (Strapline: 'He cooks, she cleans, they both work and take care of the kids. It's the perfect egalitarian marriage. There's just one problem.') clocked up 20,000 shares in its first few hours online. It was inspired by the findings of a study on chore distribution and sexual frequency, published by US sociologists Sabino Kornrich, Julie Brines and Katrina Leupp in the *American Sociological Review*. It found that 'households in which men do more traditionally male labor and women do more traditionally female labor report higher sexual frequency'. The secret to sexual chemistry, the study seems to indicate, is for men and women to stick to their gendered labour lanes.

'The more alike men and women are at some level, the less interesting we become to each other,' US sociologist Mark Regnerus commented to *Time* of the same study, adding that 'similarity is not conducive to eros'. Other commentators speculated that the effect was down to the activation of an 'incest taboo' – that domestically egalitarian partners came to see each other as siblings rather than spouses.

The furore provoked by Gottlieb's piece was straight from the 'backlash' playbook: fodder for traditionalists and a red rag to feminists ('Why do we have to keep finding something wrong with getting men to help?'; 'This was surely written to bait feminists like me to click… But hell, ya got me!').

A stock library's take on choreplay, illustrating 'Why would a man agree to more household chores?', a June 2016 story in the *Daily Mail*

In 2015, the choreplay saga took an unexpected turn, with the arrival of a quantitative study by Sharon Sassler at Cornell University. Sassler's study, which was based on a larger 1975–2012 data set – rather than Kornrich et als narrow 1980s and '90s sources – found that not only do domestically egalitarian couples have more sex, but that the sex they have is of 'better quality'. Further, the results showed specific correlations: that a higher male contribution to housework (33–65 per cent of the domestic load) leads to more sex; and a fair division of child-care correlates with better-quality sex. Explaining the findings in a 2016 briefing paper, Sassler said:

> Relationship quality and stability are generally high-est when couples divide up the household labor in a way they see as equitable or fair... It is therefore not surprising that couples with more egalitarian divisions of routine housework report being more satisfied with sexual intimacy today than they did 20 years ago.

She added, with an evident eye to print headlines: 'Sharing housework is now perceived as a sexual turn-on.'

In an article for *The New York Times*, 'How Men Can Succeed in the Boardroom and the Bedroom', arch liberal feminist Sheryl Sandberg and co-author Adam Grant weighed into the debate, with the contention that 'Couples who share chores equally have more sex... if [men] want to do something nice for their partners, instead of buying flowers, they should do laundry... Choreplay is real.' Sandberg's trite transactional drew immediate mockery from feminists, including the sharing on Twitter of a #choreplay reward chart: 'change blowout diaper = naked hula dance from yours truly... clean up throw up = BJ!!!'

In a more reflective response piece from US think tank the Council on Contemporary Families, Stephanie Coontz makes the point that data on sexual frequency from breadwinners and housewives in the 1950s and '60s, on which many of the earlier 'choreplay' panics were based, is unreliable, as they're skewed by barely consensual 'dependency sex': 'In marriages of the 1950s and 1960s, wives often reported having sex more often than they wanted because they were dependent on their husbands. Now that women feel free to say no, they are more likely to say yes when they feel the relationship is fair.'

The latest popular media consensus that housework is, in fact, an aphrodisiac ('Couples, sharing the housework leads to more satisfactory sex', *South Africa Times,* March 2018; 'Men who help with housework have more and better sex', *Telegraph,* November 2015) puts the 'choreplay' furore to bed, for now. Though it's only a matter of time until this stock horror rises, once more, like an inappropriate erection.

My favourite face of the 2010s backlash against feminism is the male complaint of being too sensitive to contribute to housework and childcare. In a January 2019 interview for the *Sunday Times Magazine,* notorious ex-lothario, media personality and spiritualist Russell Brand describes himself at length, to interviewer Decca Aitkenhead, as a sensitive New Age dad, before going on to argue that he is in fact *too sensitive* to contribute to the parenting labour load.

Has he spent 24 hours in sole charge of his children? Aitkenhead asks.

'No. She [Brand's wife] wouldn't go away for 24 hours... She respects and cares for their safety too much. Yes, I'm very, very focused on the mystical connotations of [his daughter] Mabel's beauty and grace. Not so good on the nappies and making sure they eat food.'

Aitkenhead pushes: Why doesn't he do more of the practical parenting?

'I'm still of a romantic and reflective and, possibly, to give it its proper name, a religious disposition. That's my world view. That's not necessarily what you want organising pragmatic, bureaucratic, managerial stuff,' Brand opines. Like sticking the nappy-rash cream and breadsticks under the buggy?

After a bit of back-pedalling – 'I feel like I'm doing a f****** probation interview' – Brand doubles down on the spiritual sexism: 'I'm sensitive and awake and aware, so I have to dial a lot of shit down to go through normal life.'

Yet the complaint of spiritualist sensitivity is little more than a refined take on the logic of Crap Dad: *I'm no good at diary management/remembering which way up my son goes/cooking dinner without setting fire to my feet... But you, sensible, mature woman/wife thing, are my saviour.* (*'Congratulations, darling*, Suzy breathes into your ear. *You're a Real Woman.*) Naturalized sex roles are like that: as malleable as a Vileda SuperMop.

Or, of course, the patriarchy.

In 2009, I spent a day at the Delhi villa of a rich Punjabi industrialist, who we'll call Vaish. Then in his late thirties, Vaish was heir to a dairy manufacturing empire and had just married Tiffany, a Texan former beauty queen who drifted silkily around their palatial home in a gem-bedizened pink saree. Directed by Tiffany, servants trailed in our wake bearing platters of silver-leaf sweets as Vaish gave me a tour of the house. I'd come to chat to the couple about the trials and pleasures of cross-cultural marriage for a British women's magazine. The story had been commissioned in response to a report on the rise of 'assortative mating', or the tendency for heterosexual couples to marry within their race, class, education and income brackets. The couple, my newspaper editor had romantically believed, represented something contrary to this trend: two hearts from opposite poles, brought together by the peculiar glue of romantic love.

After the tour, we took a seat in Vaish's architectural pride and joy: a pub he'd fallen in love with on a trip to Britain. He had offered the bemused British landlord £10,000 on the spot and, after a 4,000-mile journey, its mahogany interior had pride of place on the third floor of his plush South Delhi home – sticky benches, drip trays and all.

Vaish poured me a foaming pale ale, and Tiffany diffidently arranged her jewel-laden hem across the red-upholstered bench. Emboldened by ale or perhaps the rare opportunity to reflect on his life, Vaish became unexpectedly confessional. He would quite liked to have been a poet, he confided, but as the inheriting son of a prominent industrialist the expectation weighed heavily upon him to 'be a *man*'. Or, he corrected, 'a man amongst men', which entailed the following: working long hours for the family business, bulking out in his home gym, and seeking out and marrying a pretty wife who'd be, as his mother put it, a 'testament'. Vaish's entire childhood, he now saw, had been designed to socialize him into this hyper-masculine, go-getting role.

'My education was not an option: economics, politics and sport,' he said. 'There were values I needed to take on to run the business – masculinity, strength, ruthlessness. And there were things I couldn't be: artistic – you know, soft.'

Tiffany sat there, smiling and silent, playing with her hem as if it were so many brilliant diamonds cascading through her manicured fingers. Far from two hearts from opposite poles, I thought, here were two souls brought together by complementary gender strategies.

A few years later, I read a paper on sex-role socialization amongst the world's super-rich. It talked of the global elite's imperviousness to the shifts in gender norms seen, in the late 20th century, in the rich world's middle classes. Traditional attitudes to gender, the paper argued, had come to define this rarefied global class: with men groomed to inherit businesses and marry traditional, feminine wives, and daughters raised to be marriageable within elite circles rather than to assume the reins of business.

I thought, of course, of Vaish and Tiffany. And I wondered, too, how these trends might map onto growing global inequalities and the fact that the rich are growing richer and increasingly calling upon the middle classes to perform morphing categories of domestic labour: as highly paid personal assistants, housekeepers, social diary managers and present-buyers.

The predominance of binarized gender roles amongst the super-rich is often blamed on the new oligarchy: that cohort of flashy Russians who accrued their wealth in the resources grab that followed the collapse of the USSR (and who have been blamed, variously, for subsequent Russian social collapse and the plummeting of working-class male life expectancy). Russian president Vladimir Putin, of course, is a peculiar model in this regard: a former KGB intelligence officer who – posing, for example, on horseback with his top off and wearing spurs and reflective sunglasses – embodies a version of masculinity best described as 'sublimated homoerotic Wild West' (or, as Tim's brother puts it, 'ageing techno raving dad on his way to an off-grid festival'). Putin is silent on his attitudes to nappy-changing, though I think we can guess where he might lie on the scale from latte pappa to macho lug. A Moscow-based journalist friend contextualizes Putin's masculine display from a Russian point of view: 'He thinks he's a Cossack, but of course he comes across as a cock.'

Patriarchy is live and kicking amongst the plutocracy, according to the academic Elisabeth Schimpfössl. She spent five years embedding herself with the Russian super-rich for her PhD thesis, which became a book on Russian elites and their social mores: *Rich Russians: From Oligarchs to*

Bourgeoisie. In the book, Schimpfössl recounts a move away from the flashy ostentation for which the 1990s oligarchs were famed (Vogue cigarettes stubbed out in extravagant plates of caviar).* Despite such shifts, however, a strict sex-role binary pertains amongst the Russian super-rich. Women are expected to be decorative, and female demureness is prized. As one Muscovite socialite put it to Schimpfössl, 'being the talking girl is not good manners'. I think of Tiffany's pregnant silence.

Children of the Russian super-rich, according to Schimpfössl, are raised into sex-ascribed roles that Vaish would immediately recognize.

'Amongst the Russian super-rich there's a belief that if women are very successful, it won't work out on the family side,' Schimpfössl tells me, over coffee in the City of London, where much of the oligarchy's filthy money is laundered[66] and their needs, some of them lurid, are met via a circuit of Russian-speaking lawyers, property agents and escorts.

'By the "family side", I mean marrying and having children. So sons will have to study business, law or engineering, whereas women can study what they like – as, you know, it doesn't matter anyway. What is important for girls is using university to find a husband.'

This reminds me, I say, of Betty Friedan's depiction of young women in early-1960s America: women who felt compelled to become affianced at younger and younger ages to cash in on their key currencies – youth, fertility – under the exacting standards of the feminine mystique. As Friedan describes it, US universities in the 1960s became little more than marriage markets and antechambers for marriage, with teenage girls often dropping out to work as secretaries and financially support their fiancés' college degrees as soon as they had, in

* Behaviour a Russian news correspondent friend once saw in a Moscow bar – and which became, for her, a metaphor for the excesses of the oligarchy.

contemporary parlance, 'hooked' their man. Between 1955 and 1965, Friedan estimates, the average age of first marriage in the US dropped from 23 to 19 years old, and fertility rose to an average of five children per woman (from three in the post-war years).

'Yes – it's true, in a way, of rich Russian women today,' Schimpfössl agrees. 'For example, I meet 20-year-old women from rich families who are really *very* depressed because they cannot yet find a husband.'

Schimpfössl has witnessed the oligarchy marriage race at first hand. She recounts an incident from 2010, when she was at the after-party of the Champions League football final in Moscow. Manchester United had been pitched against Chelsea, owned by Russian-Israeli billionaire Roman Arkadyevich Abramovich. Attending with rich Russian friends, Schimpfössl was shocked to witness young Russian women, dressed in heels and tiny skirts, attempting to scramble into the VIP tent enclosure on their stomachs across muddy ground. 'The tragic thing being that Chelsea had lost, so Abramovich and his crew had been too miserable to attend,' she says. 'All that effort and muddy clothing, and there was no point. It was desperate.'

In polite enclaves of London's Knightsbridge and Chelsea, and on Manhattan's Upper East Side, plutocrats' patriarchal attitudes are even redesigning our built environment. An architect friend, Ben, tells me that he's worked on prominent London luxury developments that are designed with 'servant circulation' stairwells last popular in 19th-century country houses, so that their well-heeled owners don't have to come face-to-face with the growing army of feminized hired help. These buildings are hidden from curious eyes, behind glass facades, security gates and concierge desks.

Schimpfössl has heard horror stories, too: of young maids imported from the Russian-speaking Baltic and kept in abusive conditions by their rich Russian employers. While we might think that resident servants are a relic of a bygone age, or a quirk of distant cultures, there are more live-in domestic workers in London today than there were in the 1890s[67] — in large part thanks to the new, globally circulating super-rich.

'Russians are the most — how do I put it? — brutal, in their housekeeping,' Schimpfössl says. 'They explicitly ask for maids' quarters to be built in the basement with no daylight, for example. And they don't do this in Moscow — they do this in London.'

Many of us enjoy marvelling at the daft and exotic antics of the super-rich, imagining that their outrageous lifestyles have a negligible impact on our lives. Reports of rich Russians building six-storey basements beneath their Knightsbridge homes have become a stock-in-trade in London newspapers. But before we part company, Schimpfössl, who is Austrian, gives me pause for thought.

'You know, it was not just Russian women I saw running after rich Russian men… It was young English women too,' she says, carefully watching my reaction. 'As I see it, there is little difference between Russia, the US and the UK. In Austria, friends laugh at the idea that there would be such a thing as a website where women chase sugar daddies, or agencies that set up "accidental" encounters with rich men like Abramovich. But in the UK and US you have both, because both nations have extreme social inequality and little social mobility.'

I walk Schimpfössl outside into the spring chill of the city. Suited men and women occupy the pavement, eating sandwiches as they walk or miserably nursing their vape sticks.

'It is my theory that the more unequal a country, the more make-up women wear and the higher the high heels,' she adds, before striding away through the suits in her sensible boots.

What of rich men's domestic input? It's not much of a stretch to speculate that men who've been socialized into masculine traits and chosen decorative younger wives aren't wont to do the dusting after they've put their Lamborghinis to bed. A 2015 University of Warwick study led by economist Dr Clare Lyonette was, in this sense, predictable, finding an inverse link between male wealth and housework input. It showed that whilst men on lower incomes are increasingly happy to pick up the duster, higher male earners — the super-rich and the merely rich — are proving more resistant, with increasing wealth correlating with reduced domestic effort.

'We found that while men in these households do also recognize the need to help their partners, they remain reluctant to lift a finger and appear to simply throw money at the issue by hiring a cleaner instead,' Dr Lyonette said. 'And although men in general are starting to make themselves more useful around the house, regardless of income, the age-old theory remains the same — women, on the whole, are doing the most.'

It's little surprise, then, that a 2019 study from the University of North Carolina, 'Women in the One Percent: Gender Dynamics in Top Income Positions', found that 70 per cent of the men in the top 1 per cent of US earners have wives who do not work.

If social inequality continues to increase, we should ask, will the social mores of the super-rich become more visible and influential? And is high net worth always determinative of reduced male domestic inputs? Or, to put it another way, do traditional gender attitudes breed success — or does success, at least in narrow fiscal terms, in some way mobilize provider/housewife behaviours?

I chat to a hedge fund manager, Dan, who worked for many years in Hong Kong but now lives in tax exile in Jersey with his Slovenian model wife and his live-in Portuguese maid, Maria. Dan believes that the gender roles of high-net-worth individuals are conditioned, above all, by tax codes.

'Wealthy people want to pass money on to the next genera-tion,' he explains. 'In high-tax jurisdictions such as the UK and France, this wealth can only be passed over in trust, so in effect it doesn't matter how "masculine" your sons are, as they won't ever have to manage their wealth. In places with low inherit-ance tax, such as China, Hong Kong, Japan, Russia and the Middle East, sons will both inherit and be expected to manage and preserve wealth, so they're treated very differently. I've seen first-hand that sons are passed over for inheritance if they don't conform to prized masculine traits; if they're effeminate – or, frankly, a bit of an idiot.'

These super-rich social codes are rippling through our societies in the form of the return of large-scale – and often gendered – domestic servitude. Dan, in fact, sees London as being 'a bit behind' a new mood in which the global rich are unabashed about, or even flaunt, their domestic staff. 'They think nothing about making a big deal about their new European butler in Manhattan.'

Dan explains that there's a division between the rich 'around the 10-mil to 50-million-dollar mark', who'll budget £15,000 a year for a domestic staff member and recruit from a nearby nation 'with a high wage differential' and within their religious group (Christians from the Philippines; Muslims from Indonesia), and the truly super-rich. 'They have 100 mil plus and are much less "price sensitive", so they'll budget around £50,000 per head for domestic help and, well, other things come into play rather than cost.'

I ask what these other things are.

'In New York it's all about the European nanny, the French chef, and the housekeeper who runs the staff, who's like a modern butler and will often be, say, a former marketing executive.'

So these 'other things' clearly include the cachet of middle-classness and white skin. Do British butlers make the wish list?

'Yes, they do, but…' Here Dan emits a brief chuckle, like a

bicycle pump expelling air. 'Good luck finding one. It's part of the British character that we hate to serve, despite our reduced status in the world.'

I wonder if Dan, who was raised by working-class parents in rural England, finds this picture a bit grim. A new norm in which the super-rich flaunt domestic servants as status symbols feels like the social contract of the 1910s, perhaps with less paternalism towards the 'lower orders'.

Dan matter-of-factly cuts off my deliberations. He explains that live-in maid Maria is the indulgence that allows him to 'stay in the game'.

'If you work 90 hours a week, as I do and many high-net worth individuals do, the last thing you want to do is go shopping or hoover when you get back, or do chores. You're looking for the offset that will help you haul those extra hours. Once you've had domestic help for a few years it's hard to let go. To be honest, I'd rather sell my car.'

6

Power, Money, Willingness to Mop

Men don't know what dust is. I still don't see it. I don't know it's there. I know that the nirvana of non-sexist male development is dust. If I get to the dust stage, I'll know that I've really made it.

— Aspirant egalitarian male householder, quoted in Barbara Risman, *Gender Vertigo*

Man-the-hunter is basically a parasite, not a producer.

— Maria Mies, *Patriarchy and Accumulation on a World Scale*

Feminism teaches us to enquire: *where is the power?* With whom resides the power in patriarchal capitalist structures that are based on legacies of colonial exploitation? With the white woman buying a brown woman's domestic labour at an hourly rate barely above the minimum wage, eliding the centuries of exploitation implicit in this seemingly simple transaction? With a middle-class, privately educated man like Tim, who can enjoy the boons of a 64 per cent pay advantage over his female colleagues who've also opted to reproduce?[68] Second Wave feminism's radical insight was that housework is not just a relationship between a tired woman and a sink of unwashed pots. It is also a relationship between human beings: between same-sex partners, cohabitees or housesharers, but most commonly between husbands and wives. To talk about housework and its division is, as theorist Barbara Ehrenreich puts it, to talk about power.

One Friday lunchtime, I chart the shifting dynamics of power at play in the domestic sphere with a group of men who – with their Belgian beer bellies, nasal hair and natty golf pants – make for unlikely feminist radicals.

I meet the STUDS at a bistro in the bourgeois Brussels neighbourhood of Woluwe-Saint-Pierre. STUDS (or Spouses Trailing Under Duress Successfully) is a support and social group for English-speaking immigrant men who've moved to the EU administrative capital for their wives' high-powered jobs; 'trailing males', in their cheery parlance.

As STUDS president William Dantzer had explained to me via email, social support is an essential component of staying sane as a trailing spouse. Trailing males, after all, suffer the same problems the trailing wives* contend with: isolation; difficulty integrating in a new city compared to their economically active other half; the monotony of a life framed around domestic chores. 'And we've got the stigma of not being the breadwinner on top. That is a big deal in an ambitious city,' Dantzer added.

I'd first met the STUDS a few years earlier, on a work trip to Brussels. A friend whose husband was a former member had put me in touch. 'You've got to meet them; they're like your favourite cuddly uncle crossed with Fanny Cradock,' she'd said. I'd arranged to join the STUDS at one of their weekly Friday meetings: a powwow where the men drink beer, swap domestic gripes and recipes, and talk politics and sport. Younger STUDS come to the meets dandling toddlers on their knee; older STUDS come dressed for an afternoon game of golf, or toting bags after a morning's battle with the Brussels supermarket aisles. I felt that the STUDs – all of whom were in charge of the domestic smooth-running of their Brussels

---

* Who are more numerous by a ratio of nine to one.

homes, and most of whom were breadwinners in their 'former lives' – would have an interesting take on the intersection of money, power and home.

That first time I met the trailing males I'd breezed into their regular haunt – the muscularly named Le Baron brasserie – downed three 11 per cent Belgian fruit beers, and laughed along to their domestic war stories: the confused American who bought eight kilos of butter instead of eight pounds; the problems of dressing for the four daily seasons in Brussels ('so *now* I get that preppy sweater-on-your-shoulders European thing').

My second appearance at Le Baron is a different prospect. With Leo in tow, I'm late – following a spat with a Brussels cab driver about my muddy pushchair wheels (he had winced every time they banged against the pristine interior of his Prius's boot) – and 30 minutes following my arrival in Woluwe-Saint-Pierre are spent frantically pacing the pushchair around a cobbled square to get Leo to take a nap.

When I eventually park my snoring son under the bistro's hatstand and take a seat, the STUDS smile sympathetically – 'Little shits, aren't they? Thank God mine are grown up' – before quickly resuming their discussion about the best way to keep baguettes *boulangerie*-fresh.

'Put them straight into the freezer when you buy them, then warm them up in a low oven before breakfast,' says Alan from Brighton, who moved to Brussels two years ago with his pharmaceutical-boss wife.

'For sure, Belgian bread isn't like the Wonder Bread we get in Canada,' muses 52-year-old Dwayne, whose wife Carrie is a high-up at NATO. 'Wonder Bread never goes stale. I mean, NEVER. But it tastes kinda OK if you toast it. A bit like space food.'

The challenges of housekeeping in an alien environment are a central theme of STUDS ruminations. Over another *demi* of beer, the discussion ranges from where to get supermarket offers on fresh plaice (Delhaize, at €13 a kilo) to the myriad difficulties in shopping 'European-style' when you're used to British or American supermarkets.

'It's your German bread from the bakery, your French cheese from the cheese shop, your Irish beef from the butcher,' Dwayne explains, his widened eyes giving the impression of a portly Bambi. 'There's a whole right way to do things and right things to buy and I just don't get it...' Dwayne keeps himself on his toes by cooking recipes nightly from a recipe website, spending mornings scouring his neighbourhood for ingredients. Being responsible for the laundry is also a big adjustment for Dwayne. 'In Canada our washing machines are the size of an SUV. Here they're teeny-tiny, so you have to do this thing where you separate the laundry out into different colours... Man, that got to me when I first moved here...'

I'd been struck in my first encounters with the STUDS by their palpable sense of pride in keeping house. I'd met 65-year-old Colin from Hampshire, who told me that he saw his role as 'creating a nice home environment' for wife Tracey, a company executive, to come home to. That year Colin had thrown a Queen's Jubilee party 'complete with cucumber sandwiches' for the STUDS and their wives. Arin de Sousa, a 43-year-old Asian Australian who had moved to Brussels for his wife's banking job, had also spoken of a genuine pride in his new domestic role.

'They call us "house men" in Belgian legal spiel, and that pretty much sums up our role. Most of us worked before we came to Brussels and we understand the stresses of it. I like to have dinner on the table when my wife gets home.'

The epithet 'house men' reminded me of Second Wave feminists' demand for a new social category: 'housespouse'.[69] Replacing 'housewife', the term 'housespouse' would reflect a new era in which women and men would, she said, 'share the world inside the home and walk equally in the world outside the home'.

What had struck me about the STUDS small talk was that it was straight from the rosy narrative – of housework as care and succour due to the family earner – that was so trenchantly torn apart by *The Feminine Mystique*. My first afternoon with the STUDs had seemed somehow dissonant after the event: a pastiche of essential notions of the housewife of old that, as these stories always do, obscured the tedium of this daily work. Were the men tapping into these older narratives to make sense of their everyday, I wondered; or were they, from their point of male structural privilege, not subject to the sexist junk attached to the 'homemaker' role? Or more charitably, were they struggling to come to terms with their new marital dynamic?

A chance invitation from one of the STUDs had been illuminating in this regard. With three hours to kill before my train journey home, I had accepted Arin's's offer to join him on a tour of La Grand-Place. Arin's in-laws were in town from Australia, and he had arranged to take them out for an afternoon's sightseeing. Within minutes of meeting them – two sturdy Aussies wearing sun visors and money belts – I'd regretted accepting the invitation.

It was clear that father-in-law Nick roundly disapproved of Arin's worklessness, house husbandry and lunchtime rendezvous with fellow workless men. Arriving with another, youngish, woman in tow – me – proved the final straw, with the Aussie FIL delivering an invective I only remember the gist of. It was something along the lines of 'YOU'RE A FUCKING USELESS WASTE OF SPACE AND MY DAUGHTER'S SLAVING AWAY YOU FUCKING WASTE OF SPACE'. I do recall in some detail that the blood drained from the FIL's face, that Arin stared bleakly towards the spray of the Manneken Pis (the peeing-boy statue), and that the father-in-law stormed off towards La Grand-Place, money belt bouncing, in a rage as black as a bin bag. Two days later, Arin emailed me an apology:

He just blows off. He knows that I can't work for visa reasons and he takes it out on me because he can't make sense of the fact his daughter is happy to be the breadwinner. He keeps telling her she should leave me. But I have to be patient. He's an old dog really, with old ideas: you can't reason with him.

This odd exchange had evaporated much of the bonhomie of my first audience with the STUDS. It was clear that, despite the beer-warmed levity at Le Baron, many of the men fielded criticisms surrounding their domestic role. The STUDS who could blithely enjoy the cosy comforts of their support roles were the men who'd had earlier careers and were now retired, golf clubs at the ready, on a final salary pension. For the younger men, the pleasure in performing these acts of caring – in seeking out fine cheeses and reputable kindergartens – was too frequently tarnished by social and familial criticism that painted them as subordinate, or even effeminate. Their humorous tales from the trenches of Brussels *boulangeries*, and their casual acceptance of the lot of the 'house man', struck me as little more than a device to deflect this disapproval.

It all comes back, of course, to the long devaluation of the essential, feminized work of caring and keeping home. As with the STUDS and their wives, when Tim and I 'sex role flip' and Tim assumes the stay-at-home-parent role, rejection of normative definitions of women's domesticity and men's providership comes with the social penalties of the 'sad' stay-at-home dad stigma and motherly guilt.

At Le Baron with the STUDS this time around, I notice that Liam, an Irish retiree whose wife works for the EU, has refrained from the baguette deliberations, as he had from talking up the sunny upsides of his domestic day-to-day. I chat to him as we amble from the brasserie to lunch at a nearby Thai restaurant, which the STUDS have agreed upon after a heated discussion of the relative merits of its €15 menu deal ('You don't get much rice; I hate it when you just get a thimbleful of rice'; 'I like that you still get the carved carrots though; I might try to carve some carrots'). Liam grew up in the 1940s in rural County Cork, and we talk a little about the domestic arrangements that prevailed during his childhood. I had wondered, as I told Liam now, whether Ireland was somehow an exceptional historical case in terms of gendered division of housework.[70]

In 1777, as Caroline Davidson recounts, Britain levied a per-capita tax on male servants that, within a matter of years, completely changed the constitution of domestic staff in England, Scotland and Wales. The original tax – a guinea per male servant – was designed to finance the suppression of rebels during America's War of Independence, as it encouraged Irish men to eschew domestic work to join the navy. The law wasn't repealed until 1937, and during the intervening centuries it was rigorously enforced. The result of this was that domestic servitude went from being a largely ungendered concern, in which male and female servants fulfilled a mixture of domestic and non-domestic functions (such as farming and gardening), to an almost exclusively female occupation. By 1851, 89.9 per cent of domestic servants in England and Wales were female, and by 1911 it stood at 91.7 per cent.* By this point, male domestic servants were status symbols, only seen in the wealthiest homes. As Davidson shows, the domestic duties of a butler were supposed to be light, whereas it was the housemaids' duty, as the 1870 etiquette manual *The Housemaid and Her Duties and How to Perform Them* puts it, to 'keep every corner of the abode free from dust and soot, from damp and rust, from insects, bad smells, and disorder of every kind'.

In Ireland, which saw no such tax, the ratio of female to male servants remained more or less commensurate into the

---

* The UK domestic cleaning force is currently 78 per cent female.

20th century.* As Dorothea Conyers, an Irish gentlewoman, commented in the 1920s: 'Every Irish servant will do everyone else's work cheerfully, the men come in to help the maids polish the floors and shoes, and the maids are quite willing to feed the horses if the men are all out.' I wondered if the impacts of this differential history could still be felt in 1940s County Cork?

I put this to Liam, and he laughs so lustily that Leo issues a muffled yelp from the depths of his pushchair. His snood, a yellow knitted number with daft goat ears, had slipped over his face in Le Baron and I'd tried, unsuccessfully, to extract it without waking him up. I'll be keen to get a few thimblefuls of rice down my neck before trying to feed him lunch in a packed restaurant, his sturdy form wriggling on my knee as he issues his prattling entreaties: 'Take away! Don't like spicy!' (This last one was new to his two-year-old prandial patter, alongside 'yucky one' and 'Leo, more dat!')

Liam is still hooting.

'Have you ever been to Ireland? It was all mother's work. The Catholic Church hammered it into you with the catechisms and bodily guilt. And gruelling work it was too – we didn't have any fancy kitchens 'til the 1950s: no fridges, no washing machine. My mother had to tub-wash and mangle everything on a Monday, and the rest of the week was an unholy rush to cook and clean the house for Sunday, when of course it was against the doctrines to lift a finger, despite the fact there was an extended family to feed. It was blue hell for my mother looking back, what with having six idle sons.'

We walk to the clunking rhythm of buggy wheels on cobbles as I take this in. I break the silence by asking Liam how he feels about his own – current – domestic support role. Is he, like the other STUDS, happy to describe himself as a 'house man'?

---

* Around 52 per cent female to 48 per cent male.

We've reached the door of the restaurant, and hang back. It's full of lunchtime bargain-seekers and there's a kerfuffle as 11 cuddly men try to squeeze themselves onto a table of high stools in the disco-lit bar area.

'I've got a long memory,' Liam says. 'My mother died young after a tough, abused life; my cousin was cast out when she became pregnant as a teenager. When I started work as a clerk in the 1950s I was paid one pound, and the female trainees got a farthing [a quarter of the pre-decimal Irish pound] for the same work! I've lived a long life and I remember all of this and don't think it's anything like the life we live as pampered expats. So, acting like happy housewives? No, I don't think it's anything to joke about.'

In their 2013 article 'Why Study Housework? Cleaning as a Window Into Power in Couples', US sociologists Shannon Davis and Theodore Greenstein argue that housework should be seen, and studied, as a metric of relative power. And as we've seen, for all of the domestic goddess fluff, housework – excluding cookery – is routine, repetitive and generally disliked. So it follows that such shitwork might fall to the individual with the least power. And this, to an extent, is what we've seen: men, and especially wealthier men, use their relative power to negotiate housework setups more favourable to them. Dan with his non-negotiable maid; the 56 per cent of full-time working married men in our survey who admit to contributing fewer than six hours a week of housework; even Arin, scrambling to rebuild his self-worth with domestic expertise.

Davis and Greenstein also give us a useful definition of 'power' in relation to the domestic sphere. This power is broader and more invidious than the tool of a single actor who uses economic clout to shirk housework. This is the capillary power theorized by French theorist Michel Foucault: a power that is not a tool of individual arseholes but is in fact every-where; diffused and embodied in discourse, knowledge and 'regimes of truth'. Here is the disciplining power of the patriarchy we contend with when we struggle to establish non-sexist householding. Not one heterosexist man drunk on his entitlement to glug beer and watch *Top Gear*, but rather a power that bleeds through governance, social structures and 'common sense', like water through a thirsty washing-up sponge.

Economic Wo(Man)

> If a man marries his maid, all else equal, GDP would fall.
>
> – Economist Paul Samuelson

Feminism and economics have been unhappy bedfellows for much of their shared history, and feminists have long taken umbrage with the figure upon whom much of classical economics is based. As theorized by Adam Smith, *Homo economicus* ('economic man') is an idealized human being who acts rationally and with complete knowledge and who seeks, through his actions, to maximize personal utility or satisfaction. In Smith's view, these actions out of self-interest provide appetites for goods and stimulate markets.

The primary problem with *Homo economicus* for feminists is the absence of women, and the absence of the work commonly ascribed to women. Where are the many activities conducted not out of self-interest, but to keep the bodies and souls of others alive? More precisely, where is the account of the 50 billion hours of unpaid labour adult women perform, each week, around the world?[*]

'It is not from the benevolence of the butcher, the brewer, or the baker that we expect our dinner,' Smith famously wrote, 'but from their regard to their own interest.' But what about the individual who bought the ingredients for dinner and assembled

---

[*] By my angry calculation, on the back of a shopping list.

the meal? In Smithian economics, clothes are washed and meals are prepared, it seems, as if by magic.

In her 2015 book, Katrine Marçal asked *Who Cooked Adam Smith's Dinner?* The answer being: his mother. Lifelong bachelor Smith lived with his mother until her death, when his cousin Janet moved in and stepped into the domestic breach. But we've probably castigated the 18th-century economist's domestic arrangements as thoroughly as we need to.

Fast-forward 300 years, and feminism-informed economists began paying attention to the division of domestic labour. A paper presented in 2016 at the annual conference of the Royal Economic Society in Brighton, by microeconomist Alexandros Theloudis of University College London, was typical of the approach which has come to be known as 'bargaining power theory'.

In an effort to track men's domestic effort in relation to women's rising average earnings, Theloudis applied mathematical formulas to US time-use data from 1980–2009. He argued a causal result: that women's increasing income has shifted the balance, over these decades, of what the study calls 'intra-family bargaining power'. Theloudis was confident of his results:

> As women's value in the labour market has increased compared to what it was 30 years ago, that has been reflected in their bargaining power… The results suggest that the narrowing gender wage gap improved women's bargaining power in the family, resulting in a shift of household work from women to men.

Readers who've joined me on this journey so far, through the pedal bins of time and the despair-clogged sinks of the feminine cults of the domestic, might recoil at the suggestion of such an uncomplicated link between income and men's domestic effort. It certainly didn't feel that way in my childhood household, where my mother's and father's inputs — lovingly prepared casseroles and occasional egg scrambles, respectively — remained consistent from the late 1970s to the late '90s, through the fluctuations of my parents' careers.

So let's turn, with due caution, to another popular strand of economic theorizing of domestic labour: 'spousonomics'. Spousonomics attempts to apply the revelations of economic theory to the nitty-gritty of who wipes what and when. In the 2011 book of the same name, authors Paula Szuchman and Jenny Anderson interviewed 'over 80 leading economists' to glean insights that might apply to the thorny issue of division of labour in the home.

'How should you decide who does what?' the authors ask. 'Who should specialize in shopping for orange juice and who in cleaning windows?'

Their answer: apply Fordist principles of the division of labour on the production line.*

Szuchman and Anderson use the example of married couple Nancy and Eric. Nancy is better at doing the dishes and tidying up the house. She is focused and has an 'I Dream of Jeannie knack for finishing things in the blink of an eye'. Eric, however, does everything slowly and some things inexpertly. The authors suggest, following Henry Ford's insights into production-line efficiency, that Eric takes over the dishes, at which he's slightly less slow and duncey, and that Nancy tidy up six days a week (with her effortless 'knack'). Both individuals save time, although Eric is at his station longer than Nancy would be if she assumed the dish-cleaning too. So far, unobjectionable. Matters take something of a surreal turn, however, with the authors' argument for bargaining through sex.

---

* In fact this isn't the first dalliance between Fordism and the domestic. The Home Economics movement also toyed with bringing Fordist principles of the production line into domestic kitchens, in the form of task specialism and batch cooking.

Why do women have sex when they don't feel like it? Szuchman and Anderson ask women respondents.

'Answer: To get their partners to do things they don't feel like doing.'

Don't be afraid, schooled Szuchman and Anderson, to use 'incentives' to get what you want. Sex, after all, is merely a function of supply and demand. (I imagine the authors were cheering when, half a decade later, Sheryl Sandberg advised men to scrub the loo to get their wives to put out.)

Another strand of theory ventures a more nuanced take on family bargaining power. The 'divorce threat-point' model of marriage contends that bargaining within marriage on an eve-ryday level is conducted under the shadow of divorce. Each individual with a marital (or indeed cohabiting non-marital) union has a 'divorce threat-point' – the point at which they'd consider a dissolution of the marriage – that differs depend-ing upon the resources she/he/they might fall back on should the union dissolve. These fallbacks range from an individual's earning potential, to their preference for and enjoyment of being single and – grimly for those of us with a younger male partner – their likely appeal in the market for a new mate.

The drive north from Los Angeles along the Pacific Coast Highway is picture-postcard California: Pacific waves swell onto white-sand beaches full of tanned surfers; palms sway sensuously against cobalt skies. The man who overtakes us in a pickup, blaring Van Halen and drinking a Slurpie the size of a church font, does little to cramp Tim's sunshine spirits. But the sight of Van Halen man's bumper legend – 'VOTE TRUMP!' – makes my mood darken.

We're bound for the coastal college town of Santa Barbara for an audience with Shelly Lundberg, a prominent theorist of the factors that influence behaviours and bargaining power in cohabiting relationships. Secretly approaching this meeting, somewhat narcissistically, as a test of my market position as a 41-year-old straight woman, I'm feeling nervous. Tim blithely whistles 'Jump' through his teeth as we drive by the manicured greens of the University of California's Santa Barbara campus and Leo sings along: 'DUMP! DUMP!' We circle the sprawling estate for 20 minutes looking for somewhere to park.

'Oh, it's the same for me,' says Lundberg as I arrive at her office ten minutes late, disarrayed. 'We joke that these days you need to have a Nobel Prize to get a UCSB parking place!'

Shelly Lundberg's office has a view of those over-watered green lawns. I can hear the distant sound of a male student erupting into the guttural laugh that's the mating call of the male jock: all back-clapping and sweaty self-assurance.

Lundberg smiles expansively and says, 'Well? Bargaining in the marriage market, is it? Journalists are always interested in hearing about those papers.'

Her work explores a range of interactions between marital unions and economics, from the effect of the transfer of child benefit to British mothers in the 1970s (which led to much higher spending on women's and children's clothing), to the impact of a choice of environment (the city a family decides to move to, for example) on a couple's later bargaining power.

I nod apologetically and ask her if she thinks couples are aware, on some level, of their differential bargaining power when they shack up, marry, reproduce.

Lundberg smiles. 'I bet you can answer that question. One of the reasons that set of papers was so heavily cited is that we came up with a story and people said, "Oh, oh yeah."

'Power in families is a potent concept. It's not all about command of resources, though that's part of it. There are emotional and character-based reasons for dependence and differing levels of power within marriage. But economics is one source of power that we can measure, so it tends to get top billing.'

So, in the decisions and adaptations we make in the everyday, to what extent are Tim and I on some level alive to our future prospects if we separated? Do I feel the need to clean the oven more, say, because of dating-market age discrimination if I ever became single? Does Tim, who is less of an independent spirit than me, chasten himself into picking up my knickers because he's worried I'd get along just fine without him should our relationship dissolve in a flurry of accusations about overspilling washing baskets and stinking fridge drawers? (NB Tim never picks up my knickers.)

'Well, as you can guess, it isn't that simple,' Lundberg says. 'But, if you want the layperson's take, I would say, yes, it is a good idea to be aware of the effect of underlying dynamics that affect your bargaining power. Moving house is a good example. If you move house for your partner's job somewhere it's tougher for you to get work, how will this affect your future bargaining power in the household?

'Obviously it's all a bit unromantic,' she adds. 'But these forces are inescapable. And if they help us to picture a future moment when we make choices in the here and now, that's a good thing.'

In 2013's *Cohabitation and the Uneven Retreat from Marriage in the U.S., 1950–2010*, Shelly Lundberg and her collaborator, Washington University economist Robert A. Pollak, presented a picture of a socio-economically contingent retreat from marriage. To Lundberg and Pollak, the fact that lower socio-economic groups have given up on this institution is a function of economic factors: the rising educational attainment of women (surpassing that of men in lower socio-economic groups) and the falling ratio of men's to women's wages. For women with a high school education (or some college), the disappearance of the male breadwinner's earning potential means that marriage is no longer worth the costs of a potential mismatch and curtailed independence.

In 1960, around 85 per cent of white men in America aged 30–44 were currently married, with marriage similarly prevalent across socio-economic groups (84 per cent of high-school-educated white men, and 86 per cent of white men with some college – meaning any education post–high school, but not a university degree – or a university education). Predictably, the Don and Betty Draper dynamic of 'marrying up' (educationally, at least) was the norm. In this same year, 85 per cent of high-school-educated white women were married, compared to 75 per cent of university-educated women (there were vanishingly few of this latter group in 1960). Today, however, the numbers for women are reversed, with around 80 per cent of university-educated women aged 30–44 currently married, compared to 65 per cent of American women with some college and 55 per cent of women with a high school education.*

We need, of course, to beware of the trap of presenting marriage as incontrovertibly A Good Thing.** Historically, as we've seen, marriage has been the mechanism by which women's and men's life options have been tied to the brutal prescriptions of gender roles. But perhaps marriage – for all of its foul patriarchal and capitalist foundations – signifies a degree of social privilege in the 21st century; or at least in certain contexts in the West? Tim and I are not married, but this is a choice born of a rarefied point of privilege in which I can opt not to marry, out of a feminist rejection of the institution of marriage, without suffering a grave social and financial penalty.

In the UK and US, marriage is increasingly the preserve of college-educated individuals who marry later, marry each other and do so to invest in their children. But there's little to celebrate in these trends in Shelly Lundberg's view.

'The old bargain where you stay home and take care of the

---

* Or lower.
** As we do the trap of heteronormativity: these figures conceal the state of play for gay unions – marital or otherwise.

kids, and you go to work and produce the money that generated the universal lifelong marriages, has faded fast,' she tells me. 'So you have to ask: what is the glue that is holding the new marriages together? Sadly this glue is increasing inequality. Those who marry are doing so to confer status on their children in an increasingly unequal world.'

Better, perhaps, if we substitute Lundberg and Pollak's 'marriage' for the term 'stable union', for not only are non-university-educated Americans dispensing with marriage, they're also dispensing with long-term unions, typically forming a series of unstable cohabiting arrangements which emerge and dissolve over time. For this reason, Lundberg and Pollak point to a widening gap in outcomes experienced by the children of university-educated Americans – who grow up in stable households with one or both birth parents, and enjoy heavy levels of investment in their upbringing – and the children of the majority, who, as sociologist Kathryn Edin puts it, ride the vicissitudes of a 'high-speed family merry-go-round' in which parents and stepparents exit and enter through the duration of their childhood.

There are key differences between rich nations when it comes to the degree and nature of the retreat from marriage. In Northern European countries such as Sweden and the Netherlands, cohabitation has progressed further in the direction of becoming a replacement for marriage: a smaller proportion of the population ever marries; rates of cohabitation and proportions of births within cohabiting unions are much higher; and these unions are much more durable than in the US. In Southern Europe, fertility is plummeting alongside the marriage rate. We can say, however, that the general trend of a socio-economic gradient in relationship stability holds across the rich world, with low levels of education associated with more unstable forms of cohabitation and higher rates of non-marital childbearing.

A 1999 study[71] of informal caregiving in the US context – conducted by Liliana Pezzin and Barbara Steinberg Schone, an economist and a medic — predicted the societal ripple effects we can expect from this trend: that elderly fathers who played little role in their children's upbringing cannot count, as previous generations have done, on care in kind from their adult children. Lundberg calls these factors 'a ticking care time bomb'.

So, back in sunny Santa Barbara, I ask Lundberg the obvious — if unfeminist — question: is there an argument in terms of stability for the Breadwinner/Housewife model?

She thinks for a minute.

'Well, there still is specialization — right? Even in relatively non-specialized households there are things that I do and I'm best at — I do the cleaning, say, and my husband does the cooking — whether or not there's an explicit division into home and market-sphere activities. So in this sense, specialization is a tendency. But do I lament the loss of the sexist marriage models?

'No. I can't really bring myself to regret the loss of a system in which a man could condemn a woman and her children to economic penury by leaving them.'

Gary Becker, one of the earliest economists to venture into economic theories of marriage, put it another way in 1991: that even if the 'pie' is bigger when husbands and wives specialize in breadwinning or housekeeping, there's a trade-off for women between a bigger pie (more money coming in) and a larger share of a smaller pie (that comes from the economic clout of wage-earning). Notwithstanding, of course, the fact that the bigger pie is baked from the slugs, snails and puppy-dogs' tails of the patriarchy.

As Lundberg and I leave her office and walk across a campus filled with young people laughing and showing their perfect white teeth, I feel uneasy. Don-and-Betty-Draper marriages are no more, those marriages founded on the principle of economic disparity in which marriage stability is a symptom of women's absence of power or lack of real alternative to the housewife track. Today's state of affairs, however, seems similarly rife with injustices. We've got to a position in which only a small group, amongst the university-educated – and their children – enjoy both the boons of a stable union and the gains of self-determination from feminism. The rest, a full 50 years after the advent of Second Wave feminism, are left to cobble together a domestic existence from Second Wave feminism's leftovers.

The chasm between feminism's narratives and women's everyday lived reality can be heart-rending. In the 2005 book *Promises I Can Keep: Why Poor Women Put Motherhood before Marriage*, sociologists Kathryn Edin and Maria Kefalas found that economically deprived women recoil from marriage for fear of abuse and out of a concern that marriage to the fathers of their children will 'activate traditional gender roles'. The retreat from marriage is thus couched, for many of these women, as a feminist choice.

'A young mother [in a poor US community] often fears marriage will mean a loss of control – she believes that saying "I do" will suddenly transform her man into an authoritarian head of the house who insists on making all the decisions, who thinks that he "owns" her,' the authors write. 'Having her own earnings and assets buys her some "say-so" power and some freedom from a man's attempts to control her behavior... Women who rely on a man's earnings, these mothers warn, are setting themselves up to be left with nothing if the relationship ends.'

I put this point to Kerry, a single mother of two from Birmingham, who agrees that marital trends amongst working-class British mums are also based on motherly pragmatism. 'I see it as more that working-class women like me are being very cautious,' she says. 'We don't have to marry like we did in my gran's day, so that means we can bide our time and see if any man's, you know, a player, before we do something grown-up like get married. I didn't marry my daughters' dad, who was unemployed when we had our first, precisely because I wanted our home life to be stable.'

Feminism – and its effects on government policy – has given women the ability to economically support themselves and their children; yet society, miserably, hasn't produced a broader cohort of men, or indeed women, who are comfortable with men in the primary housekeeping role. Yes, feminism has given many women the agency and income to pull the plug on shitty and abusive relationships, and the language to articulate patriarchal power abuses, but economic factors have left many men foundering, with no role in either the market or the family home, yet resisting their own personal transformation. Quality non-sexist heterosexual unions are, as such, as much a socio-economic issue as a feminist one.

In her 1994 study of the origins of what she calls 'peer marriages' – egalitarian unions based on shared parenting and household duties – sociologist Pepper Schwartz points out the elephant in the kitchen when it comes to feminist idealization of such partnerships: the shortage of men who are keen on the prospect of a peer marriage with a feminist. Across much of the world, the stalled revolution is more accurately a half-revolution: women have moved on and heterosexual men are dawdling some way behind – around, say, 1974.

I think of these Time-Lagging Men as I walk through the hydrangea-filled front garden of Donna's Warwickshire home. I was at school with Donna, but we haven't crossed paths since the days we were moussing our fringes into glistening quiffs and listening to Pearl Jam. Then, out of the blue, Donna responded to my social media call-out for female breadwinners, writing: 'Breadwinner who does ALL of the housework here [facepalm emoji; eye-roll emoji].'

As a college principal, Donna earns twice her husband Dave's income as a firearms officer in the police force ('Firearms offic-ers are generally the macho knobs of the force,' Donna ventures when she tells me this). I decided to visit Donna to chew over what has been termed the Female Breadwinner Conundrum: the fact that heterosexual women who earn more or all of the house-hold income also put in proportionally more household labour.

In Dan Cassino and Yasemin Besen-Cassino's 2014 paper 'Division of House Chores and the Curious Case of Cooking', the authors show that men who earn less money than their wives do less housework than men who earn the same or more than their wives. They found, moreover, that this gender-corrective behaviour was linked to total rather than relative income (that men were threatened only by high-earning wives, regardless of their own income) and that the housework reduc-tion was particularly prevalent when it came to one category of domestic effort: cleaning. Some men made up for their cut-backs in cleaning by an increase in the amount of cooking they did; a task that the authors argue has become 'de-gendered' in recent years. Indeed, there's a ready explanation for the fact that meal preparation and, in some cases, childcare appear to be exceptions to the rule of heterosexual men's asymmetrical involvement. Cooking and childcare are high-reward chores: they are visible and accrue social brownie points, and for many people they are pleasurable tasks in their own right. Making a meal means having a meal to enjoy – a tangible outcome which may draw praise from those who share it. Likewise, taking a child to the park can be fun, and, at least for fathers, attracts approval from onlookers.

Donna's sitting room is scented by the white lilies that are arranged, artfully, in a cut-glass jar on top of her hand-restored armoire. Her coffee table bears photo books of designer homes, set out in neat piles according to colour and size. She brings me a cup of green tea with a separate saucer to dis-pense of my own teabag, and a flurry of unnecessary apologies

('Sorry, is that all right? I never know how strong people like it, I can take it out if you like? Sorry!'). Donna's four children – her son with her first husband; her son and daughter with Dave; and her stepson from Dave's first marriage who now lives with them – are all at school. There's little sign, however, these humans exist, beyond the silver-framed pictures on Donna's mantelpiece and the large wooden 'D' and 'D', separated by a wooden ampersand, on the coffee table.

Donna's house is as unruffled as the homes in the photo books. 'Oh, it's so messy – I haven't hoovered for weeks,' Donna says of the spotless hessian matting. I think of socialist Erving Goffman's concept of the domestic living room as a theatre. Here Donna is onstage, effortfully performing not making an effort. I hope for a moment that Donna has a backstage – the kitchen, maybe, or the downstairs loo – where she turns off the act and has a crafty fag.

Donna curves her small, expensively dressed form onto the bright pink accent cushions on her mid-century modern sofa. She looks exhausted as she tells me, 'To be completely honest with you, I'm exhausted. I work full-time and I do everything in the house for four kids and a lump of a husband. And I mean everything – the only thing Dave does is take the bins out and that's because the passageway gets muddy and I can't knacker my shoes and tights when I have to get to work. If I didn't nag him, he wouldn't do that.'

Dave did some housework when the couple first married. But as Donna's earnings have risen, Dave has contributed less and less to the domestic labour load. 'The rare days I'm off work are the worst, because I just see him lying there on the sofa watching TV like a toad,' she says.

Following her last job promotion, Dave took to directing her housework.

'He'll say something like, "Next time can you make sure you empty the bin in the bathroom, as when there's a used can of shaving foam in it the lid doesn't close properly."

'And of course, I'll say, "Where do you get off? Cleaning the bathroom is 50 per cent your job; childcare is 50 per cent your job and I flippin' do it all!"' Donna purses lips that sheen with peach gloss. 'And he even has the cheek to say I don't do anything for him!'

I ask how it goes when Donna raises these issues with Dave.

'He refuses to see it,' she replies. 'He always tells me that such-and-such-a-guy-at-his-station's wife has five kids and works full-time and does the housework and doesn't complain… That sort of – excuse my French – shite. There's always some woman that's apparently got more on their plate than I have…'

One thing that Dave does do is cook. Donna hates cooking, although it's a bit less of a chore now they have a new open-plan kitchen and she can chat to the kids as she chops veg. Dave says he loves to cook. That the deal is he cooks and Donna cleans. When Dave cooks – 'about once a month', Donna estimates – he assembles laborious meat dishes, uses all the kitchen's pans and baking trays, and Donna finds herself resentfully loading the dishwasher at 11 p.m.

Donna's brother lives in New York and, on his advice, she recently started seeing an American therapist via Skype to chat about the 'housework issue'. She had a few sessions with a 'life coach' in the UK but found her 'a bit damp, to be honest. She just kept asking me how I feel all the time. How do I feel???' Donna raises her fists, whether involuntarily or for pugilistic emphasis, I don't know. 'Raging bloody p'd off is how I feel!'

The new therapist, Donna confides, is better. She sends Donna women's-magazine think pieces about how to coax husbands into joining in with the housework. She's agreed Donna shouldn't put up with her double-shifting status quo. They have decided – the therapist and Donna – that Donna doesn't have to be perfect at work and perfect at home. They've come to the conclusion that Dave is a narcissist.

'So I'm trying not to let him have any impact on me, but it's tough,' says Donna, curling herself still smaller on the grey suede of the sofa. 'Especially in the mornings when I have four bodies to get dressed and out of the house before work, and he's snoring in bed.'

With this she stops abruptly. 'Shhhhhhh, he's just walked in…'

We wait, as a large body bangs through the front door, shouts 'All right, Don' and *clump-clump-clumps* up the stairs.

Worse than all of Dave's refusals to pitch in, Donna says, is the embarrassment. She doesn't talk to her friends and colleagues about the exhaustions of her Double Day. From what she hears, they mostly have husbands that pitch in, if not equally, then more than Dave.

'I'd never want anyone at work to know the situation I'm in,' she tells me. 'I'm a feminist and I'm in this house with four men and boys and I do everything for them. A few months back I was lying in bed feeling pained that my sons and stepson see me doing everything: that this is the model of relationships they're growing up with. It felt like something snapped inside me and I couldn't go on.'

In her 1971 essay for *Ms.* magazine, 'The Housewife's Moment of Truth', Jane O'Reilly speaks of the 'click!' moments of feminist epiphany. These are moments when women see their domestic arrangements in dramatic clarity: the woman who watches her husband step over a pile of toys that need to be put away before he angrily asks her why she can't keep the house tidy; the moment when a woman has a vision of herself as a snake without fangs, slithering through a house where panthers lounge around enjoying a fine meal and paying no attention to her.

I ask Donna if she's reached her click moment with Dave.

'Yep,' she says. 'I see my marriage now for what it is: a man who can't get over his macho ego shit to save our marriage. Don't get me wrong, I love him, but the housework thing is so massive for us. I don't think it will end well.'

Donna pauses as boots thud down the stairs, then whispers, 'You know I look at Dave and it feels like I'm carrying him like a baby. A big, fat, hairy baby with an attitude problem…

'But as you get older you give less fucks, don't you?'

Click.

Norm violation[72] is a recurrent theme in housework literature. And Female Breadwinner unions trigger a profound sense of norm violation: men retracting domestic effort as a means of insisting upon the primacy of gendered roles at home. Studies have also found that women working in male-typical jobs might seek to offset this by performing more traditionally 'female typed' work at home.[73] Research in India, which has one of the world's lowest rates of female paid employment (at 26 per cent),[74] has found that working women neutralize gender deviance by putting in more 'womanly' emotion work with extended family. Interestingly, however, deviance neutralization does not seem to apply when males work in traditionally 'pink collar' roles such as nursing and primary school teaching. A 2017 study by Elizabeth McClintock at the University of Notre Dame found that men working in these fields in the US also seem to perform a more gender-atypical combination and number of chores at home.[75]

Money, power, gender norms: which one is the victor in your kitchen may have little to do with your feminist hopes. In a 2003 paper drawing from data in Australia and the US,[76] Michael Bittman, Paula England et al asked 'When does gender trump money?' when it comes to division of household labour. The answer is, unexpectedly, numerically quantifiable: 49 per cent of income. Men increase their household contributions as they earn more, but only up to the point at which both partners earn an equal wage. In couples where women earn between 51 per cent and 100 per cent of the household income, traditional gender norms once more predominate, with women performing most or all of the household chores (contrary to what bargaining power theory would predict). Which makes us realize that we'd be mad to spend our feminist energies looking to an equalization of the gender wage gap as the solution to our domestic woes. Money, whatever male economists say, can't buy women a break from the labours of love.

Mother's Money, a pamphlet, Wages for Housework, 1978
What is a Housewife Worth?

Mother: nurturer, guide, seamstress, lullaby-singer, problem-solver: $10,500 a year

Cook: dietician, nutritionist: $10,500 a year

Cleaning woman: $125 per week

Secretary: hostess, bookkeeper, chauffeur, greeting card sender, party organizer and budgeter: $100 a week

Interior decorator: making a home with comforting colour schemes, plants, carpets and knickknacks: $100 a day

Wife: companion, lover, back-rubber, ego-builder, warm shoulder, loyal supporter. Cannot be replaced.

There's one theory born of Second Wave feminism's interaction with economics that's resurgent – and, for our project, salient: the care GDP. In the late 1970s, urged by feminist activism, economists and national governments began to tot up the cash value of housework. Gloria Steinem often touted the figure of $9,000. It would cost $9,000 a year, more than the income of 40 per cent of American households, to purchase a household wife's services. *Mother's Money*, a 1978 pamphlet released by Wages for Housework, estimated a housewife's worth at $41,700. A 1970 Chase Manhattan study, quoted frequently by Wages for Housework activists, estimated that a housewife worked 99.6 hours a week and that her labour was worth over $10,000 a year ($44,439 in today's money); and a UK government study in 1974 settled on a figure of £5,000 as the value women's unpaid work brought to the British Exchequer.

After four decades of dormancy, the shadow economy of care is once more in vogue. In 2016, the British government valued the UK's unpaid household service work at £1.24 trillion (larger in size than the UK's non-financial corporation sector), and estimated that overall unpaid household service work was equivalent to 63.1 per cent of GDP.

In 2012 *Forbes* magazine noted that if unpaid domestic work was included in measuring gross domestic product, GDP would have risen by 26 per cent, to 16.22 trillion, in 2010. And in 2018 the state of Victoria in Australia commissioned a study that put a dollar figure on unpaid work: AU$205 billion. It found that women in Victoria contributed 63.2 per cent of the state's unpaid work – about 1.7 times that of men. 'Putting a dollar figure on unpaid domestic and care work means we can actually value it,' Minister for Women Natalie Hutchins said when the report was published, adding, hopefully: 'When we value unpaid work, it's more likely we'll share it.'

We need to account for – and count – domestic labour.

7

The Outsourced Wife

The First World takes on a role like that of the old-fashioned male in the family — pampered, entitled, unable
to cook, clean, or find his socks. Poor countries take
on a role like that of the traditional woman within the
family — patient, nurturing and self-denying. A division
of labor feminists critiqued when it was 'local' has now,
metaphorically speaking, gone global.

— Barbara Ehrenreich and Arlie Russell Hochschild,
*Global Woman: Nannies, Maids, and Sex Workers in the
New Economy*

'Sally, there is something I have to tell you... I am
Lithuanian.'

This was the moment, in a chain coffee shop in a
down-at-heel shopping centre in South East London, that my
liberal feminist guilt ate itself.

Jurate was the fifth cleaner I'd employed as a London
householder.* Brisk, bespectacled Jurate had succeeded spry

---

* Tim told me only recently that he has always felt queasy about paying
someone to come in to our home to perform menial work, though he's
seen the sense of it with a house to maintain, two full-time jobs and a
child: 'The more time I spent with these cleaners the worse I felt. They'd
come to our homes over vast distances on the bus. The pay wasn't great.
Many of them had left their kids in another country. It seemed to be no
sort of life.'

and fidgety Chris, who'd assuaged my sense of discomfort in outsourcing my own shitwork by being male. The fact Chris was gay had, however, had a negative effect on my sense of liberal guilt.

Jurate came from an agency run by a Bulgarian woman in Lewisham and, having assumed that Jurate, too, was Bulgarian – of course, I didn't ask – I'd taught myself pigeon Bulgarian from Google Translate to make myself feel, frankly, a bit less racked with guilt.

I'd written най-добрите коледни желания! ('Best Christmas wishes!') in Bulgarian on Jurate's Christmas card in a careful hand, accompanying a box of Roses chocolates with an extra £20 in cash. I'd wondered if £20 was too little and if Roses chocolates seemed cheap, like something you'd give to a great-aunt in the 1980s. Gestures – the worry and the gift-giving – that must have made me look like a neurotic liberal.

Jurate is, in fact, Lithuanian. Talking to my London friends, most of whom also have weekly domestic cleaners, such self-flagellating overcompensations are the norm. One friend 'pre-cleans' for her cleaner; another buys a brand of ground coffee from her cleaner's native Poland; a third, more usefully, found out that the cleaner's agency was taking a 50 per cent cut of her wage and raised the amount she paid to cover this discrepancy. Did my behaviour seem weird to Jurate?

'Yes, you were weird,' Jurate acknowledges, after I translate 'weird' into Lithuanian with Google Translate.

Frankly, I have good reason for marinating myself in feminist guilt. From the point of view of Second Wave radicals such as Dalla Costa and Federici, paying another woman to do one's shitwork is feminist anathema. If housework was, to 1970s feminists, the great leveller of women,[*] handing housework down a gendered labour line was, to some radical feminists, deeply

---

[*] 'The great equalizer of women... Whatever else women did, we also did housework,' as Barbara Ehrenreich put it.

suspect. Even for those of us who've convinced ourselves that cleaning work provides employment and creates market value (and more on that point below), bitter ironies abound if we choose to delegate this shitwork to women – and more specifically to immigrant women, or to women of colour.

Bought-in domestic labour is an increasingly significant feature of middle-class home life in Europe, North America and the Antipodes. There are now 67 million domestic workers worldwide: cleaners and cooks, but also caregivers for children, the elderly and disabled. Their number is growing rapidly, as longer life expectancies combine with an economic climate in which fewer women forgo paid employment, to create a yawning global care gap. Thirty-nine per cent of respondents in our survey in the UK, US and Australia said they pay a household cleaner for at least two hours a week. Further studies in the UK find that one in three Britons now pays a domestic cleaner, in a trend led by the urban under-35s, many of whom report paying a cleaner as a means of avoiding household disputes.[77]

In my conversation with her, Silvia Federici called this a process of a 'recolonization', whereby women, primarily those from the Global South, were called upon, from the late 1970s, to solve a crisis of capitalism: the crisis of wage inflation, but also the crisis of the care gap that opened up when Western women left their domestic posts.

This move to the market, presented as a feminist solution to the era of dual-earning families, was a breath-taking reversal of what had seemed, in the post-war years, to be a modern era in which domestic servitude had all but vanished (in 1927, playwright J. B. Priestley declared domestic service to be 'as obsolete as the horse' in the era of cars). In 1980, only 5 per cent of Britons paid a cleaner, and in 1995 fewer than 10 per cent did. Britons today are more likely to pay others to clean their homes than at any other time since the 1930s. According to market researchers Mintel, the amount spent on domestic workers in the UK per annum now tops £10 billion. In 93 per cent of cases, the domestic workers are women.

For too many of us today – in the West as well as in regions such as the Middle East (where rates of domestic servitude are also soaring and abuses are rife) – bought-in domestic labour is the feminist blind spot we choose not to scrutinize. Frequently we* make sense of our privatized – and ethically dubious – bridge for the domestic labour gap by being defensive, or resorting to arguments on the basis of job creation.

> *'I loathe cleaning the flat. I see nothing wrong in paying someone to do it for me, just as I would pay someone to paint or to build a wall. It creates work.'* Single woman, 30s, UK

> *'If you can afford it, it makes total sense to pay someone to do this. It also attributes value to domestic labour.'* Single woman aged 25–33, USA

> *'Best money spent! Realizing I was cleaning the loo at 11 p.m. at night, I thought I could do with some help. Before that I'd had a cleaner during my second pregnancy and then had a break whilst building work was happening as there didn't seem any point. It is a godsend to have the house tidy and clean once a week and I am so grateful for the help.'* Woman aged 45–55, UK

> *'Domestic work has value. Outsourcing some of it frees up our time and provides employment to another person.'* White man aged 33–45, UK

In this prevailing mood of apparent ease about paying others to work in our homes, one demographic group in our

---

* Here meaning the middle classes, harried mums, working millennials…

survey stood out. Thirty-nine per cent of you said that you paid someone to clean your home, however if we compare responses grouped by sexuality the differences are stark. Forty per cent of couples in different-sex relationships pay a cleaner compared to seventy per cent of men in same-sex relationships. Women in same-sex relationships – fewer than 10 per cent of whom pay a cleaner – reported queasiness with the prospect which, in some cases, shaded into overt ethical or feminist objections.

'I feel it is problematic to rely on labour of marginalized women to prioritize my comfort. If it was possible to hire white Eton boys for paid part-time domestic help, I would probably have a different perspective.' Woman in same-sex relationship, aged 33–45, UK

'I am very much against paid help as long as those working in paid help cannot afford paid help.' Woman in same-sex relationship, aged 46–55, Sweden

'It feels wrong to me. The hierarchy and power exchange makes me uncomfortable. It's also lazy.' Woman in same sex-relationship, aged 25–32, Germany

This demographic blip leads us to the obvious question: to what extent does having an opposite-sex partner affect our take on the ethics of paying other women to scour the rotting Lollo Rosso from our salad drawer? Because, frankly, paying an Eastern European woman who's left her teenaged son overseas to do my shitwork feels instinctively wrong to me, too.

Do women in same-sex relationships have the luxury of a feminist stance on paid domestic labour that their straight female counterparts – or at least those battling the Double Day – don't enjoy? Or am I, rather, a bog-standard feminist hypocrite, espousing intersectional feminism[78] only to the extent it doesn't affect my material comfort?

For these reasons, we need to ask: is it morally and economically reprehensible to contract out our domestic labour? And if this act is dubious from the point of view of many or most feminists, can we correct for this ethical quandary by contracting, say, a male cleaner, or paying our cleaner the hourly rate we earn? As a long-time client of London cleaners, I decided I needed to experience first-hand the dirty realities of handing my shitwork down a raced and classed female labour line.

So I ask to join Jurate for a day as she cleans the homes of her clients in South London. This has to be covert: Jurate thinks her middle-class clients won't appreciate a journalist poking around their possessions. So we agree that I will wait on the street outside each home until Jurate texts me to confirm the coast is clear of her employers. We also agree that, should one of the owners come home, I'll be introduced as a fellow Lithuanian cleaner Jurate is training as a replacement for when she's ill. The clients will like that, she says. They tend to get annoyed when she heads home to her small village in western Lithuania for a month each January.

Like many cleaners with families in Eastern Europe, Jurate spent a lonely Christmas in London to avoid the surge in plane fares over the festive period ('Two thousand pounds!!' she scoffs. 'I cannot pay.'). Fearing my elbow grease will be little compensation, I pay Jurate an hourly rate for the risk she is taking – and the hassle.

In the morning, we head from the dreary coffee shop to the first house of the day: one of Jurate's least favourite gigs. The three-bed terrace is owned by a straight married couple – secondary school teachers in the state sector – who have two kids, a long-haired dog and a tendency to dump turrets of crap around the house (receipts, keys, gym shoes, sandwich wrappers). Jurate hates the dog: the hair is one thing; the tendency to fly at her mop with its teeth bared is quite another. 'Nasty dog,' she says, by way of explanation. The house has recently been done up with a new white kitchen and walls painted throughout in a shade of chalky Farrow & Ball off-white. This, Jurate says, is almost cause for her to relinquish this long-standing client, since the soft white shows up the owner's tendency to spray cooking sauce all over the kitchen walls. 'Ceiling too,' Jurate gestures upwards. 'You don't believe!'

I look up. It doesn't look too bad today – just a few weird brown striations on the cooker splashback and a grease stain resembling a map of Canada on the carpet next to an over-flowing bin. Jurate assigns me the bathroom, where in front of the sink, in full view, a non-applicator tampon adheres to the carpet with a sticky substance of unknown origin. Chewing gum? Do people use chewing gum in the bathroom? Does toothpaste go that hard? Why would you put toothpaste on a tampon? Jurate offers no answer to my querying look, and instead laughs as I pull on the set of non-latex hypoallergenic gloves I've packed for the day's work. My hands turn an immediate and angry vermillion on direct contact with detergents; even the namby-pamby eco ones. Jurate now has, she says, digits aloft, 'Hands like stone.'

I set to work on the bathroom with a bottle of Viakal and a scary bright orange cleaning fluid covered in Lithuanian writing that Jurate pulls out of her bag. Cleaning the tooth-paste-spattered mirror takes 20 minutes and is OK. Even, in a way, therapeutic. Tackling the loo, the greasy purple tidemarks on the bath and the nasty gummy tampon installation is no one's idea of fun.

This, however, is the easy gig as far as Jurate's recent career history goes. She arrived in London in 2004, shortly after Lithuania's accession to the European Union on 1 May. Back then, she lived in a large shared house in West Ham with 14 other Lithuanians and her husband, who'd come over to the UK to work on building sites. Their teenaged son, who's now grown up, remained in Lithuania with Jurate's mother. Jurate missed him so much in those early days it felt like she had rocks weighing on her heart. There was no privacy at the West Ham house, even in the small double room she shared with her husband, and it was an unpleasant adjustment after the friend-liness of village life. 'No one here looks at you; no one talks.'

On the day after her arrival, Jurate presented herself, as Lithuanian friends had told her to do, at a hole-in-the-wall employment agency in an Underground station. She was sent to work as a chambermaid at a three-star hotel in Bloomsbury, where she was expected to 'turn' three rooms – changing the bedding and cleaning up after tenants – within an hour. After a week her hands were bleeding from the desiccating effect of the starched bed linen.

One day, after being told off by her manager for not noticing that a tenant had left a used condom inside the kettle ('Why in the kettle?' Jurate pauses to ask me, as if I have the inside scoop on esoteric British sexual practices), Jurate swapped agencies and was sent to work at a five-star hotel. This was much better, she says. There was less pressure to get through the rooms, and once a resident even gave her a box of luxury chocolates. The rooms were much less dirty, too, usually just ruffled bedsheets, half-eaten strawberries and a couple of drained champagne flutes. The strawberries had really confused Jurate until a fellow cleaner told her that this was what rich people do: they bring their mistresses to these expensive hotels for just a few hours, and they nibble aphrodisiacs before the sexual act. Jurate much preferred these anonymous rich romancers over the filthy habitués of your typical three-star hotel.

Office cleaning in teams, which Jurate moved into next, was another step up: people are better behaved in their work spaces, and there's usually just coffee cups to clear up and bins to empty. The corporates paid well so there is less pressure, too, though the 5 a.m. starts, after a while, made Jurate constantly ill. You come across male cleaners more in the office-clean teams, but Jurate disliked working with male cleaners as they often assumed the easy gig of using the industrial vacuums, on the basis of their superior strength – leaving the bulk of the surfaces, or grunt work, to their female colleagues.

We leave the first house smelling of citrusy chemicals, with the turrets of crap neatly arranged and the sauce spatters wiped away, and head off to catch the bus to the next client. Jurate tells me that her job as a self-employed domestic cleaner is the best deal of all, and hard won: 'When I came, I could not speak good English so the clients pay the agency £15 an hour and I got £6. Now clients pay me direct and I decide my clients.'

Many Eastern European cleaners in the UK and Germany, she says, aspire to improve their English and then set up their own agencies to recruit women from their homeland who don't speak English, with a view to pocketing this generous agency cut. This isn't something Jurate feels she could do. Indeed, she often takes Lithuanian cleaners she meets on the London circuit under her wing, to check that they're not being paid below the minimum wage for work that she knows their agency bosses are charging the client three times as much for. The London cleaning sector, she says, feeds on naive Eastern European women.

'When I first move here it is 500 litas to £100. That is a lot of money. Lithuanians come here to send money back, and even £5 an hour you feel rich. So the girls come. Now the young girls all go to Germany as the pound is bad.' I ask Jurate if she's tempted to move to Germany. The anti–Eastern European immigrant mood that's found voice in the UK since the 2016 referendum to leave the European Union must make the UK seem, if not downright hostile, then a less welcoming place?

Jurate sighs expressively as she tells me she's too old to move to a new country, learn the language, start again. She was in her thirties when she came to London. If she goes anywhere, she says, it will be back to her small village near the city of Kaunas in Lithuania. But that won't be easy as there's a backlash against returning economic migrants; in a country with a three-to-one dependency ratio, families see these migrants as having neglected their caring duties in favour of an indulgent life in Western Europe, and even the government is making it hard for returnees by erecting bureaucratic hurdles such as the requirement that they register their residency. Why return, says Jurate, to accusations and lofty food prices? Last time she visited Kaunas, the celery and chicken — staple ingredients in *vištienos sriuba*, or Lithuanian chicken soup — were as pricey as they are in London.

The emergence of anti-immigrant populisms maps onto an already precarious picture for domestic workers in the UK — especially the estimated tens of thousands of British domestic workers who come from non-EU countries.[79] For these workers, the right to work in the UK is dependent on a visa scheme that ties them to one employer. In 2016, a damning review of the current legislation concluded that this system exposed thousands of women brought into the UK by wealthy families to conditions of slavery, trafficking and abuse. It was amended in 2017, to allow domestic workers to switch employers within the six-month term of their visa. However, according to UK domestic worker organization Kalayaan, few domestic workers at the time were aware of their right to change employers. The picture in data provided by Kalayaan to the *Guardian* makes for even grimmer reading: 85 per cent of domestic workers under the amended visa scheme reported psychological abuse; 63 per cent said they didn't have regular access to food; 83 per cent reported that their employer took their passport; and 33 per cent said that they received no wages at all. Meanwhile 38 per cent reported abuse of a sexual nature at their employers' hands.[80]

There is a difference, of course, between the structural power the employer of a domestic worker from the Philippines (the worker's visa being tied to the employer) wields over their employee, and that of a Briton hiring an Eastern European domestic cleaner who is free under law to change employers. However, in a landscape in which Eastern European cleaners are recruited to work in the UK under false pretences and are routinely defrauded by agencies out of wages, these differences are more marginal than employers – than we – might like to think. A 2018 report by the Migration Observatory at the University of Oxford found foreign-born and irregular workers are vastly overrepresented in domestic cleaning work.[81] And the conditions and pay these workers labour under are, if anything, getting worse as outsourcing suppresses wages. In a sign of how prevalent such practices are, a 2018 report revealed that cleaners at Buckingham Palace are paid below the London Living Wage,[82] thanks to the cut taken by an agency to whom the Palace has outsourced its cleaning services. In the current political climate, in which anti-immigrant sentiments are high and the UK is becoming less attractive to legal migrants from comparatively poor European countries, there's a real risk that abuses of domestic workers will increase further.

In 2018, Britain's Migration Advisory Committee (MAC) warned that the UK government's plans to expand working visa schemes in which an employee is 'tied' to a single employer to address labour shortages after Brexit offered 'considerable control' to employers and posed heightened risks of abuse. Meanwhile, a popular nationalist mood blames these migrants – the doers of our shitwork – for everything from rising crime rates to wage inequality. Women such as Jurate and Laxmi Swami, the maid whose Kuwaiti mistress tried to strangle her with a telephone cord in a luxury apartment in Knightsbridge,[83] send between 50 and 100 per cent of their wages back to their home country to prop up its economy and support family members left behind. The gig economy, which is opening up new categories of low-paid domestic labour – from on-demand babysitting via an app, to bid-for cleaning jobs – is not good news. It is now common to pay someone else to walk your dog, wrap and post your parcels, or even provide pre-chopped sets of meal ingredients. Too few of us who avail ourselves of these services stop to consider the privilege of prioritizing our time so much that we see fit to underpay someone else to perform our household chores. The lucky in society enjoy the boons of on-demand labour to secure our support in a system that debases us all.

There's something else we should acknowledge. The West's readiness to accept the domestic and caring labour of women from, in particular, the Global South is founded on a stereotype of raced womanhood that should make us all uneasy: the belief that these feminine, old-fashioned women look after their families in a way that British women do not. The tragedy being that the definition of good motherhood in the Philippines is to leave your children in your home country to clean the homes, and care for the children, of rich Westerners. Hochschild and Ehrenreich speak, movingly, of the fate of the 'left behind' children whose mothers' love has been commodified and sold to the West. Hochschild dubs these transfers the 'global heart transplant'.

I've often wondered how I profit from my current cleaner Tania's traditional attitudes to male and female roles. She's made it clear that she disapproves of the fact that I'm in paid work when my son is 'very small... too small'. She looked genuinely confused when I told her that Tim had taken a sabbatical to look after Leo, and she laughed for a full 15 minutes when she saw that Leo had been given a toddler cleaning kit – complete with mop, broom and mini dustpan-and-brush – for Christmas. She viewed the pink toy pushchair he loves to rattle his teddy along the kitchen tiles in with a mood bordering on derision: 'Why, when you have a boy?'

From London cleaning agencies to adverts for nursing homes, Western depictions of care are always gendered and often raced. In rich nations that are destinations for domestic workers, women from poorer countries — places where female identity is based on motherhood — are presented as embodying feminine qualities of nurturance, docility and eagerness to please. These qualities are played up by cleaning agencies in their choice of brand names: 'merry maids', 'home angels'. Often, Western employers are buying the labour — manual, emotional — of a woman from the imagined past, and Ehrenreich is not alone in pointing out the similarity of these discourses to those at play in the global sex trade.

Karin, a friend of mine, works as a therapist for English-speaking expats in Bangkok. Many of Karin's clients are men — British, North American, German — in their autumn years, who have come to Thailand in pursuit of the traditional womanly virtues of Thai brides; virtues they consider lost to the West. They tell her:

One: that Thai women are better than Western women because they still want to look after their men.

Two: that they fear Thai women will murder them (allegedly very common because these women rarely get prosecuted).

This trade in traditional womanly attributes is often institutionalized by these workers' home nations. Countries including Kenya, Sri Lanka and the Philippines have — or have had — state-sponsored programmes to train women to become domestic workers abroad. The Sri Lankan Bureau of Foreign Employment (SLBFE), for example, teaches young women to use a microwave oven, electric mixer and vacuum cleaner, and brokers their placement abroad. Little wonder, when remittances from foreign domestic workers represent 8 per cent of the Sri Lankan GDP (and 10 per cent of GDP in the

Philippines).[84] In the 1990s, the SLBFE even commissioned a propaganda song that became a chart hit. It was designed to sell young Sri Lankan women on the virtues of becoming domestic workers overseas:

> *After much hardship, such difficult times,*
> *How lucky am I to work in a foreign land.*
> *As the gold gathers so do many greedy flies.*
> *But our good government protects us from them.*
> *After much hardship, such difficult times,*
> *How lucky I am to work in a foreign land.*
> *I promise to return home with treasures for everyone.*

Filipino pop group Smokey Mountain's 1980s hit 'Mama' had a more plaintive take on the outflow of Filipina women – then the equivalent of 23 per cent of the female working-age population – to work as overseas domestic labourers:

> *Mama's a maid in London*
> *I want to believe that she's fine*
> *She could be lonely in London*
> *I want to know why she had to go*
> *I need her, I want to be near her*
> *I've got to be with her*
> *And see to it that we're together once more.*

In 1940s Britain, the importing of female domestic labour became a government preoccupation. Black women recruited from the Commonwealth were typically given public cleaning work – streets, bus shelters, hospitals – and distanced from British homes. In 1946, representatives from the British Ministry of Labour travelled to refugee and prisoner-of-war camps in Germany to assess the suitability of women refugees as domestic workers in British homes. White Protestant Latvians, the representatives decided, were the favourable option, though young white women from Lithuania and Estonia were also encouraged to apply under a series of 'European Voluntary Worker' schemes, which continued into the 1950s and saw over 10,000 women arriving from the Baltic states; and, later, 10,000 widowed or single German women under the 'North Sea' scheme (most of whom also went on to work in domestic service).[85] These domestics were replaced in due course by a wave of Irish and Portuguese female immigrants. Then, from the early 2000s, the accession of poor Eastern European countries to the EU again offered a ready source of women who were suitably traditional, suitably white and suitably poor, to scrub the shit from British U-bends.

In America, the status of domestic workers was similar to that in Europe: their labour remained largely invisible and was devalued by nature of its location in private homes and its association with the nonwork of housewives. It was also invisible under labour law, with benefits such as minimum wages, overtime regulations and limits upon working hours not applying to domestics, many of whom, in a grim echo of the United States' historical abuses under slavery, were African American women. Yet in the 1960s, a peculiar thing began to happen: domestic workers in the US began to organize, to challenge their lowly status and lack of legal protection. A call took shape for the derogatory term 'domestics' to be dispensed with, in favour of the title 'technicians'.

As Jessie Williams, of the domestic-worker organizing group Household Technicians of America's Alabama affiliate, told an interviewer:

> We won't go in the back door any more. We won't be told to eat scraps in the kitchen and stay out of the living room except when we are sweeping. We feel domestic work is just as professional as any other job. If people go on making it degrading, there won't be any workers doing it much longer.[86]

By the late 1960s, domestic worker associations had sprung up across the US, with demands for the status of domestic work to be upgraded and for decent working conditions and pay. The Women's Bureau within the US Department of Labor responded to these campaigns by issuing a code of standards for employers that included social security contributions, sick pay, a minimum wage and holiday entitlement. It was, however, voluntary, and barely adhered to. It took until 2010 for a Domestic Workers' Bill of Rights to come into effect to give domestic workers the right to overtime pay and days of rest.

Of course, many white, middle-class American women who were experiencing a feminist awakening were in a mistress–maid relationship with domestic workers in their own home. And this might have been an impediment to forging links of solidarity between domestic workers and white feminists. Indeed, the strand of Second Wave feminism typified by Betty Friedan – white, privileged, well educated – was, at its best, blind to issues of race and class. At its worst, it was racist: content to turn the other way as it offloaded its shitwork down the female line.

At an early conference of the Household Technicians of America, leader Edith Barksdale Sloan issued a warning to these women that, without a change in conditions for domestic workers, '"Madame" is going to have to clean her own house, and cook and serve her own meals, because *everyone* is going to quit.'

The Second Wave feminist rhetoric that positioned housework as nasty and tedious shitwork also, quite naturally, alienated domestic worker activists, just as it enrages cleaners today. (Jurate tells me that she takes pride in her work and thinks it should be seen as a skilled and 'proper job'.)

It was a testament both to the uniqueness of the time and to the strength of the feminist argument that, in the 1960s, alliances were quickly formed between the mainstream feminist and domestic worker movements. The National Organization for Women, the National Women's Political Caucus and various radical feminist groups supported the cause, fundraising for the Household Technicians of America and testifying in congressional hearings on their behalf. Domestic workers' rights became a significant issue for black feminists.

The recognition dawned for a caucus of activists in allyship that these issues were all one: that male presumption that wives and girlfriends would keep house for free kept domestics from getting their rights – and fair payment – in the labour force.

Josephine Hullett, a domestic worker activist from Ohio, made the point in an interview with *Ms.* magazine in February 1973:

> After all, there's a sense in which *all* women are household workers. And unless we stop being turned against each other, unless we organize together, we're never going to make this country see household work for what it really is – human work, not just 'woman's work'.

Sadly, this alliance between white feminists and domestic labour activists was too fragile to hold, as Having It All liberal feminism became mainstream and domestic workers more numerous. Globally, we do see some exceptions to this severing of feminist and domestic worker ties. In India, for example, domestic workers have forged powerful activist alliances with socialist feminists and sex workers, to fight for shared interests in workers' rights. But elsewhere, the rare moment of solidarity is no more, and in almost every global context these vital workers remain poorly paid, vulnerable to abuse and ill-protected by law.

Chris is waiting for me outside the restaurant: skipping from one leg to the other, a roll-up cig clenched between his right thumb and forefinger, damp from his staccato inhalations. 'Hi babes, I'll just finish this toot then I'm with you...'

Chris was the gay cleaner who'd allayed my feminist guilt when he cleaned my North London flat, pre-child, in 2015. (I now marvel that I thought I needed a cleaner before I had a child.) I fondly remember Chris: he was always full of gossipy chatter about his estate agent husband Marco ('Honestly, he does me head right in, babes. I wanted to kill him last night') and his cherished Yorkie-Chihuahua cross Charlie, who he dresses up in sequined waistcoats and spats for best-dressed-dog competitions. I miss Chris, who quite reasonably refuses to clean for anyone who lives outside his North London borough ('Another world to me, babes; another world').

My relationship with Chris occupies the liminal space between friendship and an employer/client, which Chris fosters, he tells me, to bolster his sense of self-worth about his job. He loves that his female clients see him as their gay best friend: confiding in him, feeling free enough in his presence to stand around and chat in their underwear. Chris took to cleaning after leaving the long hours and low pay of working in a well-known coffee shop, because he's 'naturally OCD'. His mum, he admits, was an 'alky obsessive compulsive', who on Sunday afternoons would get drunk and move all of the furniture in the house into different positions. From the age of 15, Chris did the same thing: regularly reconfiguring the layout of his bedroom; shifting his single bed and old wooden wardrobe against opposite walls. Sometimes the Sunday scrapes and thunks of moving furniture could be heard upstairs and down. Talk about a day of rest.

Chris has to clean when he gets home, too; Marco doesn't lift a finger. Or rather, Chris suspects, Marco doesn't see the dirt as he does – he doesn't get twitchy when there are tufts of Charlie's hair on the carpet, or plates in the sink.

In the hip King's Cross restaurant we meet up at, I order a meze plate and Chris orders a salad, which he eats very little of, instead playing with the lamb's lettuce with his fork as if it's a strange alien substance. Chris is very slim, with an almost-teenage physique and carefully gelled hair. He drinks three black coffees during my meal.

I ask him how work's going. Chris was always on the cusp of expanding his business to an agency and taking on more cleaners, but he's had a couple of false starts with two female Romanian employees, one of whom stole jewellery from a client. He'd like to find some Polish women to employ because clients like them – they are, he says 'naturally clean people' and 'wifey types'. At the moment he's trying out a Caribbean guy, Dave, who used to work in construction but was recently made redundant. Chris likes Dave: he's strong and uncomplaining and gets stuck in, like Chris. He suspects Dave will go back to a construction job when he gets one, though.

Chris's main bugbear these days are the clients he calls 'the Bridget Jones Tramps'. These are the high-earning single corporate women who leave their flash apartments looking like the aftermath of an orgy: shoes flung about, cups of spilt coffee, worn knickers cast into the corner of the bedroom with a heel. Bridget Jones Architect Tramp is the worst. She cooks meals and leaves them, half eaten, to moulder in the kitchen. Sometimes, in what Chris interprets as a stab at modesty, she covers the soft blankets of green-white fur that grow on their surface with a sheet of foil. Usually she apologizes with an abstract wave of the hand and tells Chris to 'dump the whole thing in the bin', posh crockery and all. That, too, gets Chris's goat. 'All that brand-new Jamie Oliver earthenware and a manky old sausage casserole. And "just bin it", she says!'

With the Tramps, Chris can't start cleaning until he tidies up. He prefers working for single men: not much fuss as they're out more; it's just the body hair in the plug holes and all over the carpet. There's a new category now, though, that's shaping up to be worse than the Tramps – worse, even, than the idle husbands who sit like lumps on their laptops and refuse to lift their feet so Chris can vacuum. The Eco Freaks.

Meddling with the products Chris uses is par for the course with the Eco Freaks. They don't seem to like him using anything that gets the job done: Cillit Bang, Viakal, bleach. And now one of his clients, a prominent actor couple, have taken things to a new level and started making their own cleaning products: surface cleaner from bicarbonate of soda and essential oils; some nasty vinegar thing for the windows; and a weird-smelling alcohol for the floors. 'I'm not being funny, babe – they smell nice, but they don't do nothing. You need bleach if you want to clean a manky kitchen.'

I pay the bill for an uneaten salad, five coffees and a meze plate; Chris rolls another cigarette with a rapid flick of his fingers and looks keen to get outside to smoke. Though it would put a dent in his income, Chris might drop his actor clients, he confides. There's no underwear confidentials with this pair – Chris thinks that since the husband got famous on TV they look down on him, and that makes him feel small. Chris has one rule for clients: that they treat him like a human being.

'To be honest, if I'm entering your house and cleaning your loo, I'm important in your life. You've got to show me some respect,' he says, visibly upset.

As we leave, I brave the question: 'Did I show you respect when you were my cleaner?'

Chris smiles into the flare of his Zippo flame, then regards me through a curl of smoke. 'You were one of the nervous ones, babes. You always looked like you wanted to do the cleaning yourself. And, like, I take offence with that first off. A lot of women think I'll be no good cleaning cos I'm a man, and they'll have to do it all again.'

I'm about to prattle on awkwardly about my embarrassment around hiring a cleaner, my guilt about the devaluation of feminized work, and my issue with bought-in work as a fix for our half-finished feminist revolution. Instead, as we part company, I think twice and ask Chris whether he'd ever pay anyone to clean his home.

'Nah, I'd find it a bit weird, babes,' he responds. 'Home's private, and being able to wash your own plates and tidy your own stuff up and look after yourself – there's something in it, isn't there?'

The struggle for decent wages and working conditions for domestic labourers was central to the Second Wave feminist cause. And for a fleeting moment in time, housewives, radicals and domestic workers stood shoulder to shoulder in the struggle for the common cause of elevating a category of work that was both feminized and debased. Then feminism and the domestic workers' struggles parted ways. The massive expansion of domestic labourers from the late 1980s was a means of ending some women's domestic burden in a way that didn't rock the patriarchal capitalist system. Meanwhile, the guilt that many feminists like me felt – and still feel – about employing domestic cleaners bemused many domestic workers, who grew resentful that their employers had given up on all fights but their own. For implicit in this guilt is feminists' unwillingness to make domestic labour a good job with decent payment and treatment, wedded as we are to the shitwork narrative for its own ends. How can our construction of domestic labour as 'shitwork' be anything other than offensive to those who perform this work for a living?

The day of the week my cleaner Tania visits, I return home to the smell of Dettol mixed with Tania's sweat, as well as a clean kitchen and bathroom and a drenching sense of guilt. It's the same feminist vertigo that greets me when I pick Leo up from nursery, or buy clothes from a mainstream clothing outlet that relies, as all of them do, on women garment workers in the Global South who studies have shown are at high risk of sexual and physical violence.[87] It's the trap of not knowing what's best to do, then doing the easiest thing and arguing its merits from the point of view of the most convenient feminism: the creation of paid labour; an imperfect solution to our busy lives under capitalism as two working parents.

Well, it's time to call out these half-baked arguments. In a market in which the labour of care is so routinely devalued, the argument on the basis of job creation doesn't hold. If we want to argue for that point, we need to follow it through: paying our domestic workers well (and directly) and offering them sickness and holiday pay. Feminist academic Arianne Shahvisi computes the fair-exchange price of a cleaner in the UK as follows:

> An average UK employee earns £518 each week for working an average of 37 hours. Accounting for lunch breaks and statutory paid leave — to which a cleaner is generally not entitled — this means that an average person earns £18.14 per actual working hour. Adding in £3 for a return bus fare, a cleaner should therefore be paid £21.14 to clean for an hour, or £39.28 for a two-hour session (and more for those based in London).

The average cleaner in London, however, earns just £8.89 an hour. Anything less than paying what your time is worth, says Shahvisi, is a nod to a system in which some people's leisure is worth more than other people's labour. And she adds that we must also push against the disingenuous position that paying people to clean our houses is in their best interests since it provides employment. According to this logic, all work based on economic injustices, including Bangladeshi textiles sweatshops and child-worker matchmaking factories, are justifiable on the basis that they provide work to those who would otherwise starve. And by extension, as Shahvisi points out, 'It might begin to look mean-spirited for a high-earner *not* to outsource their teeth-cleaning, handbag-tidying, and anal hygiene to a person desperate for work.'

We should remember, too, that homes in which raced and classed women clean for middle-class women and men are often homes in which children are being raised. Raised to see the labour of some women as less worthwhile than the labour and time of other women and men. To what extent is Leo learning the skills to enable him to become a feminist ally when bath-time tidemarks and tramped-in mud are magically, invisibly, taken care of?

Ideally we should form feminist alliances, and fight for better pay for all workers suffering the 'pink collar' pay and rights deficit: teachers, nurses, nursery school teachers, cleaners, care workers. And we should listen. True feminist allyship comes from listening to the points of view of those whom we cavalierly theorize. Chris, for example, would like his well-to-do middle-class clients to stop prioritizing the environment over his labour, and to treat him like a human being. Jurate would be quite happy with a pay rise, and would like to put an end to the abuses of Eastern European cleaners in London on the basis of their poor levels of English. Bobbi, an ambitious 25-year-old Bulgarian woman who cleaned for us in South London until she improved her English sufficiently to get a job in a café, thinks that agency cleaning jobs trap women in work where they can't learn English and progress to more lucrative work. She'd like to make it mandatory for agencies to give cleaners English lessons; she also thinks there should be legal implications for agencies who advertise good jobs overseas that transpire to be poorly paid when workers land in London, Düsseldorf or Milan. This is how Bobbi first arrived in Britain, and she felt angry for months afterwards.

So we need to be allies and also to accept there's no one answer to these dilemmas of privileged feminism. Globalization has supplied a cheap workforce, which has expediently allowed us to dodge the task of demanding greater male involvement; and middle-class women's emancipation from housework has come at the cost of reinscribing poor women's ties to it. Only when householding has become a quality, non-sexist enterprise – and those who work professionally in our homes are accorded the respect, pay and protections of workers in other sectors – can we contract a TaskRabbiter to wrap our presents, or an online babysitter to look after our toddler, or a cleaner to clean our homes, with a clean conscience.

8

Mrs Robot

The 'mechanical maid of the future' in Arthur Radebaugh's
techno-utopian comic strip 'Closer Than We Think' (1958–63)

In the pilot episode of the 1960s cartoon *The Jetsons*,
housewife Jane Jetson bemoans the tedium of keeping
futuristic house. 'Nothing but housework,' she sighs in
exasperation beneath her space-age hairdo. 'How I hate
washing, ironing, vacuuming… What modern-day woman has
time?'[88] The running gag of the first season of the hit series is
that Jane's day consists of little more than pushing buttons:*

---

* A gag that also pokes fun at the sudden proliferation of labour-saving
gadgets in the 1960s American home.

Jane pushes buttons to make dinner, to clean her house in the sky, and to wake her husband George so he can head off to his three-hour workday of button-pushing. Indeed, at the beginning of the first episode, we see Jane exercising her push-button fingers to the instructions of a pneumatic trainer on her 3-D TV, a gimmick that anticipated the vogue, two decades later, for Mr Motivator–style workout videos.

In an age in which drudgery has gone the way of ground-level motor cars, the answer to Jane's domestic ennui is obvious: personal humanoid robotic assistant Rosey the Robot Maid. 'Rosey cooks, cleans and still finds time to play ball with Elroy,' the narrator booms. 'Yes, this aluminium-encased, battery-powered, robotic woman is the perfect answer for any modern family!'

Jane hops in her spacecraft to U-Rent A Maid, where a moustached owner runs through her options: There's Agnes from Great Britain, a 'basic economy model' who's seen light usage at the hands of an old English teacher called, surreally from a British viewer's point of view, Mr Chips. Then there's saucy French maid-bot Blanche Cog, who has good suspension and an engine 'in the rear, where an engine belongs'. Then there's the 'old girl' Rosey, who's got 'a lot of mileage' and is 'H-O-M-E-L-Y' but still 'eager' to please.

With her fluttering eyelashes, hourglass curves and starched maid's apron, collar and cuffs, Rosey is, of course, suspect through a feminist lens. No faceless automaton, Rosey is female, servile and, as African-American journalist and sci-fi fan Erin puts it to me, 'unapologetically raced': there's a direct line from Rosey's bustling derrière and motherly attributes to *Tom and Jerry*'s heavy-set, African-American housemaid Mammy Two Shoes.

Such critiques were lost on my brother Adam and I as we settled down with our Breville toasted sandwiches – brother the customary cheese and pickle; sister cheese and tomato heated to the temperature of the earth's core – in front of our three-bar gas fire. Through my 1980s childhood, *The Jetsons* was required Saturday-morning sofa viewing. It proposed, to this 10-year-old suburbanite, a world that was at once recognizably now and tantalizingly then. *The Jetsons* gave us jetpacks and computerized dinners, but also a family that was white, middle-class and 2.4 (dog Astro was the .4, having perfected speech and being walked on a high-speed treadmill). It was also unquestioningly patriarchal, and I wondered, even then, why fictional futurism combined the technological cutting-edge with social conservativism.

Perhaps the unbridled consumerism of *The Jetsons'* American future accounted for my concurrent obsession with hanging out at the home of my childhood friend Anne-Marie. I had little in common with Anne-Marie, but her mum Pat permitted us endless boxes of microwaved chips and toasted Pop-Tarts. This was unlike my own drably old-fashioned mother, who stuck to the embarrassing oven-cooked classics, viewing the microwave we'd bought in 1985 as little more than an inadequate re-heater of forgotten cups of Nescafé. Or possibly an ornament.

By the seventies, the cultural fantasy of the female robot maid had moved from sci-fi to the workshop. In the 1970s and '80s, a range of start-ups promised to bring a feminized humanoid robot to every American home. These included Miss Honeywell, the Hamilton Beach robot 'housewife of tomorrow' (who was exhibited in New York, despite being a technological impossibility), and a robotic maid who was tellingly marketed as the 'Maid Without Tears' (and was exposed as a fraud in 1973).

In this world of hucksters and scams, Sico, a humanoid helper designed to be 'relatable', was the first genuine breakthrough. Designed by Robert Doornick, the founder of US company International Robotics, Sico still had to be controlled and voiced remotely by Doornick, but its look and functions predicted the fully functioning domestic robots that would arrive two decades later. Sico became the first non-human member of America's Screen Actors Guild after appearing in a string of movies and TV series during the eighties. The robot guest-starred in *Days of Our Lives*, entertained Ronald Reagan at a White House dinner, toured with James Brown, and shared an intimate moment with Carly Simon in the music video for her song 'My New Boyfriend'. But Sico's most famous screen outing was in 1985's *Rocky IV*, in which Rocky Balboa's brother-in-law Paulie falls in love with a coquettish Sico after reprogramming the robot to have the voice of a human woman. 'That's my girl,' he tells Rocky, pointing at the droid. 'She loves me.'

In 1972's *The Stepford Wives*, American novelist and play-wright Ira Levin satirizes the reactionary nature of 20th-century future fantasies, which frequently parlay a pliant female domesticity into the robotic age. In Levin's novel, talented New York photographer Joanna Eberhart arrives in the fictional Connecticut town of Stepford, eager to start a new life with her husband Walter and two kids. As time goes on, Eberhart becomes increasingly disturbed by the zombie-like women of Stepford, especially when she witnesses once independent-minded friends and fellow new arrivals to Stepford turning into mindless, submissive housewives. Have the town's menfolk conspired to turn their wives into robots? For Second Wave feminists, the novel was a gift, with 'Stepford Wife' quickly becoming shorthand for women who refused to have their feminist consciousness raised as they doggedly conformed to the 1950s model of docile domesticity.

In many ways, we've moved on little from those sexist imaginings of the domestic future. The labour-saving domestic robot that can interact with the family naturally, that can speak and understand commands, that can navigate domestic space with an almost-human ease, is, apparently, the robot we still long for. But what constitutes a 'robot'? Surprisingly, the term does not have an agreed-upon definition. If pressed,

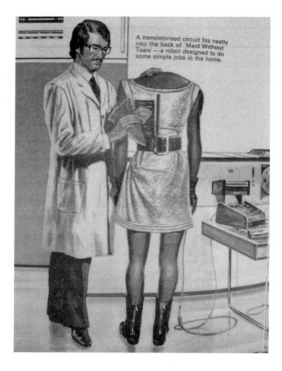

The 'Maid Without Tears', also available in top-to-toe black,
for added racist overtones[89]

you might cite the following: a 'body', an ability to move, and
intelligence. In robotics, definitions often distinguish robots
– machines that perform the functions listed above – from
'synths', or systems designed to mimic humans, e.g. online
'bots' and voice-activated personal assistants such as Alexa.
According to the podcast *Robot or Not?*, the pertinent definition hinges on who, if anyone, is controlling a given machine.
So a self-driving car is not a robot as the user designates its
destination, but an automatic vacuum cleaner is, because it's
in control of its path through space (until it collides with the
coffee table and flips itself like an unfortunate tortoise).

In contemporary fiction, female-sexed robots are, frequently, vehicles to explore matters of agency and

consciousness. Based on a Swedish precursor,[90] British/ American TV series *Humans* (2015–18) is a drama series set in an alternative near-future where humanoid robot workers and servants are widespread. In the Swedish version, robots are illicitly reprogrammed as sexbots, whereas in the UK/ US version the dual role is explicit. Consigned to a brothel, sexbot Niska struggles with her role as much as domestic servant Anita does, as each of the synths stealthily develops consciousness and an awareness of their debased social position. Their human owners simultaneously grapple with their robot servants' 'too-humanness': is Anita a slave or a member of the family? Is Anita commandeering mum Laura's role, or is mum paranoid? When at one point husband Joe asks Laura what she's doing as Anita carves the children's lunchbox fruit into swan shapes and prepares a chicken chasseur for dinner, Laura replies, bleakly: 'Oh, just standing here, being a crap mum.'

Such ethical dilemmas are the reason Tim and I decided to unplug our voice-activated Amazon Echo and consign it to the loft. How, we wondered, were Leo's increasingly impolite imperatives to Alexa – 'Alexa, play hop the bunnies song!'; 'Alexa, play "Baby Shark"!' – moulding his sense of his place and privilege in a gendered pecking order?

As the technology has evolved, the femaleness persists. Voice-activated virtual assistants Alexa, Cortana and Google Assistant were all female from their launches until 2018, when Amazon introduced a suite of six male and female voices.* The big tech giants argued that both men and women prefer the 'relatable' sound of female voices. Writing for *The Atlantic* in 2016, Adrienne LaFrance poured scorn on this convenient excuse: 'The simplest explanation is that people are conditioned to expect women, not men, to be in administrative roles

---

* Siri was the only virtual PA to buck the trend by offering male voices, in some dialects such as British English.

— and that the makers of digital assistants are influenced by these social expectations.'

Feminized servility has remained a design feature of the robot world. Japanese hospitality bot Pepper, who can perceive and respond to human emotion and is widely offered as the answer to the ticking care time bomb for ageing populations in the West, is styled as a soft-voiced girlish helpmeet: assiduous, kind and always up for chatting, but never in the way. Meanwhile, at a pizza restaurant in Pakistan, busty wheeled robots accessorized with neck scarves deliver food to diners' tables; and at a gentleman's club in Las Vegas, androids in garters perform sexy pole dances.*

From electricity to the microwave oven, 'carebots' to twin tubs, technology has been proposed as the answer to the drudgery of domestic labour — and later, to feminist complaints about this drudgery — since the dawn of the industrial age. Mrs J. G. Frazer's 1913 book *First Aid to the Servantless* answered the plight of the housewives whose cooks and maids were on the brink of disappearing into the jobs and factories of the First World War, with her breakthrough gadget the 'Ukanusa Drudgee', the name a weird feminized anthropomorphization of what was, in effect, an early easy-squeezing mop. Thanks to the Drudgee, young housewife Lucy's morning of polishing her floors with beeswax is such a carousel of carefree joy that she breaks into song:

Mop it, wipe it,
Brush it, swipe it,
Rub it, scrub it,
Till all is shiny,
Like the briny
Ocean in the sun...

---

* Pole-dancing robots are apparently a boom category in robotics, with pole-dancing robots Lexy and Tess being developed for the European market by a German robotics company, Tobit.

Technology exists in relation to that time-worn domestic labour-saver: human servitude. It forms a feedback loop that leads to differentiated patterns of global innovation. In India, low labour costs keep Delhi's human carpet-sweepers, who laboriously paddle carpets with short-handled whisks, in employment over arguably more efficient vacuum cleaners. Elizabeth Silva's 2010 paper for the *Feminist Review*, 'Maids, Machines and Morality in Brazilian Homes', shows that the low labour cost of maids and the relatively high cost of electricity and technologies in Brazil conspire to suppress the modernization of labour-saving technologies, with servants left to work in 'dirty' service kitchens and any mod cons preserved for use by the owners of the house on the maid's day off.

'It was accepted,' says Silva, of these middle-class Brazilian employers of maids, 'that electricity should not be used if it could be substituted by the labour of maids, and also it was widely perceived that maids could damage household technologies if they were allowed to use them.'

In the rich world, incentives to develop labour-saving technologies peaked with the mass exodus of the working classes from domestic servitude in the 1910s to 1930s, an era that saw the rollout of electricity to domestic dwellings and the invention of early washing machines, vacuum cleaners and electric irons; and, later, in the 1960s to 1980s, when consumer spending power was rising and women were abandoning their roles as full-time housewives for the Double Day of work and home. This later boom period introduced many of the kitchen appliances we rely on today, from dishwashers to microwaves (that futuristic and functionless item that was nevertheless displayed with pride on our 1980s faux-Edwardian kitchen countertop) to food mixers and juicers. It also saw the arrival of nearly ready products, such as ready meals and permanent-press clothing.

Despite the seemingly quick pace of these breakthroughs, especially in the late 20th century, for much of human history, innovation in the tools and technology employed in house-work has been painfully slow. The technologies of house cleaning and fabric laundering changed little from the 1600s to the 1940s. Frequently, as Caroline Davidson has recounted, new inventions were greeted with suspicion by both women householders and domestic servants. In 1923, a British, all-woman committee convened by the British Ministry of Labour responded to the crisis in the supply of female domes-tic servants by recommending that householders buy the latest labour-saving devices to make domestic service more attractive to 'educated' girls. The committee encountered resistance, however, as they made their recommendations. 'There is,' one member mused, 'a curious and quite unrea-soning hostility among maids themselves to the use of such appliances, due presumably to the conservatism of which the British race is not infrequently accused.' Even the 18th-century women's rights activist Mary Wollstonecraft was prone to such suspicions, complaining that the cutting-edge wood-burning close stoves she'd encountered on a trip to Scandinavia were 'suffocating'. Compared to the open fires then common in Britain, these fires were economical, only needed refuelling twice a day and gave out a great deal of heat – so they could have been a means of liberating women from the non-stop labour demanded of maintaining a hearth.

Wollstonecraft didn't see it, although she noted that Swedes only replenished their close stoves twice daily. 'I like a fire,' she mused, in a 1796 correspondence, 'a wood one in preference; and I am convinced that the current of air which it attracts renders this the best mode of warming rooms.'

From the ground-breaking introduction of coal, to coal gas and mains water and electricity, women's voices and expertise have been noticeably absent in the waves of technological invention that promise to ease the domestic load women have disproportionately borne. Early patents for labour-saving devices taken out by women are both thin on the ground and trivial (in the UK egg poachers and boilers were a lively category).

Women's lack of involvement in these great waves of innovation is, of course, an expression of our historic lack of structural and economic power. But the lack of women vocally advocating for the new ways also contributed to the slow uptake of technologies that had the potential to transform women's domestic lives. Coal gas and electric lighting were both developed for public use decades before their arrival in domestic dwellings.

Britain's Electrical Association of Women (EAW) is one bright spot in this otherwise bleak history. Founded in 1924 by Mabel Matthews and Caroline Haslett – two upper-middle-class women who had served as engineers in the First World War – the EAW started life as a pressure group advocating for the rollout of electricity to working- and middle-class homes, with women's emancipation in view. With support from the British

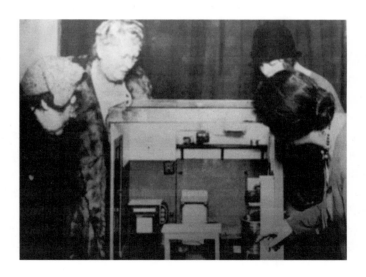

EAW members examining a model kitchen for 'working-class flats' in 1931. The kitchen features a whistling kettle, cooker, water heater and wash boiler

Electrical & Allied Manufacturers' Association and the General Electric Company, by 1933 the EAW had set up headquarters in London and soon had branch offices in Manchester, Birmingham and Glasgow. The doughty women who led the Association set about educating housewives on the benefits of 'women's best friend' through nationwide lectures, summer schools for teachers, and school visits. By the late 1930s, the EAW's electrical housecraft course – which included electricity generation and transmission, home installation of meters, fuses and switches, and components on cookery, refrigeration, kitchen planning and electrical safety – was a core module of the domestic science curriculum, and EAW members toured the country exhibiting model electrical homes to curious housewives.

At its worst, the EAW's upper-middle-class maternalism verged on battiness. The Association's 1929 propaganda book, *The Rays*, reimagines electricity as a 'magic' fairy. But their contention that electricity could be an emancipatory force for British women had merit. Homes that had introduced electricity in the 1940s – and the full range of modern appliances that made the most of this new energy source – saw their domestic workloads reduced by up to 73 per cent.[91] In Canada a similar pressure group, the Housewives Consumers Association (1937–52), focused on lobbying for state control of food and utilities prices and had some success – they are now seen as the earliest advocates for the notion of 'food security' as a political project. Sadly, by the 1980s the EAW had become a punchline – viewed, as one electricity industry administrator scathingly puts it, as 'mumsy cranks'. They disbanded in 1986 after a failed attempt to highlight nuclear power as the next breakthrough in women's empowerment, just as the non-violent protest camp against nuclear power at RAF Greenham Common (established by tens of thousands of feminists) was at its height. The EAW's legacy was forgotten.

In recent years, technology has offered us contrivances that mow our lawns, wash our windows and assemble IKEA furniture, as well as smart home systems connected to the Internet of Things (IoT) that, for example, register the contents of our fridges and reorder items that are about to run out. Coming technologies include laundry-folding robots, robot servants such as Segway's Loomo (which follows you around the supermarket carrying your shopping), and 'robotic kitchens' that cook elaborate meals from scratch and manually wash pots and pans. Christopher Atkeson, a roboticist at Carnegie Mellon University in Pennsylvania, predicts that our domestic future will be all about multi-functional 'robot arms' such as those being developed by Moley for kitchen use: inflatable robot arms that can scrub surfaces, bathe people, fold laundry and pick up clutter. Alarmingly for your author, a Silicon Valley start-up called Chowbotics recently unveiled a salad maker called Sally. 'You could call Sally a vending machine if you want, or you could call her a robot,' said Chowbotics CEO Deepak Sekar, adding, breezily, that Sally also assembles 'grain bowls' and yoghurt parfaits.

For all of their fanfare, these technologies are rarely presented as solutions to the stalled domestic revolution. Interviewed for BBC Radio 4's *The Food Programme*, Moley inventor Dr Mark Oleynik, a Russian entrepreneur and computer scientist, admits that he was inspired to invent the Moley arms by his own incompetence in the kitchen. 'You didn't think of marrying someone who could cook?' asked the female interviewer, before wondering 'what the women in your family' thought of Oleynik's invention.

'No,' Oleynik quickly answered, 'because what wife can cook food from different continents and with different techniques each night of the week?'

The greatest domestic technological advancements of the 19th century were the arrivals of mains water and gas lighting, which did away with the centuries-old labour burdens of water-fetching and lighting-up. Electricity, too, led to a big bang in terms of reduction in the hours women devoted to housework. Will robotics signal the next big bang for reduction of human-performed domestic labour?

Well, you're pretty pessimistic on this front. When we asked our survey respondents whether they thought technology would lessen the burden of chores in the future, only 22 per cent of respondents were confident it would; with 35 per cent expressing hope that it might, but thinking real impacts would be unlikely.

Do you believe that technology will lessen the future current burden of household chores?

'No — time saved will simply be filled with new chores.'
Married woman aged 33–45, US

'Change yes, but possibly not lessen. New categories of work will still be required. I think this is where tensions often lie, not the actual doing. Although interestingly, my male partner takes on more management of the house when technology is available.' Greek-Armenian heterosexual woman aged 33–45, US

'I think technologies such as dishwashers and the like are becoming more accessible to people, and more technologies that could lessen the burden will continue to be developed. But this might just create a new higher standard of household cleanliness and perfection.' White married mother, aged 25–32; UK

The fear that new technology might usher in more exacting standards, and new categories of work (we might call these categories 'digital domestic labour') is well founded.

In *The Feminine Mystique*, Betty Friedan points out that the new technology available to 1950s American housewives often made cleaning more laborious than it needed to be. Once a woman 'got an appliance going', she felt compelled to undertake cleaning that wasn't strictly necessary. The 1960s housewife, at the point of the post-war breakthrough of electric-powered domestic appliances, was spending longer each day housekeeping than she had 30 years earlier, despite spending seven times as much money on labour-saving appliances. And Caroline Davidson recounts that the spread of electric lighting illuminated dust and cobwebs under the 'merciless rays' of the 75-watt light bulb, and that women who replaced their coal gas ranges with newfangled gas stoves would cook more elaborate meals on them. Meanwhile the arrival of electric washing machines raised expectations as to the availability of freshly laundered clothes and bedsheets (until the 1950s it was only typical to wash underclothes such as underwear, shirts and blouses on a weekly basis, and bedding was washed infrequently).

Academic Ayako Kano notes in her book *Japanese Feminist Debates: A Century of Contention on Sex, Love, and Labor* that the arrival of new technologies in future-mad Japan – a country often held up as a techno-social utopia – has led to a weight of expectations placed on women, ranging from elaborate multi-course dinners cooked from scratch to a crippling focus on neatness and tasteful domestic decoration. I mention this to Diana, a journalist friend who's married to a Japanese man, has two young daughters and is based in Tokyo, and she complains of the assumption that Japanese mothers will assemble lunchtime bento boxes for their kids featuring elaborate manga-character shapes arranged on the rice in carefully cut pieces of veg. 'Achieving such feats against the clock with fumbling British fingers is, I have to say, beyond me,' she adds blackly.

We need only to register the fact that Japanese women perform 87 per cent of housework and childcare – a greater proportion than in any other rich nation in the world – to realize that Japan is not the hi-tech utopia it's often portrayed to be. Because, when it comes to all of these new technologies, we have to ask: who steps in? Who steps in when our IoT-enabled fridge mistakenly orders 3,000 kilograms of unsalted butter?

We arrive at Living Tomorrow's Brussels compound in the sheeting grey rain locals refer to as *'la drache'*. The colourlessness is in sympathy with the sight that greets us, which is more like an office in the exurbs of a second-tier city than a portal into our shared human future.

Tim has a more sinister reading. 'It looks like the sort of place where a Bond villain would go into hiding to plan the destruction of the earth,' he says, as we pile out of an Uber with our soggy buggy and soggy son.

In a hard shiny foyer we meet innovation coach Dirk Gaudeus, who greets us with a 'halloo!' and a round of back-clapping as he ushers us into a demonstration room. Here, Gaudeus fiddles with a laptop to instruct Nao, a metre-high humanoid robot, to dance Gangnam style to the Korean pop hit as we chat. Leo stares at Nao's small white windmilling robot arms and collapses into tears.

Gaudeus is all effervescent enthusiasm and tufty mad-professor hair. 'You know people get like little kids again when they meet a robot?' he says. 'We take Nao to care homes, and elderly inhabitants open up about their pain and loneliness as they never would with a human carer. It is quite, quite, quite touching.'

The Living Tomorrow organization describes itself as a 'future scenario' builder. Part-funded by Microsoft, the site includes a model care home, model restaurant, and a 'house of the future' fitted with the mod cons we'll all be cursing at when they're in our homes in 2030 and they order that 3,000 kilograms of butter following a system error. Corporations on delegate trips – European, increasingly East Asian –

troop through its rooms with inquisitive expressions. Living Tomorrow's next 'hush-hush' project is a fully operational hotel of the future, complete with room-service robots and personalized lighting, heating and entertainment settings automatically captured from guests' home settings via the Internet of Things.

Tim, Leo and I follow Gaudeus through the restaurant of the future, where Thermodyne fridges arrest food decay, and herbs are grown in in-built vertical gardens on the walls. In the house of the future, a large, open-plan living room and kitchen is ornamented with white, sensuous curving surfaces that wouldn't look out of place in an episode of *The Jetsons*. Why, I wonder, is the future always so bubble-like and 1960s?

Gaudeus explains that when the house of the future notices its residents – us – are heading home, it will 'start things happening'. The house is currently configured to Gaudeus's heat, light and music preferences. He takes a bottle of Viognier out of the curvy white fridge and the fridge – *PING!* – puts in an order for a replacement, which strikes me as a fast route to alcoholism.

Fine-tuned personalization will be the primary feature of future houses, Gaudeus says, as Tim and Leo take a seat on a curvy sofa next to a giant projected TV screen. For example, Tim could sit on the sofa enjoying a glacial breeze while I chop vegetables in tropical 25-degree heat a few metres away, as I curse at the fridge. Granted, temperature preferences are a bone of contention in our home: I routinely dress for bed as if I'm preparing for the slopes at Chamonix, whereas Tim can't sleep unless he's as nature intended, right leg resplendent on top of the duvet like a felled log. But I'm not sure enjoying our ideal heat settings to a fraction of a degree will be the breakthrough Gaudeus promises in terms of family accord. We could end up even more isolated in our individual ambient micro-zones. Why have a hug, for example, when you'd risk a head cold? And, more to the point, why am I over there chopping veg in Gaudeus's brave new world?

The house of the future's other advancements – such as the Tubie, which irons shirts by inflating them with high-pressure air into weird puffed-up torsos that resemble decapitated superheroes – are, well, unconvincing. And I'm not sure, either, that I'll take to printing my own lawnmower or the replacement parts for my broken fence on a home 3-D printer; not when my permanently jammed, bog-standard black-and-white paper printer is the source of so much rage. But mocking the future – all those dinners as pills and triangular foil dresses – has always been an own goal. Cheap humour that masks the fact that the joke is usually on us.

The Tubie, Gaudeus admits, is soon to be relegated to the scrapheap of futures past. It failed to find appeal after a prototype was introduced onto the market a couple of years ago. 'That's the problem with the future,' Gaudeus muses, 'it moves so fast.' There are always teething problems, too: Google glasses that contravene privacy laws; virtual reality devices that cause seasickness. They're only just working out how to get driverless cars to navigate human error and manholes, Gaudeus says. For all of this, domestic life will look very different in a few short years. 'It's all coming, it's all coming!' he briskly adds, with mad professorial glee, as we step across the wet forecourt into a Škoda.

Later, in a nicotine-stained Brussels café that's unchanged since the days when gas lamps were the *dernier cri* in domestic technology, Tim and I dissect our odd experience at Living Tomorrow. Before we left, Gaudeus had launched into a jeremiad about how much he enjoys whispering to horses as an escape from the grind of his digital working day. It had undermined his future-eulogizing a bit.

Tim drinks a slug of a dark Trappist beer. A beer mat sticks to the bottom of his glass.

'To be honest, all of it freaks me out,' he admits. 'Alexa, self-ordering fridges – it all feels a bit like people are outsourcing their brains. And those robot cooking arms: do they chop veg, or do they stab you in the side of the head when you tell them off?'

I laugh. Leo grabs a knuckleful of duck-fat *frites* and laughs too, although I suspect he's laughing at his dad's impersonation of stabbing robot arms, which give the impression of someone drunkenly juggling invisible balls rather than Tim's Luddite complaints.

Tim has a suspicion. He thinks that our current fascination with domestic technology is all about our self-aggrandizing notions of how busy we are.

'Are we really too busy to use an iron or to pop to the shop and buy a bottle of wine?' he says. 'I mean, God – will we all be sitting around waiting for machines to blow our noses in a few years?'

Then: 'Hang on, you're not writing that thing about nose-blowing machines down in your notebook, are you?'

The breakthrough technology I recall most fondly from 1980s Solihull is the arrival of the microwave and its exotic, palate-scalding 'hot spots'. We washed up by hand, and salad spinners were a thing of, other, more middle-class homes. The Breville sandwich toaster – also a game of chicken with its incendiary melted tomato – was more of a fad than a time-saving alternative for a meal cooked on our four-ring upright gas stove (a gas stove I remember being as ashamed of as I was my father's old Maestro when a middle-class friend from sixth-form college paid a visit to my family home in the early '90s). In Tim's childhood home, the microwave oven arrived with a figurative and literal bang, when his dad memorably continued microwaving a sausage until it caught fire, perplexed as to why it wasn't turning brown.

A few weeks after our visit to Brussels, I visit Home Futures, an exhibition at the London Design Museum that explores the domestic future as it was conceived of in our recent past. Walking through the rooms of modular furniture and self-assembly electric lamps, I'm struck by how close some of the trappings of this imagined past are to our present. In some ways, the present is more dystopian than the modernists imagined: the nomadism that designers of the past thrilled for has become today's digital nomadism, in which homes are adaptable and multifunctional because capitalism has inveigled itself into the domestic space through the expectation that we're always working. The new great hope of domestic labour-saving is ultra-connectivity and personalization, which – as sci-fi author Bruce Sterling argued in a 2004 lecture at SIGGRAPH, an annual computer graphics conference – can be seen as a sordid power grab for data dressed up as the future, by tech companies with skin in the game (Google, Facebook, Amazon, Apple and Microsoft). Dr Orla Lynskey, who teaches and conducts research in the areas of data protection, technology regulation, digital rights and EU law, says of start-ups in the Internet of Things that even if they talk of serving social goods such as closing the gender labour gap and reversing global warming, they are, above all, capitalist ventures chasing the next round of investment.

At Home Futures, a haunting video runs on loop against a bare white wall. It features a man who lives from featureless hotel room to featureless hotel room because he has turned his smart Copenhagen apartment into his income on Airbnb. 'What is home? I can't afford my home to be more than these four walls,' this modern man says, waving at his drab single hotel room. It unsettles me for several hours. 'Home', in this dystopian vision of the capitalist 'sharing economy', is the new frontier to be commodified and sold back to a given buyer as a temporary home-from-home. In cities, architecture is changing: compressing us, as a gesture of modernity, into ever-smaller spaces. In global cities such as London and New York, homes divided into rooms, as we've known them for five centuries, are disappearing as we squeeze our human functions into smaller and smaller open-plan spaces.

Of course, home was never a precious retreat from the demands on our bodies made by capitalism, especially for women, but there's a sense that our homes – if these trends and fragmentations continue – will lose more than walls and discrete divisions of use and space. What are the demands made on humans to operate in cramped spaces where we're seamlessly producing and reproducing for capital? Who occupies the toddler when dad's patching into his virtual office in a cardboard box in the corner – another innovation Gaudeus had shown us – because his business can no longer afford a bricks-and-mortar office space? Won't turning a bedroom into a playroom by pissing about with adaptable modular furniture become just another new category of feminized work?

At the end of *The Jetsons* first episode, Jane's choice of the budget model Rosey, the 'old girl' with 'a lot of mileage', has backfired. The robot has cost husband George his job after plonking a pineapple upside-down cake on his boss Mr Spacely's head. The new family member has proved, in the end, too un-robotic: exacting revenge on old buffoon Spacely like a faithful family dog. Rosey embodies the disquiet that comes in all of our navigations of help, whether robotic or flesh-and-blood: our need for this intimate work of care to be made human; to be anthropomorphized and feminized. To be just like faithful old Mammy Two Shoes.

It's a characteristically human trait that the more gadgets we have, the more we elevate our notions of household efficiency and cleanliness: we take it for granted that our wardrobes will always be filled with clean clothes; that our gardens boast well-maintained flowerbeds; and that our shiny kitchen appliances will make it possible to enjoy a diverse, tasty and even exotic menu. The march of technological advancement, after all, has done little to curb human desires.

New domestic technologies have had, at best, a neutral effect on the patriarchal status quo. At their worst they entrench private, patriarchal modes of housekeeping: the three-bed semi with the lone wife at her post at the sink, watching the kids in the garden through the double-glazed panes, as my mother did, behind the floral roman blind that was shadowed by grease stains. These old-fashioned modes of housekeeping disadvantage women and domestic workers, and sustain the assumption that the domestic arena is a self-sufficient unit maintained by a wife (or feminized care/sexbot). For all of the trends, articles and cartoonish sci-fi, for all of the robot maids and self-driving cars, the biggest domestic labour saver in post-war history happened more by accident than design. It *was* white and curvaceously smooth-edged, though.

It was the contraceptive pill.

9

Marketing Yummy Mummy (or The New Sexed Sell)

Faye's subtly tanned legs are crossed decorously, mid-shin. The 41-year-old plays with the paper straw in her limoncello mimosa as she discusses, with friend Gloria, the pros and cons of having fat harvested from her 'mummy tummy' and injected into her face to make it smoother, plumper, and 'more *me*'. The problem, she complains, is 'resting bitch face', or the tendency of the sagging of early-middle-aged skin to give one's face the aspect of petulance.

'It's just too bloody exhausting to have to grin all the time, so you don't – you know – look like a gargoyle.'

I politely raise objections. Faye looks more like a '70s Bond girl than a gargoyle: her hair is long and straw-blonde, her lips sheen with gloss, her dress is tight and uncompromisingly white.

The five women gathered at this Kensington restaurant call themselves the Chelsea Yums: partly a tongue-in-cheek nod to 'yummy mummy', the popular term for expensively maintained stay-at-home wives; and partly, I suspect, as a vague ambition for living. But the term is also a source of succour. The women report having grown apart from old friends since they gave up work to become full-time mothers and housekeepers.

Gloria is also expensively turned out. Her husband is a partner at a London law firm and they have three kids. On bad days, the 39-year-old feels frivolous and disapproved of.

'Even women who can afford to stay at home with their kids have to justify it these days by becoming "mumpreneurs",' she says. 'I bloody hate that word. The world doesn't need any more "sexy" breastfeeding dresses with zips that make your nipples bleed, or, I don't know, £7 jars of organic compote.'

It's hard enough, Gloria adds, living up to the relentless press of expectations that come with upper-middle-class modern parenting: checking your kid's friend's allergy requirements when they come for playdates before you bake sugar and wheat-free cakes (a bought-in cake, even from Dominique Ansel, just doesn't say a 'mother's love'); finding Mandarin and music tutors; topping up your LOs (little ones) with organic, zinc-free sunscreen.

I've come to Kensington to explore a new demographic. After four decades in which the number of stay-at-home mothers (SAHMs) consistently declined, the 2000s saw an overall rise in their number in the US[92] (from a 1999 low of 23 per cent, to 28 per cent of mothers in 2014). In the UK, the number of middle-class mothers in work has broadly remained stable at around 75 per cent, but amongst the wealthier upper-middle-class cohort of heterosexual women, represented by my well-heeled white companions, stay-at-home motherhood is making a comeback. In part reflecting this latter group, London now has the lowest rate of working women of reproductive age in the UK, with 26 per cent of women aged between 25 and 54 not working for pay.

Most of the Yums have two or more children* and none of them, as a badge of maternal honour, have nannies. Their help is mostly, as Faye quips, 'below stairs' – Polish women clean for them and Australian men are sought-after to tend

---

* Unfashionably in a country in which women now average 1.8 births.

their gardens. When you have a large house, there's a lot to manage. Whole new categories of labour, in fact. Who, Gloria hypothetically asks, needed someone to curate their domestic art collections 20 years ago, say? Which of the Yums' mothers were expected to know the provenance, gluten content and organic pedigree of their groceries so their kid's friends' mums didn't go off-the-wall at a drop-off playdate? Who, in those simpler times, had to consider the Instagram friendliness of their daughter's birthday bash?

Being at home can be lonely, and the assumption that they live off their husbands makes Snell, a small elfin woman with a husband working in finance and a fifth child on the way, feel 'like a piece of shit'. So, she explains, the Yums 'cling together like refugees on a lifeboat'.

'Hang on, can I say that?' she glances around, warily. 'Does it make me sound *racist*?'

So far in this book we have explored factors that might influence women's retreat from paid labour: disillusionment with the emancipatory promise of paid work; persistent patriarchal attitudes that land women with the Double Day; policies inimical to working parenthood. This reversion has roots, too, in the current incarnation of the feminist backlash we saw in Chapter Five, which reifies women's essential roles as domestic carers, even as the project of emancipation in the public sphere – at least in some quarters – ostensibly holds.

But the work of Dr Shani Orgad[93] of the London School of Economics finds that this puzzle of highly educated women who make what's seen to be the retrograde choice – leaving careers for the ignominy of the 'mummy track' – is for the most part a reaction to the failed promises of equality. Women who enter highly paid roles in the corporate world find that these worlds foster a culture of 16-hour days and stigmatize workers who have care needs. Or, worse, pay lip service to flexi and parenting policies and fail to follow through. Many women, Orgad found in her 2019 study of the stay-at-home wives of top earners, had opted out of the working world out of disillusionment rather than choice.

What most intrigues me about the Yummy Mummy phenomenon is its attendant cultural rehabilitation – glamorization, even – of the stay-at-home mother. At the height of the 1980s and '90s Having It All cult, stay-at-home mothers were, as Deirdre Johnston and Debra Swanson discovered in their 2003 content analysis of US women's magazines of the 1980s and '90s, frequently demonized as lazy mums on benefits (or 'welfare queens', if they were poor); or submissive, 'zombified' and bitchy 'Stepford Wives' suffering from such complaints as 'mommy mush brain', if they were wealthy.

In Australia, economist Greg Jericho notes that stay-at-home wives were most typically portrayed in this period as a 'drain on the economy'. In the UK, similarly, early-21st-century discourses positioned SAHMs as vain, lazy, indulgent and over-pampered. An eviscerating 2007 op-ed in the *Telegraph* outlined the average day of the 'hideously parasitic' stay-at-home wife, a woman who is wealthy by marriage, having commuted her 'trophy' status to a life of idle self-indulgence:

5.30 a.m.: Husband leaves for London.

7.45 a.m.: Filipina brings wife tea in bed.

8 a.m.: Nanny takes children to school.

8.30 a.m.: Breakfast, Sudoku and the papers.

9.30 a.m.–4 p.m.: God knows; possibly gym, spa, shopping, boozy lunch with friends, nap or massage.

4 p.m.: Nanny collects children from school.

5.30 p.m.: Nanny gives children tea and goes home.

7 p.m.: Filipina gives children bath.

7.30 p.m.: Wife disappears off to book group.

9 p.m.: Husband returns and roots around for an M&S ready-meal.

10.30 p.m.: Wife returns. Bed.

10.35 p.m.: Sex? In your dreams.

The piece argues that 'the transition from trophy wife to toxic wife is as fast as the end result is furious'.

In Japan, these discourses became combative. The postwar 'Housewife Debate' began with the rise of Japanese consumerism in the 1950s. As feminist academic Ayako Kano recounts it, the attack on housewives positioned them, in their role as consumers under capitalism, as idle gluttons enjoying the time-saving boons of washing machines and rice steamers. Gone, claimed these arguments, were the hard-working housewives of a Golden Age, who maintained extended families and cottage industries such as weaving cloth and producing soy sauce from scratch. In the 1960s, these feminist debates rehabilitated the housewife and, similarly to feminist narratives in the West, called for women to be remunerated for their labour in the home to improve their social status.

By the 2000s, the debate had become fractious. Ichihara Rosa's essay 'Go to Hell, Full-time Housewives' caused a sensation. It refers to stay-at-home wives as 'cattle': 'They hoist their dreams on children whom they treat as dress up dolls. They spend more time than is necessary on housework, treating their homes as if they were model display rooms.'

In her 2004 novel *The Howl of the Losing Dog*, Sakai Junko explored the competing – and equally unfeminist discourse – which positions single career women such as Sakai as 'loser dogs' and 'snarling demon hags' who are crazed by unarticulated jealousy of their counterparts, the 'winner dog' married women. 'Society doesn't like loser dogs,' Sakai says. 'Society likes the housewife who waits at home with a vat of miso soup for her husband and kids.'

There's something intrinsic to the Yummy Mummy – and her pornified alter egos, the Hot Mom and the MILF* – that was absent in earlier cultural representations of the stay-at-home wife. The 19th-century Good Housekeeper and the 1950s Modern Homemaker and, in the US, the Perfect Wife in her Ideal Home were all required to be expert and indefatigable carers, feeders and sweepers – as it fell to them to maintain neat and pleasing-looking children and a neat and decorous personal appearance. They were, however, generally exempt from the requirement to be yummy and (MIL)fuckable.

For those visiting the *Daily Mail* Ideal Home Exhibition in Olympia in March 1947,[94] the publicity brochure for furniture-makers James Broderick & Co. left little doubt as to the expectations placed upon housewives that they should be domestically adept and neatly turned out. The section 'What every newlywed should know' included a day-to day plan for new brides:

Monday. Is not essentially a day for laundry. Scour the kitchen after week-end catering activities, check upon on rations and shop for vegetables, canned foods and breakfast cereals for a few days ahead.

Tuesday. Manage the light personal laundry, leaving the sheets and bath towels. Get all items dried and ironed during the day whenever possible.

Wednesday. Clean thoroughly bedrooms and bathrooms and use early afternoon for silver cleaning.

Thursday. Change bedlinen, launder 'heavies'. While they dry, clean the lounge. Iron early afternoon.

---

* The unlovely porn/pop-cultural acronym for 'Mother I'd Like to Fuck'.

Friday. Plan meals for week-end, making provision for Monday 'left-overs'. Shop. Give dining room or dining alcove a thorough clean and polish.

Saturday. Keep this free for the family as far as possible. Prepare vegetables for Sunday and manage some cooking in the morning. Then relax.

Sunday. Belongs to you and those who share the home with you. Confine all essential cooking to early part of morning.

It continued: 'What you wear in the house for the working hours is important. Crisp, easily removed gay overalls, smocks, nylon or spongeable plastic aprons look attractive. Wear your hair as you would do for the man-of-the-house's homecoming.'

A survey of women's domestic workwear from the 17th to 20th centuries highlights this ongoing onus on a practical – if attractive – appearance for houseworking women. In the 1700s and early 1800s, short house gowns, worn by women of all classes, allowed for freedom of movement and were often complemented by 'pockets', which could be tied on and used to carry small tools such as scissors, needles and thimbles. These house gowns were replaced in the 20th century by ready-to-wear house dresses such as those designed by Nell Donnelly Reed, whose simple yet feminine $1 dress (with its pretty scalloped neckline) made her a fortune in the interwar years in the US (no mean feat when these years coincided with the Great Depression).

Of her success, Irish immigrant Reed told a US newspaper that she'd been inspired to 'make women look pretty when they are washing dishes'.

In a similar vein of glamorizing the domestic, female Hollywood film stars of the 1930s and '40s recorded showreel films where they were filmed 'at home' (in stylized domestic settings or the studio), applying make-up, rustling up light meals, and sashaying around in a still-more-glamorous take on the house dress: the flowing peignoir (a light dressing gown).

I ask the Chelsea Yums what they wear about the house in their day-to-day lives. 'Designer yoga pants,' says C, after a beat. The other women nod. Expensive yoga wear – signalling wholesome sexiness and fashion-brand awareness – is the new house dress.

'I take my kids to school in my Lululemons [yoga pants],' adds M. 'But I wouldn't go out without my hair blow-dried, even if I'm in casuals. Although of course I wouldn't want to look *too* blow-dried, either...'

In their 2018 paper 'The Escalating Price of Motherhood: Aesthetic Labour in Popular Representations of "Stay-at-Home" Mothers', Sara De Benedictis and Shani Orgad find that 21st-century representations of the 'good mother' frequently praise and celebrate her for her 'hot' look. These expectations weigh heavily on women who put in the Double Day and are also required to be (MIL)fuckable: an attractive appearance being a central requirement of 'coping' with dual workloads and projecting the image of a successful working mother. Women in the working world have always been expected to 'perform sexuality' as part of the capitalist social contract.[95] The hegemonic look of women in the corporate sphere – killer heels, trim waistlines and impeccably flattened hair – is a style a former City-working female friend refers to as 'the Iron Maiden', after the restrictive torture and execution device rather than the British heavy metal band. It's also in direct descent from the Iron Lady, Margaret Thatcher, whose skirt suits and immovable hairdo defined the 1980s corporate woman: not a hair out of place, nor an errant ruffle, nor a moment of 'feminine' weakness.

What's new, in De Benedictis and Orgad's view, is the extension of this requirement of 'hotness' to stay-at-home mothers, who were historically, as we've seen, exempted from the 'sexual contract' imposed on single and working women: the social requirement to perform sexuality.

Unlike in the 1990s or 2000s, when the Have It All career woman reigned as the cultural ideal, the stay-at-home mother is, De Benedictis and Orgad argue, endorsed as a valid personal choice, as long as she satisfies the requirements of being: a) not on benefits; b) middle class; and c) effortlessly sexual or 'yummy'. 'Mediated figures such as the yummy mummy and pregnant beauty emphasise how maternal identities are reliant upon and articulated through beauty practices and body projects such as dieting and exercise and cosmetic surgery, [which are] entrenched in self-regulation.'

This is true of the Chelsea Yums, who add to their rosters of high-octane 21st-century housekeeping and parenting a rigorous regime of activities or 'body projects', designed to slim, depilate and keep preternaturally youthful their outward appearances, whilst simultaneously concealing the practices that achieve this 'yummy' look.

For the apparently wholesome yoga-panted mum who just slung on her Lululemons for the school run, the labour required to achieve the idealized Yummy Mummy image – to remain slim, body-hair- and baby-puke-free; to have your hair styled, but not too styled; to carefully maintain a natural-looking year-round tan – is masked, and its concomitant practices of self-surveillance, self-disciplining and self-regulation are denied, if not at the Yums conspiratorial brunches (where strange and painful-sounding surgical interventions and harsh diets are discussed frankly), then at least to the outside world.

Gloria would prefer the playground mums to think she'd been home-baking granola snack bars for her 'LOs' at 6 a.m. rather than doing battle with her straighteners, or putting in a 4 a.m. fat-busting 10k before the school run.

A survey of the popular figureheads of Yummy Mummyhood tells us much about the shifting ideals and nuances of the domestic maternal. In the UK, Jools Oliver, whose publicist rebuffed an approach to be interviewed for this book, is the Yummy Mummy par excellence: upper middle class (by wealth), fertile, effortlessly 'yummy', and portrayed as a stay-at-home mother by choice.

I'd always been unsettled by Jools's self-description on her social media feeds: 'mum @ jamieoliver.com'.

The maternal, of course, is a stock descriptive on Twitter and Instagram – 'mother of two terrors!', 'proud mum of three', 'sports mom' – but Jools's blurb goes beyond this: folding, as it does, minimization of the self into the capitalist endeavour of her husband's identity/brand. A feminist friend puts it this way: 'Why doesn't she just cut the crap and say "Jamie Oliver's womb"?' But Jools is more than a womb. She's both naturally yummy and corporate mummy: manifesting and personifying stay-at-home motherhood, whilst selling the new stay-at-home motherhood as a commodity.

The Olivers came into fame in the late 1990s with Jamie's TV show *The Naked Chef* (1999–2001). The hit Channel 4 series (and subsequent shows) made much of the narratives of Jamie's working-class Essex roots, his meritocratic rise through the ranks of London's top restaurant kitchens, and his photogenic and growing traditional family. Although Jools Oliver had worked as a TV researcher before the couple met and had their first child, this was rarely discussed in the acres of glossy magazine coverage soon devoted to the young marrieds. Instead, Jools was repeatedly presented as a 'former model', a career she'd pursued briefly in her youth, and as a mother. In her oft-repeated self-account, 'I wanted the babies, the baking and the roses round the door.'

And as Jamie said of Jools in a 2002 interview, still trotted out ad nauseum in magazine profiles: '[She] hasn't got a mission, she just wants to be married to someone she loves and have a family and that's the end of it, end of story... It baffled me for ages, I almost felt she had a part of her life missing, then I thought, it's sweet and quite refreshing.'

Jools's good looks – naturally glamorous, wholesomely sexy, quick to slim after the birth of each of her five children – are depicted as more the function of 'good genes' than effort, self-regulation and bodywork. Of course we all know, when we take a minute to interrogate the Yummy Mummy mystique, that 'good genes' do not sponge baby sick from a woman's shoulder, or compensate for perinatal hair loss with a swishy hairdo that lands in place as if freshly styled by a salon.

It's easy to bridle at this uncomplicated and apolitical celebration of baking and breeding and 'roses round the door'. But this media-generated New Housewife presents a feminist quandary. To revile Oliver for choosing to be a stay-at-home mother would be unfeminist. The best of feminism, after all, is about giving women choice: the choice to pursue careers and have children; the choice to be full-time mothers dependent on a wage-earner or the state; the choice to throw in the towel on the whole capitalist-patriarchal shit-work shitshow, and set up a feminist separatist community in rural Oregon. But that doesn't mean we should benignly accept this projection of stay-at-home motherhood as an apolitical, post-feminist 'natural' lifestyle. After all, the figure of Jools Oliver as stay-at-home mother is as much a hollow capitalist construction as the Having It All mum or the Perfect Housewife. As 'mum @ jamieoliver.com', Jools and her nature-born mothering practices are relentlessly commodified: in the Little Bird children's clothing brand she designs for Mothercare, the children's books she authors, the constant family snapshots on Instagram. Feted on mothering forums as a 'proud SAHM', Jools apparently has no qualms about heading up a corporate brand that sells this naturalized, effortless and, for most, unattainable motherhood to other mothers and the market.

The labour in these capitalist efforts, the beauty treatments and dieting that women like Oliver undertake to stay 'hot' is invisibilized. To the extent that the public buys its effortlessness.

'I like Jools because she always looks natural and like she couldn't give a damn about celebrity,' says one fan on Facebook group The Mum Group.

The figure of the Yummy (stay-at-home) Mummy is what Arlie Hochschild might call a 'cultural cover-up': a cloak of glamour around an unpalatable truth about the nature of inter-family power dynamics and histories of oppression and abuse. Forget the shitty nappies and the shitty status, it seems to say: you can choose to become a natural-born, naturally beautiful mother-woman; a figure who seems to occupy a space above and beyond the dirty grub of feminism or the laborious domestic day-to-day. In a sleight of stardust, stay-at home motherhood is thus rebranded as a post-feminist choice for the rich and effortlessly beautiful. How different, we have to ask, is this new construction to Friedan's desperate 1950s housewives, for whom motherly fulfilment was also defined as a 'total way of life'?

The marketing of 'yumminess' and the creep of capital into our notions and expressions of good motherhood has happened so rapidly it seems as if it were always there. Today the launching of a mothering lifestyle brand – in the vein of Jools Oliver – is an automatic next step for many women who've achieved a certain level of fame and have also reproduced. Amongst the mum-'me' brands launched in recent years, Elizabeth Banks's portal, ElizabethBanks.com, offers 'Yummy stuff' and 'Mommy stuff', including recipes and product endorsements; actress Jessica Alba's honest.com offers 'safe, eco-friendly, beautiful, convenient, and affordable' baby and home products, from nappies to mouthwash and candles; and actress Brooke Burke's Baboosh (a tribute to her infant daughter's pet name) pedals postpartum belly wraps to help 'shrink your tummy back into shape', as well as workout DVDs and organic stretch-mark prevention oil.

The most famous of these mothering lifestyle brands, of course, is Goop – founded by the waspishly wholesome

Hollywood actress Gwyneth Paltrow when her children Apple and Moses were, respectively, four and two, as a 'homespun weekly newsletter' from her kitchen table. In the 12 years since its founding, Goop has offered mystical-ecological advice on everything from vaginal steaming, to the use of jade vagina eggs to balance women's hormones, to the range of everyday family products in which 'toxins' can be found; from child sunscreens to soya beans to salad dressing.* One male columnist for the *Evening Standard* didn't hold back in his assessment of Paltrow's 'new age claptrap':

> [She's] a human yoga mat, a walking pilates class, a kale smoothie in female form. She glows. She swooshes. Her chi is so centred she could drag the fillings out of your teeth just by frowning slightly. That's her brand. And she uses that brand, unfortunately, to make staggering amounts of money peddling nonsense to idiots.'[96]

The latest arrival in this shouting match of mothering advisories are the Instagram influencer mothers, or Instamoms/ mums. This strand, typically positioned in contrast to starry celebrity mothers as 'everywoman' and 'relatable', began with the 'mommy blog' boom of the mid-2000s. One of the most popular mommy blogs in the US was Dooce, founded by Mormon mother-of-two Heather Armstrong, which billed itself as 'dishing on the agony and ecstasy of raising two daughters'. A typical post from the peak of Armstrong's output reads 'Feeling guilty – For blaming my farts on the baby', alongside portrayals of collapsed cakes and eccentric fancy-dress costumes that illustrate a lightly comic take on a heteronormative, white family life, where mom bakes the wonky cupcakes and stitches on the angel wings and husband Jon is largely invis-

---

* All gleefully denounced as nonsense by gynaecologist Jen Gunter, who wrote a series of articles on her blog that fact-checked Goop's claims.

ible, except on his parallel blog Blurbomat (the couple have now divorced, having announced their separation on their respective blogs).

In the 2010s, mommy blogging evolved into an 'influencer' version: image-driven and carefully curated, yet still projecting itself as 'normal'. Doyen of the Instamoms is 'relatable influencer' Amber Fillerup Clark, or Barefoot Blonde. A 26-year-old Mormon mother of two (Mormons are overrepresented in the confessional blogosphere, as their Church encourages its adherents to keep journals), Barefoot Blonde chronicles Fillerup Clark's marriage to the similarly wholesome David, her children's births and infancies, and her everyday 'domestic bliss'. Fillerup Clark – whom *The Atlantic* referred to as '[a woman] with the golden locks, lithe frame and wholesome femininity associated with prom queens who date quarterbacks' – poses with her two children and husband, on her blog and Instagram feed, in idealized domestic settings wearing designer clothes. The images are salted with click-through links to clothing and homeware items followers can buy (and for which Fillerup Clark earns a commission). Other posts are what's called in the influencer world 'native advertising'. In these, explicit product placements are packaged as Fillerup Clark's endorsements. A typical example, sponsored by a chlorine-free nappy brand, pictures the family picking berries, with the toddlers outfitted in the brand's nappies and Hunter boots (another sponsor-partner).

Today, myriad 'mom' influencers crowd social media, pushing everything from their own brand (Mother Trucker baseball caps for working mums); to their own children as model brand ambassadors (@taylensmom who charged up to $5,000 for a sponsored post pictured with her preschool daughters and now runs an account under her elder daughter's name, @taylenbiggs); to everything from hotel resorts to home gym equipment (@diaryofafitmommyofficial, who poses in gym wear with a toddler in one arm and dumbbells in the other on the #fitmom hashtag). A rare case of a highly paid Momfluencer who didn't echo the wall-to-wall white hetero norm was WeGotKidz, who – as one women's magazine write-up said of her at the 2013 height of her blogging career – 'flaunts #BlackGirlMagic as she embraces her natural hair and teaches her daughter to do the same'.

Karen Robinovitz, co-founder of Digital Brand Architects (the agency that represents Fillerup Clark) claims that mom bloggers at the most successful level can earn between $1 million and $6 million a year, and *Money* magazine estimates that influencer marketing is now a $10 billion industry. Mom bloggers in the upper echelons, who boast brand deals with major corporations such as Procter and Gamble and Minute Maid, are disproportionately white, married, American, conventionally pretty and straight.*

It seems odd that, before the mid-2000s, it was unusual to find moms as brands anywhere other than the furthest recesses of US cable TV. 'It was always kinda naff,' confirms African-American journalist Erin when I put this hunch to her over Facebook Messenger. She's referring to the Martha Stewart era of TV moms. 'All fake smiles and nasty dishes with marshmallows and string cheese.' But now, she admits, the sector has gone 'nuts'. In April 2019, the annual Mom 2.0 Summit – a paid-for event, started in 2009, where would-be momfluencers pay to 'meet brands' and get tips from women who've made it in the mom blogosphere – was staged in Austin, Texas.

In 2018, a new category of mom bloggers appeared on the scene. I first heard about them when a journalist contact messaged me, as follows:

Cleaning is now #careergoals thanks to influencers such as @mrshinchhome. Mind. Blown.

---

* An exception to this: LaShawn Wiltz, or Everyday Eye Candy, an African-American mom blogger with a Minute Maid deal.

Doyenne of the 'cleanfluencers' is @mrshinch, Essex-based hairdresser Sophie Hinchcliffe, whose video logs (or 'vlogs') of cleaning instruction – in which she refers to her cleaning mops, hoover and brushes by human names (her mop is called Vera, her hoover is Sharon, and her cloths and sponges are Minkeh, Pinkeh, Buddy and Brian) and cleans in a full set of acrylic nails – have been credited with leading to a boom in sales of the cloths and disinfectant products she recommends. Hinchcliffe's Instagram account has 2.6 million followers and her book *Hinch Yourself Happy: All The Best Cleaning Tips To Shine Your Sink And Soothe Your Soul* became a number-one bestseller in the first week of its release in April 2019. Hinch's legion of online fans, the #hincharmy, swap selfies in which they proudly tote Dettol cans in all-grey sitting rooms modelled on Hinchcliffe's own.

Much is made, in magazine and TV interviews with the unlikely star, of Hinchcliffe's back story. The 29-year-old claims she took to obsessive cleaning to cure clinical anxiety. 'There's no worse feeling than when you're sat there and you get that heat in your chest and you start worrying, panicking for no reason,' she mused on the ITV *This Morning* sofa in April 2019. 'For me, I'll get up, I might grab my mop or my hoover and I'll get going. When you feel you're [at] your most weakest you're still achieving something.'

The following month, @MrsHinch recommended a range of metallic pink and black loo and washing-up brushes. The £2–£5 products immediately sold out, with one online Hincher commenting of the coveted items: 'Rose gold AND hinching combined: I'll feel like a lady when I'm doing the loo.' Another fan said, simply: 'I'll match when I'm cleaning.'

In comparison to the Zoflora-scented cult that's grown up around @MrsHinch, Lynsey Crombie, aka @lynsey_queenofclean, a blonde 40-year-old cleanfluencer based in Peterborough, offers a cosier roster of domestic aphorisms. Crombie's 150,000 followers on Instagram lapup chemical-free and natural cleaning tips such as: 'Get rid of water marks and traces of limescale from your draining boards, taps and shower screens by simply cutting a lemon in half, covering with a thin layer of bicarb then adding a light squeeze for ultimate cleaning power.'

'What makes you smile?' another post asks the reader, with Lynsey going on to answer her own question:

1. Clean sheets
2. Empty laundry basket
3. Clean bathroom
4. Vacuum lines

Joining the ranks are mumfluencers who reposition expert housework as a means of controlling and reordering a chaotic world. They include Gemma Bray, 'The Organised Mum' (163,000 followers); Melissa Maker from Toronto, whose Clean My Space YouTube channel has more than a million subscribers; and Becky Rapinchuk from Chicago, aka Clean Mama (361,000 followers on Instagram), who soothingly advises: 'it's okay to not have a cleaning routine and to feel overwhelmed with everyday life. I'm here to help you sort it all out… Cleaning IS more enjoyable when you have products that really work, are easy on the eyes and better yet, safe for you and your family!'

Then there's Marie Kondo. The diminutive 34-year-old Japanese tidying expert has tapped middle-class metropolitan neuroses around the domestic to the same degree as Mrs Hinch has animated disgruntled women in the British suburbs. The KonMari Method, first set out for English-speaking audiences in the 2014 translation of Kondo's book, *The Life-Changing Magic of Tidying Up,* and now a hit US reality TV show, advocates an approach to arranging your material possessions that combines a fetish for pared-back Japanese aesthetics with an unflinching attitude to shedding your clothes, books, paperwork and miscellaneous tat (the latter a category Kondo calls 'komono'). Kondo sees her widely acclaimed process of folding, throwing things out and seeking domestic order as a 'tidying festival'; as in: 'I can't this weekend, sorry, I'm having a tidying festival.' Her book famously advises that adherents spiritually commune with their possessions, from dog-eared books to pairs of socks 'cruelly' balled in the back of the cupboard. Of these sundry items, Kondo enjoins us to enquire 'Does it *spark joy*?'

It's easy to mock Kondo's claims of a life-changing spiritual awakening through sending a bag of tatty leggings to the charity shop. After all, the introduction to her book glowingly trumpets case studies who've launched businesses, saved marriages and lost 'three kilos' since 'putting their houses in order'. And Kondo's book is rife with gender generalizations. The 'male instinct to be ready for action in response to danger and the female instinct to protect the home' manifests itself, apparently, 'in their treatment of loose change'.*

But the proper feminist response to the KonMari cult would be to ask: *where is the work and who is doing it?* I don't doubt that some of Kondo's followers find spiritual succour in winnowing down their shirt collections. Pinterest, after all, bristles with pastel-hued Marie Kondo 'daily checklists' and seductive images of her vertical folding technique in action in impossibly neat bedroom cupboards. But with 78 per cent of Marie Kondo's online followers[97] being female, and the average Kondo clear-out (start with your items, then move on to your husband's and children's) demanding a full day, KonMari strikes me as another — albeit artistically rarefied — distraction from the politics of housework; another post-feminist con. Never mind the fact that, as Japanese academic Yuina Uno put it in an email to me, 'behind closed doors the Japanese are as messy as anyone', KonMari is domestic self-help interiors

---

* Since you ask, men pocket it and women stick it in a drawer.

porn for Western liberals who like a nice Feng Shui'd hotel room with a view of a bamboo-shaded pool. It's an alluring construct. But we need to interrogate our valorizing of the lot of the Japanese woman – who, as we saw earlier, performs a greater percentage of the housework and childcare than women in any other rich nation in the world.

Virginia Nicholson, author of the history of the 1950s housewife *Perfect Wives in Ideal Homes*, interprets the arrival of social-media cleaning gurus as symptomatic of a retreat to a glorified version of the-domestic-as-feminine-domain last seen in the aftermath of the Second World War.

'There is a huge amount of uncertainty in society, which is similar to the post-war period of the Fifties when housework and housewives were similarly glamorised,' she told *Stylist* magazine, in a 2019 piece that asked: 'Is this newfound passion for housework a step backwards?'

'Whenever we're dealing with traumatic upheaval and uncertainty in our lives, we retreat to our four safe walls... There was a similar glossiness to the housewives of the Fifties as there is with cleanfluencers – perish the thought that anyone doing housework would feel discontent at their task.'

A German feminist friend, Rebecca, tells me that the social-media cleaning guru trend is echoed, in Germany, in the rise of *Putzwahn*, a pop-cultural term that refers to a 'cleaning madness' or a mania for cleaning one's home. Search #putzwahn on Twitter and Instagram and you'll find before and after shots of German women's homes after an energetic bout of 'putzwahning', alongside artsy pictures of dustpans and brushes on spotless wooden floors.

Tim and Leo agreed to spend a day following the bright domestic advisories of the cleanfluencers, celebrity mums and Instamoms. First, we followed Jools Oliver's top mothering tips excavated from interviews and her Instagram feed. Oliver advises we stock up on anti-bacterial wipes and broccoli. Jools 'hasn't been on a journey as a mum', she claims on her

Instagram page, in which she hasn't needed the high-tensile polyester sheets that are blamed for clogging up sewers and choking jellyfish and turtles.*

Tim: I suppose she's trying to sound normal, even though the pictures show her posing with a weird half-pout and her kids are lolling on cushions looking a bit glum. I think they're mainly used by adults to wipe their own bums, aren't they? Isn't that why we have so many fatbergs in London?

Leo: Bum-bum-bum-bum... BUMHOLE!

Leo and Tim flatly refuse my offer, per Gwyneth Paltrow's 2010 'daily diary' for Goop, of a 7 a.m. dose of lemon-flavoured flax oil. At 11 a.m. I try, as Paltrow also advises, to work out with Leo 'crawling' about the room.

'There have been countless times where I've worked out with my kids crawling around all over the place,' Paltrow schools. 'You just make it work, and if it's important to you, it'll be important to them.'

After spending 10 minutes mimicking my leg kicks and squats and laughing uproariously, Leo heaves his sizeable mass onto my back when I'm in yogic 'tabletop' position and refuses to budge, shouting 'Mummy! Mummy! Mummy! Stop! Mummy' moistly into my ear. My post-baby waistline is clearly less important to him than Paltrow might hope.

At 5 p.m. I float Paltrow's suggestion that the family all pile into the tub for an evening bath together before rubbing each other's feet, another recommendation from 2010's day in a mothering life on Goop.

Tim had a few things to say about this plan.

'This says more about her level of privilege than anything else. How big is her bath? And where was Chris Martin when

---

* Two loveable creatures chosen for effect. They also garrote dogfish.

all of this was going on? He's never mentioned. Was he down the tap end?'

Tim throws in the towel, literally and figuratively, and Leo and I get into the tub together. In the first 18 months of motherhood I enjoyed bathing with my soft-skinned and giggly infant son. But by the time Leo reached the age of two, the water displacement and incessant stomping made the experience more like a Turner nautical-storm scene than a portrait of mothering bliss.

Me: Leo, don't stand up in the bath; the bath's slippery. Sit down.

Leo: I done a farters! I done a farters! Wha dat!

Me: That's mummy's vagina.

10 seconds later...

Me: No, that's the fingernail brush; we don't use the fingernail brush on mummy's vagina.

Leo: JY–NER!

15 seconds later ...

Leo: I done a farters.

You get the gist.

Mrs Hinch's tips to remove limescale from shower panes are most impressive for being performed in two-inch false nails. Yet, as Tim and I both suffer from contact dermatitis, her portfolio of products – seven for a bathroom-cleaning job alone – would be, at best, a recipe for livid red skin and light asphyxiation. For followers whose self-worth is tied to winning the battle against bathroom tidemarks (do these women exist outside of advertisers' wet dreams?), there might be some value in these 'cleaning hacks', but to what end? Such cultural representations do little more than take the hackneyed depictions of advertising mums – waging their indefatigable wars against dirty collars and greasy hob tops – and migrate them to social media, where they're out of the reach of regulatory bodies such as the ASA. Little surprise, too, that these clean-fluencers combine domestic labour with the labour of the feminine aesthetic: @mrshinchhome and @lynsey_queenof-clean are both heavily made-up blondes.

It's easy to be unsettled by glamourized depictions of normative mothering: of cheery white photogenic families and effortless meals that appear on summery patios as if conjured with the click of Jeannie's fingers; of fathers at the margins (Fillerup Clark's husband is often pictured in the background awkwardly sucking in his belly) and mothers commodifying their picture-perfect looks, their children and their children's childhoods.

But these carefully curated, 'relatably' glamorous images tell us more about capitalism than the realities of modern parenting. The meeting of the domestic and the digital could have been a force for candour and for revolution. And, granted, un-airbrushed mothers also populate the digital space. British Comedy duo the Scummy Mummies represent such an example, although they use the medium of audio podcasts for their 'look at the scummier side of parenting', rather than the inexorably youth-, beauty- and whiteness-driven social media platforms where the influencer moms ply their trade. There's also the problem, articulated by a British-Italian journalist friend Simone, who describes herself as the 'original scummy mummy blogger' (she wrote for a leading mothering website in the mid-2000s), of sheep in wolves' jogging pants.

'It drives me mad that you get lots of pretty young women claiming to be scummy these days where they're yummy,' she says. 'In the early days, scummy was a retaliation against all that BS.'

Simone describes her take on 'scummy' mummyhood this way: 'The mum who is not organized, who has not sorted out the baked goods for the school or nursery sale, the one in scruffy clothes and unwashed hair, the one who is usually a home-worker so has no clothes to dazzle in at the school gates.'

A description of scumminess which, although it seeks to give women permission to fall short of the expectation that they carry the domestic load whilst simultaneously remaining 'hot', does little to challenge the nature of these expectations.

In 2015, 'Queen of the Mommy Bloggers' Heather Armstrong closed her blog, Dooce. Her embittered farewell post, thrillingly, lifted the veil on capitalism's control of the mommy blogosphere.

'Living online for us looks completely different now than it did when we set out to build this community, and the emotional and physical toll of it is rapidly becoming a health hazard,' she wrote. She went on to call out the intrusive demands of the 'brands' and corporate sponsors – which led to Armstrong being asked to dress her daughters in brand-sponsored cloth-ing and push them, through tears, into undertaking outings for brand-sponsored posts.

> At the beginning, it was, 'We're just gonna put the logo at the end of the post. Write something around this.' And then it was, 'Well, actually, we need you to show pictures of the product.' And then it was, 'We need you to show the product.' And then it was, 'We need your kids involved in the post.'

The woman who'd made so much money as a mom blogger that her husband gave up work to manage her busi-ness signed off on her 14-year career with the simple phrase 'I cannot be that person'.

Back in Kensington, I put these new popular paragons of aesthetic mothering to the Yums. Do they follow the cleanflu-encers and Instamoms?

'Ugh,' winces Gloria, 'who wants to be cold-sold cheap lipstick and Dettol?'

Snell admits she follows a few of the Instagram influencers, though mainly the 'fashion mums' such as former fashion editor Erica Davies, whose Instagram thread is all filtered pictures of interiors, shoes and babies in photogenic clothing. Davies' recent blurb described her like this: 'Writer, stylist, interior designer and mother. SHOP MY QVC line!'

Snell enjoys the fashion and house-decor tips, though on bad days these shining mums with their magazine homes make her feel gloomy.

'They can make you feel fat and messy,' she says. 'But that's the way with all of the airbrushing these days, isn't it?'

None of the women, including Snell, has taken anything by mouth other than liquid during our two-hour audience. On a shiny marble table, a tasty-looking plate of herb-encrusted pretzels sits untouched. But even these mothers – who diet and self-surveil and frantically hunt for Mandarin tutors – feel uneasy with these social media projections of perfect, purchasable motherhood. Or perhaps these women, more than many, experience the intimate costs of this ideal.

Faye tells me a grim story about another friend, a young mother who spent so much time on Instagram she became convinced she had to 'drop the baby bulge' at breakneck pace and bought fat-stripping tablets on the internet.

'Basically, you know, speed. She was breastfeeding her son and wondering why he wasn't sleeping for longer than 20 minutes at a time. He was off his head on amphetamines.'

Mothering has long existed in intimate relation to capitalism. The needs of industrial capitalism gave us the concept of the 'housewife' and mother as the Modern Homemaker. But what's new to the digital age is the creep of capitalism into the furthest dusty nooks and neuroses of our mothering. These digital-capitalist ideologies, frequently posing as 'normal' and 'relatable', package heteronormative, primarily white and certainly exclusionary modes of mothering as a product to be bought with a quick click-through.

Amelia, a young South Asian journalist, bemoans the calcification of the influencer scene as 'a lost opportunity'. 'When the [influencer] trend came out, we had high hopes that influencers would challenge the white voices that dominate mainstream media. What we're finding is the same shit prevails: whiteness sells and white people get to speak.'

For all of the crap that adheres to the ideology of motherhood – women's natural-born subordinate role; unpaid labour ascribed to us on the basis of the urge of some of us to reproduce; desires which are hyper-powered in late capitalism's digital space – we do not want to forgo or deny the qualities and experience mothering affords to some women. The right of parents to care for children full-time, if they wish, is a right we should support. But we need to disavow the digital distortions of stay-at-home parenthood, a choice that's only endorsed in the narrow form of a glamorously wholesome, white, heterosexual, married, middle-class stay-at-home mother by choice.

A placard at a 2018 rally against right-wing lawmakers' assault on abortion rights in the US read: 'Get your politics the hell out of my vagina'. We might repurpose this bon mot as: *Get capitalism the fuck out of my (non-sexist) householding.*

10

A Case for the Commons (and Why Separatists Still Struggle with Who Scrubs the Loo)

Oregon Women's Land Trust meeting 1970

I struggle to feel that clutter in the home doesn't reflect poorly on my character. I have come to realize that the expectations I put on myself are unrealistic and reflect a value system I have long ago abandoned. But still, I struggle. Not least because in the country an uncluttered home is an impossibility.'

These complaints could have been penned by an 18th-century parson's wife. But they were written by the founding member of a radical feminist separatist community in rural Oregon, as she reflected on the unexpected trials of two decades of feminist separatist living.

Jean was amongst the thousands of American, European and Antipodean women who were inspired by the Women's Movement and feminist consciousness-raising groups to take part in a radical experiment in feminist living: Women's – or Womyn's[98] – Lands. In 1994, when she wrote the words above, former housewife Jean had been living in Rootworks, the community she co-founded with partner Ruth in rural southern Oregon, for 16 years.

At the Women's Movement's 1970s height, thousands of women lived in these intentional feminist communities, most of which were in the rural US and Mexico, but also Australia, New Zealand and Western Europe. Loosely affiliated to the American back-to-the-land movement,[99] Womyn's Lands sought to establish practical ways of living beyond the oppressions of the patriarchy, through rural self-sufficiency.

Many Womyn's Land inhabitants – the 'land dykes', as they came to call themselves – were homosexual by political choice. 'Feminism is the theory and lesbianism is the practice,' radical feminist author Jill Johnston said of this reasoning in 1973's *Lesbian Nation*. The land dykes shared the belief that the pursuit of formal equality within the patriarchy was impossible and that true autonomy for women, when it came to such matters as social equality and division of labour, could only be achieved by breaking away from the capitalist-patriarchal system and founding a new society in the absence of men.

Jean and Ruth took the shared surname 'Mountaingrove' from the first of the separatist communities they lived in (many land dykes relinquished their 'father's names'). In 1974, the couple founded the feminist-spiritualist magazine *WomenSpirit*, which became a mouthpiece of the revolutionary womyn's land movement, aiming to recruit women to the utopian project, connect communities, and share skills and knowledge. Its first issue outlined the movement's utopian hopes:

> When we realize the political implications of all our struggles, we know that patriarchy cannot withstand our changes; something is going to happen. We are feeling stirrings inside us that tell us that what we are making is nothing less than a new culture.

Rootworks was one of at least nine formal womyn's lands established in rural Oregon in the mid-to-late 1970s (there were also communities that 'preferred to fly under the radar', historian Heather Burmeister notes), which also included the mystically named Rainbow's End, Raven Song, Steppingwoods, WomanShare, Cabbage Lane, Copperland and Fly Away Home.

The reality of founding new communities in hardscrabble rural locations, where locals might not thrill to the prospect of an encampment of lesbians and where cheaply bought land could be tough to farm, was challenging. In another of the movement's publications, *Country Women*, women's land community member Jeanne Tetrault wrote plaintively of the skills she had to teach herself from scratch because she had not been allowed to take 'woodshop class' in high school; and Nelly, a resident of Fly Away Home, wrote that her biggest obstacle in adapting to community life was 'learning to tell the difference between what is real danger and what is fear: fear due to the conditioned intimidation women have been taught to feel around dangerous tools...'

Historian and queer feminist artist Leah DeVun spent five years documenting the waning days of the Womyn's Lands, most of which had disbanded by the late 1990s, for *Our Hands on Each Other*, a photo series that poses women topless amid the tumbledown remains of wood stacks and log cabins. The series was a tribute to Ruth Mountaingrove's photographs from the 1970s, which pictured topless land dykes performing manual labour at Womyn's Land sites: building walls and floors, digging ditches and planting gardens. The women DeVun met in the late 1990s and early 2000s were in their fifties and sixties, DeVun told me, and had the sunbaked stoicism of souls who'd led a hard, outdoors life.

'These women had to be tough: they built their own houses, they downed trees with chainsaws and they ran people off their land with shotguns – that was called for in rural settings, where the local townspeople were often homophobic. Doing "men's work" was a badge of honour.'

More troubled was the land dykes' relationship to the labour that had traditionally fallen to women under patriarchy: the work of caring, cooking and keeping house. Division of domestic labour and child-rearing, not least the thorny issue of the place of male children in feminist separatist communities, were live and contentious debates within the wider feminist separatist movement. A revolution in 'women's work' was, for many of these communities, a founding principle.

In Oregon, the WomanShare collective agonized over an appropriate division of necessary domestic work, claims LGBT historian Shelley Grosjean. They wondered: should all such work be rejected for a focus on the bare minimum of labour to maintain life? In the absence of the unspoken gendered division of labour they had grown up with, domestic work in some womyn's lands was unintentionally divided along class lines. A WomanShare resident from a middle-class background, Carol, recalled her initial resistance to pitching in with kitchen work, and other members' displeasure with being left to cook for and clean up after her.

'I had been fighting to maintain a privileged place within our women's commune… a middle-class woman with servants. My sisters had lost their patience. Especially Billie and

Diane who had been struggling with my kitchen phobia for two years.'[100]

Through a series of consciousness-raising workshops, WomanShare came up with a practical solution. The community itemized essential chores and required community members to sign up to a rotating task on a weekly basis. Tasks were all equivalent and were intended to be stripped of gendered and classed connotations. Academic Catherine B. Kleiner remarked of a visit to WomanShare in the late '90s: 'Sign-up sheets for weekly chores ... such as garbage and recycling runs, wood-cutting, gardening chores, cleaning the main house, grocery shopping, and meal preparation are still tacked to the community bulletin board in the kitchen.'

Such solutions required vigilance, ongoing effort and collective discussion. Complaints of an unfair division of everyday chores were rife in communities with a high member turnover. 'We struggle against our natures to shirk; or we take on, out of a conditioned need to please, too much work,' one Womyn's Land member lamented to a feminist researcher in 1981.

In some Womyn's Lands, issues around division of domestic labour were deflected through an onus on solo dwellings within the communal project. In an unpublished manuscript, *The Little Houses on Women's Lands*, lesbian artist Tee Corinne documents the typical dwellings in three rural Womyn's Lands in Oregon that were active from 1972 to 1995.

'They represented a negation of traditional womanly roles,' Corinne writes. 'They were not built to accommodate child-rearing or large-scale entertaining. Often lovers lived in separate buildings thus reinforcing the autonomy and independence which were the cornerstones of this community... What could better symbolize the separation from patriarchy than tiny buildings where women crafted individual lives?'[101]

The Womyn's Lands were a radical attempt to translate the insights of Second Wave feminism into lived reality. The effort to carve out feminist life may have been more materially difficult than many hoped: sustaining community finances was difficult, with many members of these communities having to work for a wage (and therefore within the patriarchal market economy they were trying to reject). As exponents of the 1960s and '70s feminist movement aged, communities struggled to attract new members. One former Womyn's Land member, Pelican Lee, wrote with regret when the once-thriving community she lived in disbanded in the 1990s. In this she echoed Jean Mountaingrove's reflections on the unexpected challenges in living a radical life in which they couldn't fully escape the expectations of the 1950s housewives they had been raised to become.

'We were very hard on ourselves with our idealistic politics,' said Lee. 'We could not emotionally handle living the ways we believed in politically. Our endless meetings trying to deal with everything in a politically correct way caused too much trauma and upheaval, and eventually burned us out... Sisterhood was not enough, and even working hard to work things out was not enough. Growing up in capitalistic patriarchal America had not prepared us for living the kind of life we desired.'

Of the nine or so Womyn's Lands set up in southern Oregon in the late 70s, only We'Moon Land continues in any residential capacity, and it is now home to a small community of women making a living from selling spiritualist calendars. A current member, in her sixties, told me that such communities often feel under siege from new feminisms — accused of being TERFs* due to their onus on separatist, women-only membership. These sores have been aggravated by talk of legal challenges to remaining Womyn's Lands under the 1968 Civil Rights Act, which prohibited discrimination concerning the provision of housing on the basis of race, religion, national origin and (as of 1974) biological sex. 'It's a depressing case of

---

* Meaning 'trans-exclusionary radical feminists', a loaded term that's much bandied about in the transfeminism debates.

feminism eating itself,' as one unapologetic radical feminist[102] describes the mood.

Yet in showing that, with effort and will, naturalized attitudes to work — and women's work — could be rewritten through practice, the history of Womyn's Lands has much to teach us; not least the effort required to achieve such goals.

What do you take when you're invited for dinner at a non-binary houseshare? It's a question I never thought I'd have to ask myself, especially against the clock and on Leyton High Road, where my choices entail a) Romanian supermarkets selling unpronounceable baked goods and b) workaday supermarket chains. Booze is out: 20-something Britons barely booze anyway, not least on a Tuesday night. After 15 minutes of dithering along the aisles of a mainstream supermarket, I settle on own-brand carrot cake slices. Relatively healthy and a bit veggie, I reason.

Ten minutes later, 26-year-old Fern greets this offering with qualified thanks.

'Oh, thanks. I'm totally non-packaging so I'd *never* buy anything in cardboard *and* plastic. So this is a *real treat*.'

Valerie, a well-fed feline who is 'Queen of Number 45', eyes me witheringly.

Number 45 is a millennial and Gen Y community that occupies a Victorian townhouse in the old East End. Like many London houseshares, it has cycle paraphernalia blocking the hallway and walls painted a lively colour (in this case, sunset orange) that probably seemed like a good idea at the time. But here the resemblances end. The household is a radical experiment in householding, established along the lines of conscious gender non-binarism. Four of its five inhabitants identify as neither male nor female. At 35, Susan, the sole gender-identifying member, is older than the other inhabitants and describes herself as a 'run-of-the-mill lesbian woman'.

Tonight the household is gathered in the kitchen – a cosy dining and cooking space that's dominated by a large pine trestle table and, on the wall, a sizeable whiteboard. The whiteboard features a table and a wheel. On the table, under the heading 'Dishes', there are rows for each weekday. The wheel has five segments and clockwise arrows under the heading 'Weekend jobs', with the segments titled: 'Dishes', 'Kitchen', 'Hoover + lounge', 'Laundry' and 'Bathroom'. Moveable coloured magnets, Fern explains, refer to each of the household members. Number 45 is a strictly labour-egalitarian, as well as non-gendered, home.

Over a communal supper of veg Thai curry, these 'conscious housemates' explain the system. Three of the members have a history of living in communal houseshares, and this new rota was an effort, Fern tells me, to correct earlier failings.

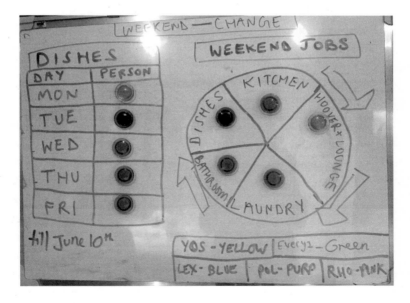

The chore chart and wheel at Number 45, a non-binary household

Susan once lived in a commune where two of the members supplied the commune's fruit and veg from their allotment. 'That didn't work out,' she says, 'cos they thought it absolved them from any other housework, which was news to the rest of us.' Wall and Fern once lived in a co-op where they had a very elaborate tasks wheel on the wall, which 'frankly, no one really understood', says Fern. Absenteeism can be ruinous too. If housemates are coming and going or away a lot, systems quickly slip. 'So we choose housemates who are homebodies,' Fern adds.

Fern once dated fellow Number 45 housemate Wall, who's also non-binary but then identified as male. Fern claims that rigidity in task allocation is essential, as is an effort to 'curate' household members.

'They have to, like, *get it*,' says Fern, who asks to be referred to with the pronoun 'they'. 'And by "get it" I mean understand that jobs in the house are consciously ungendered. Tidying up boys' mess is one of the only things that makes me feel like a woman. That and being sexually harassed, of course.'

Fern wanted their non-binary name to be derived from the world of flora. Fern has tattoos of climbing roses on their thighs and dandelions climbing across their left calf. They hope soon to have a fern rendered across their chest, to realize the ambition of turning themself into a 'human garden'.

Are there any struggles, I ask, when it comes to shedding the expectations of gendered labour? As the group guiltily unwrap the carrot cake slices – cardboard, plastic film, plastic tray – and tuck in, I tell them about the melancholic realization of the 1970s land dyke communities: that sex-role socialization was, after all, a corset that few of them could wriggle out of.

'What's difficult for me is how I respond if a room's messy,' offers Wall, quietly. 'I'm on the autism spectrum and mess really bugs me, but can I mention this to a housemate who was once a woman and not risk seeming like the worst sort of cis man? And I still struggle with the fact, even though I'm no longer male-identifying, that housework is emasculating.'

This point elicits widened eyes from Fern and Z, a Mancunian who, at the age of 23, is the household's youngest member.

For Fern, too, the struggle is within. Fern was raised by a feminist mother from the old 1970s and '80s radical school — 'A total TERF, she really can't help it. And she also prefers men to women' — and I wonder how the division of labour in their childhood home differed from this household's experiments.

'Well, my mum was one of those women who interpreted strong womanhood as being about controlling everything,' Fern says. 'And that's how I struggle now. I just can't help but be the household controller. I know when we're out of loo roll and soap. And I do all the banking and finances, although that's more a fault of the Co-op Bank, who can't get their head around communes, than anyone in the house.'

'Fern's definitely the "mum brain",' says Z, patting the crown of Fern's head.

'We tell them off, but they still take it on,' adds Susan, with a note of sadness. By my feet, cat Valerie (who's 'definitely a she') rigorously cleans her anus with a coiled pink tongue.

For all these blips, the division of labour at Number 45 works out well. Susan suspects this is because the housemates are, as much as possible, invested in conscious householding. 'And we're all nice,' she adds. 'This sort of set-up doesn't work if you're not a nice person. Niceness is important.'

Curious, I ask the housemates whether they plan to have children.

Fern, who works as a 'queer nanny' to the children of an older lesbian couple, breathes in sharply.

'This is something I'm really conflicted about,' they say. 'On the one hand, I really love kids. On the other, climate change is a big issue. What will I say to my kid when they ask me where the bees have all gone and why is summer six months long?'

That said, Fern couldn't imagine raising a child in any domestic setting other than a communal one.

'I couldn't raise a child in a house with less than three parents,' they say. 'I mean, how would you get everything done? I would TOTALLY BURN OUT in that nuclear family thing.'

Z looks out of the window, dreamily. 'Would the baby arrive on the doorstep here, like, in a bassinet?'

'Sure, it could do,' I respond carefully, struggling a little with this hypothetical.

'I would be overjoyed,' Z says, 'and then I would probably think, *Shit! How do I keep this thing alive?*' They ponder for a moment. 'But, on the other hand, it would be good being at home with a kid as I'm agoraphobic and don't like to go out much.'

Susan glances up at the house chore board. 'We'd have to do a rota for who would wake up with the kid though...'

'Yeah, not me in the mornings,' Fern says.

'No, me neither,' adds Z.

I ask what the Number 45ers consider the best age, these days, to have a child. After all, by Barbara Risman's calculations their late-millennial/Gen Z generation will reproduce with much less gusto, and much later, than the generations that preceded them.

'I don't know... 36 to 45?' says Z. 'It's not like the other generations where you had, like, no uni debt and could buy a house for £15,000. Our lives are kinda financially precarious.' Z currently works at a vegan café whose owners reduced their wage from £10 an hour to the UK minimum wage on their last payslip without telling them.

I leave the radical householders to their shared pot of camomile tea, but realize, on the way home, that I've forgotten to ask them something important. I send a message to the WhatsApp group Susan set up to plan the supper. It's named 'Domestic Arrangements'.

Do you see yourselves, I type, *as a feminist household?*

Ping!

Fern has quickly responded. *I think feminism should be a doing word rather than an adjective... Like that famous quote I've forgotten.*

There's a vogue in academic feminism that I call the 'argument from utopias'. This is the tendency for academic papers that theorize gender oppressions, often with grim finesse, to propose an upbeat means of emancipation at the paper's close; like the cheery news shorts at the end of local TV news bulletins. For a while in the 1990s, the internet was a popular upbeat conclusion to feminist papers, promising emancipation through feminist networking and the collapse of hierarchical knowledge production (aka 'it's all right, the world wide web will save us as we collectivize and push for the redistribution of power'). Women grassroots activists are perennial flag-bearers of feminist succour. Currently fashionable are calls for a return to the pre-capitalist commons, investing hope in leftist collectives – such as Central American female 'land defenders' and First Nations women activists fighting mineral extraction – who work to manage land and resources for the common good, outside of the state or market. The social practice of 'commoning', or managing resources as communal (sometimes now theorized to include the internet 'commons'), is also clung to as evidence of our bright, post-capitalist, post-patriarchal future.

At our current impasse, when narratives of women's proper domestic roles are ascendant, domestic-labour asymmetries resistant and revolutionary calls, at least on the domestic front, long forgotten, it is time we asked ourselves whether new and radical ways of living – or indeed old and radical ways of living – might offer a route out of the cul-de-sac of our stalled domestic revolution.

The distant past has more to teach us than we might think about our feminist projects of the present day. Not least a sense of renewed feminist camaraderie. Companionship was often intrinsic to household chores in the centuries before capitalism privatized these tasks and assigned them, unambiguously, to women. Water-fetching, baking and washing clothes were all once communal, and often convivial.

'Country women who had... joined forces by the river on wash-day, found they spent far more time indoors when they moved to town. They also found that most of their time was spent on cleaning,' Caroline Davidson says of the great urban migration of the early Industrial Revolution.

The communal washing culture of rural Scottish women in the 1800s was particularly ebullient. 'They normally washed in groups,' Davidson notes, 'two women to a tub, supporting themselves with their arms thrown over each other's shoulders, while they danced up and down and sang rousing songs.'

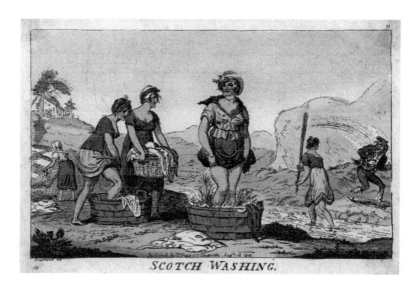

SCOTCH WASHING.

Artist Isaac Cruikshank's eroticized take on the communal tradition of 'Scotch washing', 1810

Silvia Federici, when I visited her at her pleasingly chaotic Brooklyn apartment, told me the attack on communalism that coincided with the rise of capitalism was intertwined with the attack on women's forms of common knowledge such as midwifery and women's claims to land. 'It is in the course of the anti-feudal struggle we find the first grassroots women's movement that offered alternative models of communal life.'

This social function of the commons – the coming together and sharing of resources and land – was especially important to women peasants, and hastened women's social degradation in the era of enclosure, when common land was forcibly taken into private hands and women could no longer grow or gather food. At the same time, the rise of the male wage economy foreclosed women's avenues to paid labour, forcing them into the home.

Federici wonders if the commons might not be reclaimed as a space for solidarity for women: the conspiratorial communal washes, for instance, or the space for social interaction that comes from ruddlestoning our terrace stoops.

For some Victorian reformers, a return to communal labour was the answer to housewives' increased drudgery under capitalism. In the 1894 pamphlet *Democracy in the Kitchen*, English writer and women's rights activist Edith Mary Oldham Ellis demanded the rollout of municipal domestic service facilities as a means of freeing both servants' and women's hands and intellects from the daily grind:

If every woman could have a minimum instead of a maximum domestic spider-threads tugging at her brain year-in, year-out, through the municipalisation of laundries, bake-houses, kitchens and restaurants, worked well under well-trained and methodical civil servants, just imagine for a moment what a new life would be on this earth.

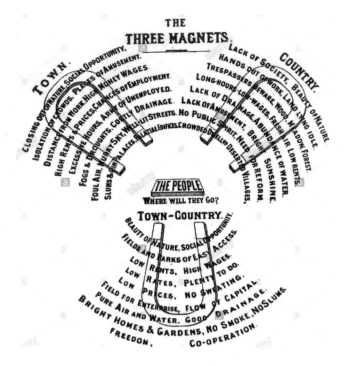

Ebenezer Howard's 'Three Magnets' diagram

Twenty years later, a radical American First Wave feminist was having similar ideas. Alice Constance Austin was the Chicago-born daughter of a railroad investor. Somehow, she came into contact with the theories of British social reformer and urban planner Ebenezer Howard.* In his 1898 book *To-morrow: A Peaceful Path to Real Reform* (later republished as *Garden Cities of To-morrow*), Howard advocated the construction of a new kind of town, summed up in his 'Three Magnets' diagram. These planned communities would combine the advantages of cities (efficiency and access to services) and of the countryside (greenery and open spaces), while eliminating disadvantages

---

* Records show Austin visited London in the 1890s, but there is no record of Austin and Howard crossing paths.

such as pollution and isolation. His ideas were mocked in the press but struck a chord with many, especially members of the emergent Arts and Crafts movement and the Quaker reformists (then building their own planned ideal communities, such as Birmingham's Bournville). Howard's projects were realized in the planned communities Letchworth in Hampshire (1903) and Welwyn Garden City in Hertfordshire (1920).

Austin saw in Howard's socialist urban planning not just a means of bettering the health of the working classes[*] but, importantly, improving the lowly lot of women. In 1915, Austin, by now a self-taught architect, was commissioned to design a socially egalitarian city on a plot of land north of Los Angeles: Llano del Rio. Her client was the controversial minister and Socialist Party candidate Job Harriman, who'd recently lost a mayoral election and wanted to make his political mark. Austin's 1935 book, *The Next Step: How to Plan for Beauty, Comfort, and Peace with Great Savings Affected by the Reduction of Waste*, laid out her feminist design ethos. Traditional nuclear homes were, she said hotly, a 'Procrustean bed', where women were 'drilled from babyhood into isolation in the home' and 'each feminine personality must be made to conform… by whatever maiming or fatal spiritual or intellectual oppression'.

Much like Ellis and the suffragists who later picked up the mantle of communalizing laundry, Austin did not challenge the assumption that this labour should fall to women. Instead, she sought liberation from the drudgery of domestic labour for leisure through efficiency: good town planning, technology and the socialization of this work.

Austin's designs for Llano del Rio feature a radial layout of 'kitchenless houses'. Her homes are connected by a system of underground tunnels used for commuting, laundry and hot meal collection and delivery (from a large centralized city

---

* Howard's stated aim, although most of the residents of the garden city projects that were realized at Letchworth and Welwyn were middle-class.

kitchen and laundry), as well as the transportation of supplies and goods. Railway cars bring cooked food and laundered clothing via these tunnels from the centre of the city to 'hubs', from which small electric cars are dispatched to the basement of each house. Austin designed the homes with sightlines to allow for children playing outdoors to be minded communally and – radically for the time – with built-in furniture, roll-away beds, heated tile floors and windows freed from dust-gathering curtains; all innovations intended to reduce the labour of floor-cleaning, laundering and setting fires. Austin said, of her design for Llano del Rio, that she hoped women would be relieved 'of the thankless and unending drudgery of an inconceivably stupid and inefficient system, by which her labors are confiscated'.

Nine hundred members signed up to join Austin and Harriman's utopian socialist community, each family paying a $1,000 membership fee. Alas, the dream of a feminist utopia as Austin designed it was never fully realized. A number of structures were built on the site according to Austin's design: a meeting house, a hotel, a granite viaduct and a water tank. However, after a disastrous 1916 dry season in which the site proved itself unsuitable for building and the soil too poor for agriculture, the community collapsed into 'dreary factionalism' and the site was abandoned in 1918.* Its few structures remain today, as an eerie desert mausoleum to utopian dreams.

Other socialist – if not explicitly feminist – communitarian communities came into being in Austin's day. These included the Shaker community at New Lebanon in New York, with its shared laundries and kitchen gardens; and the communes of the Oneida communalists, which had been influential to Austin and sought, as founding member John Humphrey Noyes put it, to get 'beyond the little man-and-wife circle' through the prac-

---

* Austin's proposals for low-maintenance heated tile floors and curtainless windows were, however, adopted by housing projects in Pennsylvania and New Jersey.

tice of 'complex marriage' (or free love) and raising children and working communally. From the point of view of the era, the Oneida communities (by 1878 there were five branches in New York, Vermont, Connecticut and New Jersey) represented a radical project to change female roles: women shaped commune policy, their right to sexual gratification was recognized, and they were free to assume male roles in business and sales or as artisans or craftsmen. Domestic duties, however, remained a female purlieu; and women's right to refuse sexual overtures, in this culture of mandatory free love, was limited.

The same decade saw a radical experiment in the socialization of domestic labour we can claim, less problematically, as feminist. The Cambridge Cooperative Housekeeping Society in Cambridge, Massachusetts, was an experimental housework co-operative that ran from 1870 to 1873. Melusina Fay Peirce, a well-to-do housewife, founded the organization to challenge the site of women's oppression as she saw it: the never-ending drudgery of unpaid and unspecialized housework and housekeeping. Women's reluctance to organize themselves against this unfair state of affairs was an issue that enraged Peirce. In her 1880 tract *Co-operative Housekeeping: How not to do it, and how to do it,* she summarized the average housewife's fate as an unceasing carousel of 'fighting the dirt', 'sweeping, dusting, scrubbing, dish and kettle-washing, laundering, what is it all but "fighting the dirt"?'

Peirce marvelled:

> The extraordinary social fact remains that in the face of all of the progress and enlightenment of the nineteenth century, that women have not as yet gone outside the home and joined hands and brains for the better charge of their functions toward the home.

Peirce established a system of co-operative housekeeping in her small Massachusetts community, through which women undertook domestic chores together and profited from their labour by requesting payment from their husbands. Homes of participating women were reorganized to allow for specialization in discrete skills such as cooking, baking and laundering.

Astutely, Peirce had understood that household services were on the cusp of capitalist expansion, and that women, in their role as consumers, were ideally placed to take charge of the new sectors that grew up, from ready-made food production to distribution. The Cambridge co-op lasted for three years, and although the women were cruelly caricatured in the contemporary press, there was also public support for their experiment.* Peirce also called for the construction of multi-family apartment houses with single centralized kitchens and laundries for the more efficient application of her principles of co-operative housekeeping, although nothing came of these grander plans.

Their ideas resurfaced in the 1970s, when various schemes were proposed – also in the US – through which homemakers could hire each other to perform domestic services and pay each other a daily wage from their husbands' earnings.** Jessie Hartline, a Rutgers University economist who proposed such a 'trade-a-maid' scheme, dismissed accusations that these ideas were an attention-grabbing gimmick. 'If I put an ad in the paper to hire a housecleaner, and it turns out that the lady across the street answers the ad, that's fine, right?'[103]

Amongst the Edwardian advocates of bold new ways of living to improve women's lot, one figure looms large. Born in Connecticut in 1860, Charlotte Perkins Gilman was raised by her mother and a phalanx of aunts, including suffragist Isabella Beecher Hooker, anti-slavery campaigner (and author

---

* These projects of communalization, of course, issued their challenge to household organization, rather than men.
** As these women workers also qualified for the social security and employment benefits denied to housewives.

of *Uncle Tom's Cabin*) Harriet Beecher Stowe, and women's education advocate Catharine Beecher. She began her career as a speaker on behalf of Nationalism, a political movement inspired by the utopian socialist vision of Edward Bellamy's bestselling novel *Looking Backward* (1888). In the novel, Bellamy proposes a society in which men and women are economic equals and commerce is conducted via 'credit', which is equally distributed to females and males.

Quickly, Gilman took to writing her own utopian socialist novels and essays, in which she advocated – rather than for socialist economic parity as a route to utopia – for an ideal society born of women's 'mother instincts' and the 'self-sacrificing ethics of the larger motherhood'.

Gilman's seminal utopian fantasy, 1916's *Herland*, was part of a trilogy that hangs on the fantastical premise of a land inhabited only by women. In Herland, inhabitants reproduce 'parthenogenetically',* raise children communally and have eliminated the domestication of animals. When three bold male scientists lead an expedition to Herland, which is located on a remote mountain range, they're easily outrun by the bloomers-wearing Herlandians, who promptly chloroform the young men and put them under house arrest in a fortress. As the men resign themselves to captivity, they encounter a peaceable, highly efficient agrarian community in which competition, crime and antisocial behaviour are unknown.

Herland was rediscovered in the 1970s and immediately hailed as a First Wave feminist classic, although many Second Wave feminists found fault with its gender essentialism, white racism and flirtation with eugenics (whilst all Herlandians can reproduce parthenogenetically, only an elite is entrusted with birthing children, in the aim of improving the 'race'). Historian

---

* Occurring in some insects and flowers, this is a form of reproduction in which the unfertilized ovum develops directly into a new individual.

Michael Robertson[104] notes that *Herland*'s utopian vision seems – from our present moment – presciently, well, dystopian:

> Four decades after its rediscovery, *Herland* no longer seems the purely playful, light-hearted speculative fiction it once did. Nor does its central theme of collective child-rearing seem that different from the gendered regimes animating *The Handmaid's Tale* – which, with an unabashed sexist and racist in the White House, serves as a powerful cautionary tale for progressives.

When Gilman was diagnosed with incurable breast cancer, she followed through on her belief in euthanasia for the terminally ill and committed suicide using the romantic means that had fascinated her in fiction: overdose by chloroform.

Despite her problematic take on race, and we have to acknowledge that elements of Gilman's worldview are wonky, her broader work offers an interrogation of women's naturalized domestic role, and the oppressions wrought by Victorian and Edwardian cults of the domestic, that's ahead of its time.

In *The Home, Its Work and Influence* (1903), Gilman argues that exclusion in the 'small dark place' of the domestic sphere 'crippled' women with its 'too continuous' demands.

The American homes at the dawn of the Edwardian age were, she says, 'bloated buildings stuffed with a thousand superfluities wherein the priceless energies of women are poured out in endless foolishness; in work that meets no real need'.

In *Women and Economics* (1899), Gilman elaborated on her plans. If domestic life fosters 'an elaborate devotion to individuals and their personal needs', obstructs women's collective interests and renders them, in their 'docile acquiescence', ill-equipped to engage with public life, is it not time, Gilman asks – echoing Peirce – that 'the principles of industry' were applied to the home? Communities of houses and apartments should, she said, be built without kitchens and should be connected to professionally run and communal childcare facilities, kitchens, laundries and dining rooms. Families can either eat in communal restaurants supplied by a central kitchen, or have food sent to the home. Clothes-laundering should be devolved to a 'suitable workshop' where domestic tasks were in the hands of 'skilled professionals'. These ideas were certainly influential to Alice Constance Austin at Llano del Rio.

Design historian Dolores Hayden, author of *The Grand Domestic Revolution: A History of Feminist Designs for American Homes, Neighborhoods, and Cities*, wrote that the late 19th and early 20th centuries saw arguments for women's emancipation from domestic labour similar to those that would preoccupy Second Wave feminism in the 1970s. (Hayden was writing in 1981, when the Wages for Housework campaign was live.) 'They demanded economic remuneration for women's unpaid household labor. They proposed a complete transformation of the spatial design and material culture of American homes, neighborhoods, and cities'.

In the 1910s, efforts to socialize women's work were led by the suffragettes,[105] who established communal kitchens and a nursery called 'the Mother's Arms', intended to care for the children of women working at the suffragists' co-operative toy factory at Bow. The two nurseries the suffragettes went on to run in the East End – which ran from the outbreak of the First World War – were early adopters of the Montessori method, although they disbanded after the franchise was achieved in 1921.

The between-war and post-war periods, of course, saw the great experiments in communalization of the socialist states. Soviet Russia and Mao's China both saw the rollout of communal kitchens, mess halls and nurseries: technologies of the state intended to free women to work productively by passing women's labour to selected women. Women, according to Mao, 'hold up half the sky', but they were also expected to wash the dishes for the great project of class emancipation: the aim of these state interventions being class liberation rather than the liberation of women.

In neither of these socialist states was gender, or the ascribing of labour based on gendered lines, problematized. And Russian and Chinese state socialism has left an inadvertent legacy that could be claimed as feminist: comprehensive and affordable state nursery-school provision. In the kibbutzim, the collective agricultural communities established in Israel in the early 20th century,* childcare, laundries and food preparation are socialized. In the absence of an enquiry into the workings of structural sexism, however, these labours remained women's work – and power, relatedly, was in men's hands. The 1930s also saw flirtations with communalism in the West. In Manhattan, apartment blocks were built with dumb waiters to ferry food to units from centralized kitchens; and in Vienna (the Vienna School of Architecture), apartments were built with communal nurseries and laundries.

The world the feminist utopianists envisaged came to pass, if only in a limited sense: ready meals and nearly ready foods crowd our cupboards, and carpetless floors and curtainless windows are a common feature of our homes today. Sadly, these women's more radical call – for a wholesale reorganization of the households to professionalize domestic labour – has been lost to the soap suds of 100 intervening years.

Modern minds might recoil at the drab Soviet-era connotations of communal kitchens and laundries – Tim mutters about 'grey underpants' and being 'forcefed rissoles' when I

---

* And which were at their height in the 1920s to 1950s.

float the idea. But could we reclaim something, for our present moment, from this forgotten impetus to communalize domestic labour?

The Number 45 communalists certainly think so. But what about larger-scale communes, or those that are home to biologically related adults and kids? It's a question I put to members of Diggers and Dreamers, an online group for people living in – or aspiring to set up – communes in the UK.

Annie, who's currently a member of a co-housing project in Sussex – where residents have their own homes but share some facilities, including a dining hall where communal meals are held several times a week – has lived in a number of large-scale alternative communities in the UK and Europe. She's circumspect about the prospect of seeing a new communalism as a great feminist hope.

'There's a lot to be said for intentional communities in that they attract people who want to talk about things and try a new way of life,' she tells me. 'Communal cooking and laundry doesn't tend to work out that well as an ongoing thing, though. It might have been cool in the 1970s when they all ate bean cassoulets, but people these days are just too fussy about what and when they want to eat. And, of course, you get sexist dicks everywhere, who don't want to do their bit.'

A woman who only wants to be referred to as 'JB' sounds a cautionary note: 'Most communities are far from feminist IMO. Vulnerable women are attracted to these alternative communities seeking safety and are frequently preyed upon by abusive others; mainly men.'

We need to dispense with utopian fantasies and 1970s Golden Ageism. Communalizing the work that is routinely ascribed to women on the basis of the shape of their genitals is no panacea. As at Number 45, sexed roles need to be interrogated as part of any emancipatory project. Even in leftist separatist communities, the shadows of class, race and childhood socialization loom large, requiring daily vigilance and adjustment. Without such efforts, the call to socialized labour is merely another adaptation to an unfair state of affairs.

I'd like to hope we can incorporate the best of the communalists' insights into homes and communities that meet our modern needs. Many of us are stuck with housing stock from the height of the housewife cults – Victorian terraces designed for servants and Good Housekeepers; three-bed post-war semis where the housewife was expected to assume her station at the kitchen sink, observing kids playing on the strip of garden lawn. But could we set up non-sexist housework co-operatives on our streets? Or lobby for a radical feminist house-building policy? Communities that offer spaces where we can cook and eat communally; centralized laundries in new-build apartment blocks where we can socialize as we wash our smalls and reduce our ecological imprint?

In a 2019 article for architecture website Dezeen, Phineas Harper, chief curator of the Oslo Architecture Triennale, talks of architecture's responsibility to take a stand against the 'stifling' and 'deterministic' hegemony of the nuclear family home: '[which] is designed to enforce a particular social structure [and] hardwires divisions in labour, gender and class into the built fabric of our cities.' These uniform homes, Harper adds, are isolating and inefficient as well as being an ecological horror show. 'Equipping every house with its own domestic infrastructure, from washing machines to power drills, is a boon for consumerism but requires vast resources,' he says, before going on to ask of the architectural community: 'Is it time for domestic nuclear deproliferation?'

The market-founded sharing economy – the rise of 'home-sharing' sites such as Airbnb and 'car-sharing' sites such as Lyft and Uber – is rightly criticized for profiteering, and for hiding abusive employment practices behind a shiny, happy veneer of 'community'. But we shouldn't dismiss the potential impacts of either state-led or grassroots iterations of the sharing economy, such as the UK's Local Exchange Trading Systems, through which members barter tools and skills such as the use of tumble dryers or clothes-mending. Projects that share the capacity of municipal kitchen facilities in the US and projects of 'collaborative consumption', such as MamaBake and BakeSw@p in Australia, which promote the communal cooking and sharing of meals between families, are on the rise. Social sharing initiatives such as timebanking[106] and freecycling[107] are also, cheeringly, emergent on a global scale.

In *No Is Not Enough*, her 2017 response to the election of Trump and its societal and ecological implications, author Naomi Klein wonders if transformative change can only occur in unique points in human history, when crises, such as the Great Crash of 1929 or the wreckage of the Second World War, unfold alongside explosions of utopian imagination – 'times when people dared to dream big, out loud, in public'. Are we at such a moment? Maybe not yet, but its earliest formations are perhaps coming into view in women-led movements to protect the environment and battle climate change, and large-scale yearning for new ways of life.

In August 2017 I spent a week in Athens, exploring the Greek capital's alternative, 'post-capitalist' communities. During the country's great economic crisis of 2011–17 women were laid off from paid jobs at twice the rate that men were but were also expected to pick up the shards of a collapsed social and welfare state through their unpaid labour: stepping in to care for grandchildren, friends' children and the elderly and frail, as the cash-strapped state failed to meet basic social needs. Here I found the first glimmerings of something quite interesting: an ecosystem of socialized services outside of the state – nurseries, community centres and canteens – whose doors were thrown open to Athens natives as well as the thousands of refugees who've arrived in the city from the Middle East and Africa since the great refugee migration of 2015 (many fleeing grim conditions in refugee reception camps in Turkey and on the Greek islands).

'We see communal labour as solidarity,' as one young Greek woman put it to me when I visited City Plaza, a former hotel that had been squatted as an intentional community, with a communal kitchen and childcare facilities, by leftists and refugees. These projects were inchoate, unfunded, and struggling, in many cases, to square leftist revolutionary values with the cultural values of residents from staunchly patriarchal countries (including Greece). A workshop at City Plaza, led by a tattooed young feminist anarchist from Spain, on Western feminist insights and male involvement in commune affairs, riled residents from predominantly Muslim nations. 'Who is she to tell me that my culture is wrong?' one Afghan woman refugee complained. But the commune's bustling kitchen, where a pot of Syrian lentil soup simmered aromatically on the hob, was a model of non-sexist, cross-cultural collaboration. These are reasons for cheer.

The impetus of Womyn's Lands, too, is not lost. At a hipster Brooklyn café, Leah DeVun tells me that a new generation of 'queerlands' – countryside communities set up as experimental communities by lesbian, gay, trans and non-binary individuals – are taking up the mantle of rural experiments in feminist living. A network of camping sites and retreats, queerlands communalize labour, but, unlike Womyn's Lands, emphasize non-dogmatic acceptance or rejection of the trappings of the capitalist patriarchy: residents are free to express their gender identities and sexualities as they wish, as long as they abide by community rules and pitch in with daily duties. 'I predict we'll see much more of this as cities become more expensive and push young people out,' DeVun says.

Queer feminist writer Vanessa Friedman says the following of her nine-month residency at a queerland campsite in southern Oregon:

'I want [feminists] to exist in a space that is just a little bit out of the patriarchy's grasp. I want Diva Cups and skipping showers to be the norm, but tampons and deodorant not to be scorned if that's what you want to use; I want communal cooking and intergenerational learning and late-night slumber parties and impromptu sing-a-longs and love, so much love.'

In 1891 Oscar Wilde, another queer traveller, wrote: 'A map of the world that does not include Utopia is not worth even glancing at, for it leaves out the one country at which Humanity is always landing. And when Humanity lands there, it looks out, and, seeing a better country, sets sail.'

Such alternative communities might be a marginal enterprise, or they might not, but we should take comfort in the fact that feminists are once more finding space to dream.

11

Don't Iron While the Strike is Hot!

'When women stop, everything stops,' the posters read.

On 24 October 1975, 90 per cent of Iceland's adult female population left their jobs, their children and their homes, and took to the streets for a general strike that was billed 'Women's Day Off'.

Guðrún Ögmund, now 68, attended the march. 'It was Women's Day Off from our work as lowly paid workers under men bosses, but it was also Women's Day Off from housework, childcare and all the other thankless work women did,' she tells me. Toting a placard that read 'A Day Off – and Then?', Guðrún joined the sea of women who took to Reykjavík's streets (30,000 of them, with 10 marches elsewhere in this nation of 220,000 souls). The day was unseasonably mild and spirits were high. A group of marchers broke into the campaign song written for the day ('*Why Women's Day Off? / Women are joyous now / They ask for unity*'); they listened to speeches and chatted about what could be done to improve women's lot in this small and unequal Nordic country. As they marched up the arterial Laugavegur, or 'Wash Road',* a women's brass

---

* Named for the medieval springs where Reykjavík's women used to bring their laundry for communal washes.

band played the marching tune from *Shoulder to Shoulder*, a British TV series about the suffragettes which had recently been shown in Iceland.

'I was quite ecstatic,' Guðrún recalls.

For men, conversely, the day became known as 'the Long Friday'. With no women to staff desks and tills, banks, factories and shops were forced to close, as were schools and nurseries – leaving fathers with no choice but to take their children to work. There were reports of men arming themselves with sweets and colouring crayons to entertain the swarms of little humans in their workplaces, or bribing their older offspring to look after their siblings. Sausages (easy to cook, of course, and a hit with kids the world over) were in such demand that shops sold out. Children, Guðrún remembers, could be heard giggling in the background while newsreaders reported the march on the radio.

At the Reykjavík event, a flyer became a paper baton, held aloft. It asked: 'Why a Day off for Women?'

- Because when someone is needed for a bad-status, low-paid job, the advert specifies a woman.

- Because the average wages of women in trade and commerce are only 75 per cent of the average wages of men doing the same jobs.

- Because it is commonly said about a housewife: 'She is not working, she is just keeping house.'

- Because the work experience of a housewife is not considered of any value in the labour market.

The general conclusion is that women's contribution to the community is underestimated.

The closing speech of the day was given by Aðalheiður Bjarnfreðsdóttir, head of the union that represented Icelandic women cleaners, kitchen workers and laundry staff.

'Men have governed the world since time immemorial and what has the world been like?' Bjarnfreðsdóttir stormed. 'It's been a world soaked in blood, an earth polluted and exploited to the point of ruin.'

Guðrún was reduced to tears. 'It was one of those moments when your mind thinks *YES!* and your heart soars,' she says.

Many of the greatest successes of feminism have come in moments when boots were on the ground – our bodies elsewhere to the posts ascribed to women by patriarchal capitalism. In the UK, public reaction to the sexual violence meted out against the 300 women who marched to the Houses of Parliament demanding women's suffrage on 18 November 1910, the day that became known as 'Black Friday', was instrumental in gaining the franchise for women. The 1968 strike by Ford's women sewing machinists at Dagenham, which was followed in 1970 by a strike by women clothing workers in Leeds, was a landmark labour-relations dispute that triggered the passing of the Equal Pay Act 1970.

The 1975 event in Iceland was the most successful of a series of strikes that were called to draw attention to women's unpaid and devalued domestic labour at the height of the 1970s Women's Movement. Its stroke of genius was to bill the strike as 'Women's Day Off', thus uniting a broad coalition of women's organizations, women workers, housewives and unions, and pre-empting employers' and husbands' complaints. Women could be sacked for striking, but not for taking a day off.

A year after the strike, equal gender pay rights were enshrined in Icelandic law; and in 1980, citizens voted in Vigdís Finnbogadóttir as the world's first democratically elected female head of state. In 2018, Iceland ranked top in the World Economic Forum's *Global Gender Gap Report* – an index that examines educational opportunities, life expectancy, pay equity and the average time spent each day on housework – for the 10th year running. The gender pay gap is due to close in Iceland in 2022. It will take another 202 years[108] to close the gap globally, and an estimated 60 years in the UK.[109]

What about the division of domestic labour in the world's most gender-equal nation? Well, single Icelandic men put in 14 hours a week of housework compared to single women's 9, but when heterosexual couples cohabit this picture reverses, with women contributing 14 hours a week to men's 4. Clearly there's still some way to go, even in the most equal country on earth.

In 2009, Iceland's first female prime minister and the world's first openly lesbian head of government, Jóhanna Sigurðardóttir, was sworn in. In a 2019 interview with the BBC, a few years after leaving office, Sigurðardóttir advised caution in positioning Iceland as a model of feminist governance. 'If we were truly an equal nation I would not have been the first [woman] Icelandic prime minister,' she quipped. 'However there are two things we get right: universal high-quality childcare, without which basic right no nation is feminist, and three months' use-it-or-lose-it parental leave for men.'[110]

Five years before the Icelandic women's strike, on 26 August 1970,* over 100,000 American women left their jobs and homes and gathered for the largest women's march since the suffrage campaigns of the 1910s. Billed as the 'Women's Strike for Equality', the day became the visible marker of the strength of the new Women's Movement: 50,000 turned out to march down Fifth Avenue in New York, 5,000 in Boston and 8,000 in LA. The marchers had three explicit demands: free abortion on demand, equal opportunity in jobs and education, and free 24-hour childcare as a right.**

The marchers were adroit propagandists, carrying placards calling out the oppressions of 'women's work': 'Housewives are

---

* Chosen to mark the 50th anniversary of American women gaining the right to vote.
** To emphasize the latter point, strikers set up ad hoc solidarity crèches for the day of the actions.

Unpaid Slave Labourers! Tell Him What to Do with the Broom!!' read a poster carried by a young woman in New York. In Los Angeles, marchers wearing Richard Nixon masks counter-heckled the men who'd gathered to jeer and throw pennies at the marchers: 'Go do the dishes, go do the dishes!' they cried. In Detroit, women staged a sit-in at a men's restroom, and in Minneapolis there was a 'guerrilla theatre' of stereotypical women's roles in American society, in which women mutely washed dishes and obsequiously doted on their husbands, wearing heels and aprons. The day's slogan, brilliantly, was 'Don't Iron While the Strike Is Hot!'

Fifty years later, have these Second Wave feminist strikers' demands been met? Well, the record, sadly, is patchier than Iceland's. The early decades of the 1970s saw a series of legislative landmarks when it came to women's equality in the US public sphere. The passage of Title IX in 1972 forbade sex discrimination in any educational program that received federal financial assistance; and in 1980, the Equal Employment Opportunity Commission recognized policies banning sexual harassment. In 1973, through the Supreme Court ruling *Roe v. Wade*, abortion was legalized in all 50 states (although the decision only protected a woman's right to terminate an unwanted pregnancy during the first trimester). In the late 1970s and early 1980s American women also gained, thanks to Second Wave feminist campaigning, financial rights within marriage and the recognition of homemakers' contributions in divorce settlements.

Yet when it comes to the last of the US marchers' demands – for the right to free universal childcare – the response has been tepid. In 1971, the United States Congress passed the Comprehensive Child Development Bill, which would have set up local daycare centres for children on a sliding scale based on family income, but President Richard Nixon then vetoed the bill. Today, infant childcare, at a US-wide average of $850 a month, prices an estimated 48.4 per cent of primary-caring parents out of work.[111] And, as we've seen, women still disproportionately shoulder the burden of the labour American capitalism devalues and underpays. It's a case of a few legislative gains masking failures and reversals elsewhere.

The intervening decades have seen periodic flurries of women's direct action: the Global Women's Strike on 8 March 2000, in which women across 60 countries marched for (amongst other demands) payment for caring work. In 2004, the reproductive rights March for Women's Lives saw a million women descending on the National Mall in Washington, DC; and the Women's Marches that followed the January 2017 inauguration of Donald Trump witnessed millions marching worldwide against bigotry, discrimination and sexual assault. A black feminist academic friend, Dina, refers to these recent events, somewhat scathingly, as 'liberal feminist identity marches', and worrying reports surfaced after the London Women's March on 21 January 2017 of women of colour feeling marginalized – in some cases even elbowed to one side – in the predominantly white crowd.

Perhaps feminists' demands are becoming increasingly disparate and complex. Many Republican pundits in the US commented of the 2017 Women's Marches that marchers 'did not know what they were marching for'. This argument riled US journalist Jessica Valenti. In an episode of her podcast *What Would a Feminist Do?*, recorded in the aftermath of the 2017 Women's Marches, she attributed such analyses to media pundits' lazy miscomprehension of the nuances of the modern feminist movement. It was true, she said, that women's marchers did not have a set list of demands or a policy proposal, but that's not to say that they didn't have common aims.

'We care about reproductive rights and justice but also racial justice and how those things connect. We want violence against women to stop, and we want trans rights front and centre and we want to talk about how those things inform each other.' These are not issues that can be summed up in a five-second media soundbite, Valenti admitted. 'But that's OK... That doesn't mean that we don't know what we're fighting for. It's that you don't care enough to do a deep dive to find out.'

In countries with an ascendant antisystem left, the picture is somewhat different. In Spain, marches to mark International Women's Day (8 March) have increasingly been positioned as strikes against the housework and care burdens ascribed to Spanish women. In 2018, the 24-hour strike's organizers, the 8M Commission, articulated their call to action in a country where women put in 26.5 hours of weekly domestic labour to men's average of 14[112] in a manifesto.

> The care strike today is meant to make visible a set of daily tasks that nobody wants to acknowledge, neither as free work at home, nor as an undervalued employment. We claim that the care work should be recognised as a social good of first order and we demand the equal redistribution of these kind of tasks.

Organizers called for an inclusive and intersectional strike: 'We are migrants, students, butches,* journalists, housewives, trans, artists, self-employed, doctors, lawyers and much, much more...' And their hope was realized in the sight of women in hijab dotting a crowd of middle-aged workers and millennials.

8M also set up a network of collective soup kitchens and nurseries – or 'care points' – across Spain, which in Madrid were staffed by 'a network of feminist men in solidarity', as they told a newspaper reporter. Almost 6 million Spanish women joined the 2018 Day Without Women, including Madrid's mayor Manuela Carmena and actress Penélope Cruz, and it in part prompted the Spanish government to draft, in 2019, legislation titled 'Royal Decree-Law 6/2019, of 1 March, on urgent measures to

---

* Butch women.

guarantee equal treatment and opportunities between women and men in employment and occupation'. The draft legislation announced that it would equalise parental leave, with earmarked paternity leave of 16 weeks to be introduced by 2021.

The visual symbol of the strike was the old-fashioned mother's apron, sewn at get-togethers in advance of the march, strung from balconies and thrown as the women marched.

Much of the strength of the 2018 Spanish care strikes resulted from the support of Spain's confederation of radical labour unions, the National Confederation of Labour (CNT). Such feminist strikes with labour-movement support have been seen, too, in countries such as Argentina, where in 2015 and 2016 hundreds of thousands of women took to the streets to unite under the slogan *Ni una menos* ('Not one less') after police inaction after the rape and murder of a series of women. Selma James, the co-founder of Wages for Housework and the organizer of the 2000 Global Women's Strike (through the

Aprons hang from balconies in Galicia in 2018 to mark the women's general strike against 'invisible' unpaid labour

network International Women's Strike), points out that as the power of unions dwindles, the climate in some Western countries is less hospitable to such gestures of withdrawn labour, even as feminist identity strikes gain broader support. Without the level of union protection for women's strikes that is seen in Spain, women who strike from paid work risk losing their jobs; and without social acknowledgement of the validity of strikes, these gestures can fall flat. In such conditions, redoubled by a climate of precarious, freelance and zero-hours work and the exorbitant cost of private childcare, striking from work often exacts its greatest toll on the woman striker. Doubly so when we factor in the penalties exacted by race and class discrimination and single parenthood. To the single mum on the breadline, women's marches can seem the preoccupation of privileged white feminists.

Speaking to *VICE News* in 2017, black feminist activist Chardine Taylor-Stone was withering about the climate for such direct action in the UK, expecting most young feminists marking International Women's Day in the same year as the Spanish marchers to make their revolutionary gestures via social media posts.

'Even though it's called a strike, it's not the same as those organized by train workers,' she said. 'We're post-Thatcherism and a lot of people aren't even unionized so can't afford to take time off, so we're thinking of different ways people can do something. Symbolism is important, not everyone's going to read Marx by next week, but people connect with symbolism.'

Domestic labour has always been a tricky injustice to organize around. It takes place in the privacy of the home, making it difficult for women to see each other doing this work and to collectively acknowledge the injustice that men do not share equally in its burden. For successive waves of feminist activism, domestic labour has been a sidelined issue, easy to see as less important than women's waged work and the inequalities they face in the paid workforce, such as sexual harassment, pay

Poster from the 2019 Walthamstow mums' strike

inequity and pregnancy discrimination. How far symbolism will get us when it comes to the material issues of who wipes arses and cleans loos, and how society treats these workers, is a matter of debate.

There are early glimmerings of direct action against labour injustices in the Anglo-Saxon West: 8 March 2019 saw a smattering of mums' strikes for International Women's Day in parts of leftie London, including an event in Walthamstow where mothers brought their children to workshops to teach them about International Women's Day, with paid male childminders on hand, and a Hackney mums' strike, which offered a free ready-prepared dinner ('Bring Your Takeaway Containers'). In October 2018, the Women's Strike Assembly, an antifascist group set up by young British feminist activists with the founding motto 'It is impossible, that is why it is necessary', called for a 'social reproduction assembly' to discuss ways in which volunteers from the left could rally to offer help with childcare, cooking and 'other forms of reproductive labour' so Women's

Strike Assembly members could counter-demonstrate against the rally of far-right group the DFLA (Democratic Football Lads Alliance).[113] The organization, who promoted the 2019 mums' strikes, is busy creating transnational coalitions with groups such as sex workers, cleaners' unions and advocates for Universal Basic Income, and in June 2019 it staged a series of feminist educational events in London, Bristol and Cardiff, including 'WTF is Reproduction #2: They say it's love but is it actually unpaid work?' And 'The Fight for Childcare is ON!'

And direct actions are also being seen in unlikely countries such as Switzerland, where on 14 June 2019, tens of thousands of women — in what the Swiss media referred to as a 'purple wave' of pram marches, whistle concerts and giant picnics — abandoned work and caring commitments to strike against the slow progress towards gender equality.[114] Along with broader anger over sexism and workplace inequality, many demonstrators demanded higher pay for cleaners, teachers and care workers. In Zurich, marchers strode through the city with a giant pink clitoris mounted on a float and in Basel they projected a clenched fist onto the headquarters of Roche, a leading Swiss corporate.

It is impossible, that is why it is necessary… There's an evergreen dilemma for women strikers who care for the young and vulnerable: how can you strike if you risk endangering those you care for?

I've attended women's day marches, the 2017 London Women's March the day after Trump's inauguration and numerous marches of the left: for the climate, and against war and university tuition fees. But I've never downed tools, domestic or otherwise. So on 8 March 2018, the day 5.6 million women went on strike to draw attention to women's invisible labour in

Spain, I decided to withdraw my own paid and reproductive labour. But 8 March, I quickly realized, would be no good. I was in charge of Leo for the day, with Tim at work and no childcare on hand. Striking on this day would constitute child neglect and, as I scrambled around for untested sitters, also supplant my day's labour with a mental load of administrative chores. The point would be, I supposed, to tell Tim I was striking and that he'd have to find a sitter, but, as he'd do so through gritted teeth and in a state of distrustful panic (new sitters gave him the 'heebie-jeebies'), this would land me, however much I tried to evade it, with a different variety of common-or-garden mental load.

And so I came to an intimate realization of one of Second Wave feminism's insights: unpaid labour works as a form of blackmail against the capacity for struggle.

As my Madrid sisters marched, I took Leo to a hellish soft-play centre in Central London and watched as he got lodged in a padded slide, performed a backflip and broke out in a voluminous nosebleed. I decided instead on a 9 March private direct action: a home strike! There would be a 24-hour delay in my solidarity, but solidarity doesn't spoil!

In May 1977, *Ms.* magazine featured a story on a housewife who sent a letter of resignation to her family:

> This is to inform you that I am no longer running this household. The cupboards, the Lysol, the linoleum, the washer, the dryer, the marketing – they're all yours. I HEREBY RESIGN AS KEEPER OF THIS HOUSE, AS YOUR LIVE-IN MAID/COOK/MENTOR/NURSEMAID.
>
> You can fend for yourselves. Best of luck.
>
> Mom[115]

The accompanying article advised women countenancing a housework strike to set up a chart of housework chores, or a detailed list of work to be shared between household members in the mother/housewife's absence (clearly, our striking moms wouldn't be fully exempt from housework's mental load). Such charts became the vogue in the 1970s, with sample chore lists printed in feminist magazines.

The article went on to recommend that other readers — housewives, working wives and mothers — followed suit with small-scale direct actions against the tyranny of women's work. Drop the pots, put your feet up on the pouffe, strike up a menthol ciggie.

The day I decided to resign from being a 21st-century heterosexual mother was, propitiously, a day that Leo was at nursery. Tim was working at a 9 a.m. to 6.30 p.m. lawyering gig he darkly referred to as 'contracting his anus', and I was due to work at home, filing an article on the social cost of the UK's IVF 'postcode lottery' as I simultaneously packed our flat up for an impending house move and rustled up the family's evening meals. With Tim at work beyond 6 p.m., I realized I'd have to jump through hoops to find someone to collect Leo from nursery at 5 p.m. This simple task would require procuring a photograph of the person undertaking this pick-up and sending it to the nursery to clear their safety checks. Tim couldn't do this as he wasn't listed as primary carer, so even if I relinquished this task to him I'd first have to contact the nursery to tell them that Tim would then contact them to arrange the photograph and sitter clearance in a never-ending vortex of administrative hell. For these reasons, my strike would extend from 8 a.m. to 5 p.m., then from 7.15 p.m. on.

My small-scale act of resistance went like this: two hours of worrying about overstepping my article deadline; another sundry hour or so trying not to trip over empty packing boxes and attempting to find things that had already been packed; many minutes of being annoyed about living in filth as I couldn't clear up the kitchen; and, eventually, at 3 p.m., going out to a coffee shop to avoid all of the 'domestic spider threads tugging at [my] brain'. I then stomped off for the nursery pick-up and returned home to cook for and feed Leo, before striking from preparing an adult dinner even though, frankly by this point, I was a bit peckish. Tim returned from work to a manic flat, put Leo to bed and prepared our dinner, which we ate at 9.30 p.m. before I shuffled off to bed accompanied by sour sensations of annoyance and indigestion. I didn't tell Tim why the flat had descended into chaos until the following evening, when he confided he'd been quite pleased to cook pasta and eat at a continental hour, but had wondered about the half-drunk cup of tea on top of the loo and why the bedroom floor was 'even more festooned than usual' with my knickers and pairs of 70-denier tights. Also why Leo went to bed, that night, in a toddler sleeping bag that smelled 'more than faintly of piss'.

Tell me an anecdote about domestic labour in your home when you were a child.

'Once, when I was a teenager, my mother went on strike for a few days. I don't remember the outcome, but I vividly remember the strike. I don't think anything changed much.' Single female aged 56–64, UK

Perhaps my domestic set-up is too egalitarian for a targeted strike to have the effect it might have had in a home that's closer to the Breadwinner/Housewife model? After all, my principal beef is with the system that expects of me a Double Day while also nudging me into unpaid labour through my role as a mother and the inflexibility of my partner's corporate job. The British corporate in question staged a 'family fun day' in 2017, to which partners or paid carers were allowed/ expected to bring the staff's children. At this family fun day, the staff in question were permitted to leave their desks and 'join the family fun!' for 90 minutes.

Striking against the system, as we've seen, requires collective action. Or is this all a callow excuse? Am I simply too timid to upset the precarious tower of cards of favours, understandings and borrowed time upon which our family life teeters?

American home-economy blogger Katie Berry is an advocate for periodic 'wife strikes' in contexts such as hers, in which older kids and husbands act, as she puts it, as if you had 'nothing else to do besides clean and cook for them'.

On her website, Housewife How-To's, Berry talks of the moment that inspired the first of her now routine strikes:

> One evening while I was making dinner, my daughter brought down a load of dirty dishes from her room and dumped them in the sink. She was on her phone the entire time and only paused long enough to say, 'Happy now? I cleaned my room.'
>
> My son, meanwhile, came and grabbed a handful of the cheese I'd shredded for dinner, then went back to playing his video game. He left a trail of cheese on the floor behind him.
>
> Then my husband got home from the nine holes of golf he'd decided to play after work and collapsed in front of the TV where he napped until I called him for dinner.
>
> Once we'd eaten, everyone disappeared. My daughter went back to her phone, my son went back to his game, and my husband went back to his recliner to watch football all night. Me? I was stuck in the kitchen putting away the meal I'd made and doing the dishes. After that, I still had a load of laundry to fold and put away.

Halfway through that unappreciated pile of dishes, Berry snapped, throwing the dishcloth into the sink and loudly announcing: 'I AM ON STRIKE!'

She called a house meeting to set out the terms of her strike, a tactic I now realize might have made my direct action more of a strike and less of a damp squib.

'I promised to get them to a doctor if they got sick,' Berry says, 'but otherwise, they had to take care of themselves. They needed to wake themselves up, pick out their clothes, make their breakfasts, pack their lunches, and work together to make dinner. They'd have to do the dishes, laundry, and other household chores. They'd have to do their homework without being reminded. They'd have to referee their arguments.'

Berry went on strike for a week, claiming that that first action taught her teenagers new domestic skills such as how to launder their jeans in the washing machine and cook dinner, and that it 'restored gratitude' in her household.

'When I went on strike, my kids figured out that meals don't just appear on the table: someone puts effort into cooking,' she continues. 'They decided they wanted spaghetti for dinner. It took them nearly two hours; then they had to wash dishes after. When they realized bedtime was in 30 minutes, they just about lost it.'

Berry is silent about the effect her periodic strikes have on her husband's domestic involvement and golf escapades, and clearly her actions are less a grand gesture of feminist resistance than a throwing down of the (tea) towel in exasperation. But, in their bid to make Berry's labour visible, at least to her teen children, they prove that the withdrawing of labour, on however small a scale and however contingently, can have outcomes we might claim as feminist.

Tell me an anecdote about domestic labour in your home when you were a child.

'Once, at some point in the 1980s, my mum got exasperated with my dad and put Post-it notes around the kitchen pointing out things he never noticed like dishes

that needed washing or bins that needed taking out. The Post-it notes said "LOOK!" with eyes in the Os. He started noticing things more after that.' White British woman aged 33–45, UK

In the absence of women's ability to strike against their situations – where support from labour organizations is not forthcoming, or where withdrawing labour will endanger others or lose women their jobs – Selma James calls for a constellation of 'small resistances'.

We can protest our situation as women, she says, by 'returning from lunch even 10 minutes late, banging pots in the streets or at the window, as women in Spain did against the 2003 Iraq war'.

An unnamed representative for the International Women's Strike echoed this call in an interview with VICE News in advance of 2018's a Day Without Women in Spain: 'Do a part-time strike, or put a broom outside [your] front door, do a shopping strike, wear black or red, block roads, put a poster up in [your] house.'

Small acts of resistance to patriarchy have a long heritage. Think of the women of the past who were subjected to the ignominies of scold's bridles, or the body of literature that argues that the symptoms of neurasthenia – the portfolio of non-existent 'conditions of the nerves' that rendered Victorian women fashionably bed-bound with lassitude and fatigue – were unarticulated forms of bodily resistance against their position under the corsetry (literal and metaphorical) of the Domestic Cult.

An episode of the US sitcom *I Love Lucy* which aired in 1952 hangs on a housekeeping wheeze of Lucy's husband Ricky. After Lucy takes so long to get dressed that they miss a dinner with his new boss (frothy wives and exacting bosses are the stock-in-trade of mid-century sitcoms), he puts his wife on an exacting domestic schedule. Smilingly, Lucy enacts her revenge, handing Ricky frozen coffee and a precooked egg at the breakfast table, saying 'I knew I wouldn't have time to cook it this morning'. When two other husbands decide they'd like to follow patriarch Ricky's housekeeping example, Lucy invites these couples for dinner, serving a spread that their wives whip away before they can eat it, tapping their watches because 'we're trying to stay on schedule!' Similarly, Elizabeth Silva shows us that domestic workers in Brazil resist their lowly status through small routine acts of insubordination, or theft: refusing to cook meals to schedule, or taking cuts of meat from the dinner joint for themselves.

Recently, there has been a form of resistance argued for (often by childless young feminists) that I call the tactic of wilful incompetence. In her now-defunct feminist newsletter *Lenny Letter*, actress, screenwriter and millennial tastemaker Lena Dunham suggested that every woman should consider having part of American writer Shel Silverstein's poem 'How Not To Have To Dry the Dishes' tattooed onto their arms:

If you have to dry the dishes
And you drop one on the floor –
Maybe they won't let you
Dry the dishes any more

By flagrantly burning the toast and leaving the sink smeared with toothpaste, we – like Kate Moss all those years ago – push aside the humble pie and have another fag instead. Through wilful incompetence, we refuse the old and patriarchal expectations to be expert homemakers.

Arlie Hochschild and sociologist Ann Oakley, author of the seminal observational text on British housework, 1974's *The Sociology of Housework*, argue, rather, for 'cutting back' strategies against the heterosexist labour asymmetry. This was the tactic taken by several of Hochschild's disillusioned women interviewees in *The Second Shift*, who 'cut back what had to be done at home by redefining what the house, the marriage and, sometimes, what the child needs. One woman described a fairly common pattern: 'I do my half. I do half of his half, and the rest doesn't get done.'

The logic is seductive. Men not pitching in their 50 per cent? Fine: reduce your 50 per cent by not washing those curtains or tucking in those hospital corners, or by letting the dishes pile up until tomorrow. Give yourself a break from that growing list of expectations that fall most weightily on heterosexual cohabiting mothers' shoulders. After all, will your daughter suffer if you don't help her to bake a Victoria sponge for a teacher's birthday? Will anything life-threatening happen if you don't take the detour to the shop that does the nice organic bread and instead plump for a supermarket loaf? (These are the scenarios imagined from middle-class privilege, but you get the gist.)

When I visit Arlie Hochschild at her polite hilltop home in Berkeley, California in the spring of 2019, it is my second audience with her. At our first meeting, in 2013, I quoted her own book back to her as the work of another author, so I arrive in an apologetic guise. Since then, Hochschild has published a book, *Strangers in Their Own Land*, which looks at how white blue-collar workers have begun to see their demise under globalization as attributable to identity groups – immigrants, uppity women – queue-cutting, and therefore taking white male Americans' due.

The University of California sociologist – a Democrat supporter – has just returned from speaking at a congressional Democratic retreat in Virginia, and the party is struggling to agree its message for the 2020 presidential election. How do you counter the divisive right-wing populism of Donald Trump?

Do you aim high and ignore the debasements of populist politics, Hochschild wonders, or do you address the grievances of the Trump-voting constituencies in a fresh way, talking of healthcare and jobs? The experience has left Hochchild anxious and a little dismayed. She sips a glass of water in her beautiful book-lined study, where floor-to-ceiling windows frame views of the deep-green Berkeley Hills, and shakes her head.

I ask Hochschild – as the author of 1989's *The Second Shift*, the book that first articulated the working lot of women in the age of Having It All liberal feminism – what she thinks of the current state of play in the private sphere. Are we in a position she might have predicted 30 years ago?

'Well, we're seeing a stalled revolution. In a small proportion of society, the upper middle class, the ideal of a sharing male partner has caught on; and that is new. But men have also taken a huge financial hit: their jobs are more precarious and their wages are down,' she says. 'What we didn't predict was the total disappearance of these men from the domestic sphere. But blue-collar guys are much more likely to not be living with the mother of the kid than they were in the 1960s, and much less likely to be involved in their children's care. So the question is not: are men lightening the load with the second shift? These men are *not even there.*'

She tells me that she sees much of the current mood as being a backlash against the presence of women in the workplace and positions of power. 'Women in the workplace are not yet seen as [simply] a *person who is doing a job.*'

But Hochschild is trying to be optimistic. 'You know, we have to hang together. We have to reach out to the 8 million people who voted for Obama in 2008, then switched to Trump for 2016. We need a *renewal* on the left. A new message, one that doesn't vilify black people, immigrants or women. New common ground.'

Then she takes another sip of water and regards me levelly. 'So, tell me about Brexit…'

These times – when a stalled revolution is flanked by a land grab on women's rights – call for efforts, perhaps, more strenuous than 'cutting back'.

There's a lot to be said for giving yourself a break from the unfeminist internal critic. For letting hairs choke the plughole and dust settle on the blinds to protect your own sanity. But strategic incompetence doesn't hold up to scrutiny if it fails, as it must, to address the myriad underlying factors and systems that lead to our domestic labour asymmetries. It strikes me as too similar to the evasive tactics – those 'you're just better at it, babe' moments feminists have dubbed 'learned incompetence' – that we revile in some men. Men who shrug winsomely and claim themselves 'terrible cooks'; men who mix the laundry loads and shrink the woollens and stain the whites that tell-tale sepia-pink-grey. (As I write this, Tim, Leo and I are staying in a house-swap in Oregon where he's just informed me that he 'better not put the laundry on' as he doesn't know 'how to work' these massive upright American washers. He adds, shamefacedly: 'Not as a sexist thing, you understand.')

In an opinion piece for British newspaper *Metro*, Miranda Larbi asks:

> Is conscious male incompetence a form of misogyny? If you labour the point that you can't cook, then chances are that you won't be made to cook. If you make a hash out of doing the laundry or hoovering, you're forcing someone else to take over...
>
> But those who choose to remain ignorant and then ask their girlfriends, wives, partners to do it for them are participating in a very subtle form of misogyny that burdens women with low-level emotional labour.

Is this expectation, in fact, worse for young, unattached women than for 'mothers', wonders young, unattached Larbi:*

---

* The answer, of course, is no.

'The expectation that you're supposed to have your own shit together as a young woman *and* be able to look after a fully grown man with whom you have no familial attachment is draining.'

She importunes male readers:

> So next time you ask your girlfriend if they could give your shirt a quick iron because you're 'rubbish at it', just stop and have a think.
>
> Are you really that thick? Or are you just offloading your laziness onto someone who traditionally has been made responsible for male incompetence?

Through wilful incompetence, we – like Larbi's hapless male – become infantile, and by 'cutting back', as Marjorie DeVault notes in her 1991 book *Feeding the Family*, we fail to address inequality and also risk undermining necessary levels of care.

For all this, I have sympathy with another emergent argument: the reclamation of 'domestic sluttishness' as a statement. In a story for *Lenny Letter*, author Tatum Dooley asks, 'Should I commit to messiness in the name of Simone de Beauvoir?'

Dooley quotes de Beauvoir's famous invective against the pointlessness of housework:

> The housewife wears herself out running on the spot; she does nothing; she only perpetuates the present; she never gains the sense that she is conquering a positive Good, but struggles indefinitely against Evil.

Messiness, says Dooley, should be cleansed of its patina of laziness. 'For me, the level of my mess is in direct correlation to productivity in other areas of my life.'

This argument speaks to our moment, in which housework jostles for woman-hours with the demands of productive work, leisure and self-care. Such gestures invariably become more complex when caring responsibilities, cohabitation and differential gendered earning potentials enter the equation. Could, more powerfully, 'domestic sluttery'[116] perform the work of terms such as 'bitch' and 'queer'? Reclaimed linguistic territory from the argots of sexism and homophobia that provoke, and issue challenges to, the heterosexist status quo?

This reminds me of the most ribald take on that 18th-century nursery rhyme:

They that wash on Monday
  Have all the week to dry;
They that wash on Tuesday
  Are not so much awry;
They that wash on Wednesday
  Are not so much to blame;
They that wash on Thursday,
  Wash for very shame;
They that wash on Friday,
  Must only wash in need;
And they that wash on Saturday,
  Are lazy sluts indeed.

Maybe we should become lazy sluts indeed. Sluts in deed.

We might also take our cue from Second Wave feminism's avant-garde. The height of Second Wave feminism saw an explosion of such agitprop art, which was designed to draw attention to feminist insights. American artist Shirley Boccaccio's *Fuck Housework* depicts a woman snarling as she breaks a witch-style broom, under the banner 'Fuck Housework', rendered in an Old English font. It was reproduced on posters that sold across the USA in the early 1970s, and it allowed the single mother artist to feed her three children until a large poster company stole the design.* Socialist-feminist art collective the Hackney Flashers, who formed in London in 1974,

---

* Boccaccio's attempt to enforce her intellectual property rights was thrown out after a judge declared the image 'patently obscene'.

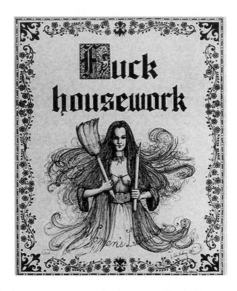

Shirley Boccaccio's 1971 poster, *Fuck Housework*

aimed — through exhibitions such as *Women and Work* (1975) and *Who's Holding the Baby* (1978) — to document women's work in and out of the home and 'make the invisible visible'. A pervasive sense of stay-at-home mothers' isolation and loneliness and anger looms large in *Who's Holding the Baby*, which is currently housed in the Reina Sofía Museum in Madrid. The exhibition made a rousing argument, through art, for decent state childcare provision and services such as well-maintained city parks — the last another forgotten fight of feminism's Second Wave.

Most dramatically, the 1970s and '80s saw a series of bombings and arson attacks at the hands of West German far-left feminism organization Rote Zora, targeting ideological enemies involved in the exploitation of women and enforcement of patriarchal society.[117] The organization took its name from Kurt Held's 1941 book *Die Rote Zora und ihre Bande*, about a Croatian girl named Rote Zora who leads a gang of orphans in a fight against social injustice. In 1978, Rote Zora

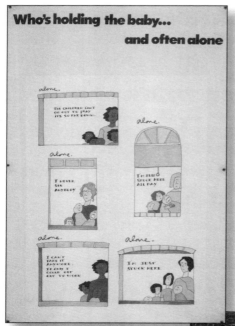

Panels from *Who's Holding the Baby*, a 1978 exhibition by the Hackney Flashers Collective

committed arson attacks against sex shops in Cologne; in 1983 they carried out four bomb attacks against a recruitment agency that was bringing in foreign workers for, amongst other low-skilled jobs, domestic work; and in 1987 they attempted to bomb a clothing factory in Bavaria that under-paid its women staff. Rote Zora's activists were known in the German press as 'after-work terrorists', because they were commonly working women who dabbled in direct action.* In 2007, Adrienne Gershäuser – a qualified radio technician who had helped, under the code name 'Lea', to build Rote Zora's bombs – turned herself in and stood trial for two attempted bombings. She received a suspended two-year sentence, and no further Rote Zora members were caught or prosecuted.

If all else fails, a German feminist friend tells me, there's always rage-cleaning. Karen uses cleaning as a therapeutic method for dispensing with her feminist ire.

'I just take out all the patriarchal shit on my bathtub,' she says. 'Then I have a nice clean bathtub.' After talking to Karen about *Putzwahn*, that German notion of 'cleaning mania', I think that it would be a great word to scream, full of glottals and indignation, as you frantically cleaned your Berlin *Altbau*.

Similarly, a British friend drinks a pint of coffee before setting to it with a sponge scrubber and the Ecover. 'I would say I more use my feminist rage to get myself to clean more effectively,' she muses. But 'rage cleaning', of course, loses most of its tactical potency if a shirking heterosexual man is the chief beneficiary of our therapeutic diversions. And if all this sounds a little tame – cleaning efficiently as a means of taking out your anger against a system that ascribes you the labour of clean-ing efficiently – there's always feminist 'rage-breaking'. One internet advocate advises me, in the course of my hearty bout of feminist cleaning, to 'rage break a fugly vase: fuck yeh!!!! It's

---

* It helped perceptions, of course, that no one died as a result of Rote Zora's actions.

literally the best catharsis.' But I wonder whether cleaning can be both productive and strategically destructive? Who cares about whether I rage-break a vase, fugly or otherwise, if I have to gather up the broken pieces afterwards? And who bears witness to this gesture? Should I buy a fugly vase to break, and leave it shattered across the dining table for Tim to clear up, stained in blood (or, I don't know, ketchup posing as blood)?

I ask Tim what he would conclude from my actions if I did this, and he answers: 'I'd think you'd been watching too many ITV murder mysteries in which strange warnings like dead birds are left on doorsteps by unknown parties.'

Direct action against material injustices can backfire. Rote Zora's action drew opprobrium in the German press and hardened some commentators against the *verrückt* ('crazy') excesses of Second Wave feminism. In response to the 1970 Women's Strike for Equality, a faction of American women, in the Fascinating Womanhood vein, called for a 'National Celebration of Womanhood' – a day dedicated to women dressing in 'frilly', feminine clothing, singing while doing the laundry, and making breakfast in bed for their husbands. It gained press coverage but there was little take-up.

In Spain, a vocal lobby of women – many of whom are allied with extreme-right populist party Vox – countered the feminist narratives of a Day Without Women with the campaign *'No hables en mi nombre!'* ('Don't speak in my name!'), which featured a series of clips posted to social media with the hashtag #nohablesenminombre. The footage explained how much these women enjoyed housework and looking after their families. And a campaign video released by Las mujeres de Vos ('The women of Vox') in advance of the 2018 strike features sun-lit images of smiling young women. 'The women of Vox say,

"Do not speak in my name",' says Vox party co-founder and businesswoman Rocío Monsterio San Martín, to camera. 'We say to the feminists: "I am a woman, but I am not a victim." We say "do not speak in my name" because we do not believe in the totalitarian doctrines of feminism. Doctrines that are against men.'[118]

Vox is rapidly gaining support amongst men who, as my Spanish journalist friend Maruxa puts it, 'fear feminism'. 'There is an old argument in Spain that Vox repeats constantly: "The laws of domestic violence are unfair for men." They are winning seats. It's not funny at all.'

On 28 April 2019 in the Spanish general election, Vox won 24 parliamentary seats: the most significant victory by a far-right party since the end of Franco's dictatorship. We need to be vigilant of the tactics of rising nationalist populisms as we plot our direct actions, as much as we need to persist.

Every five years, on the anniversary of Women's Day Off, Icelandic women stop work early as a tribute to the women who went before them. In 1975, the women strikers marched at 2.05 p.m. In 2005, they left their desks at 2.08 p.m., reflecting the progress made towards gender equality in the intervening 30 years. In 2010 they left their labours at 2.25 p.m., and in 2016 at 2.38 p.m. That year they raided their kitchens for pots and pans to bang together as they marched. Icelandic women persist.

It's in the global rising-up of the women who clean our loos and stitch our clothes and teach our children and care for our elderly that we see the seeds of resistance against gender inequities in the private sphere. Next year I will march for International Women's Day alongside the Women's Strike Movement and a faction of workers from Kalayaan, the overseas domestic workers' union in the UK. Kalayaan are marching for recognition of their work as work, and for stronger rights to escape abusive British employers.

I hope Jurate will join me, if she's keen. (Tim has been put on notice.)

Conclusion

Home Truths

It was domestic work that first animated my feminist consciousness; although I only realize this now, with the hindsight of three decades. As a Brownie in the early 1980s I was thrilled to receive my flower-arranging and tea-making badges, the latter requiring that I slopped a teabag 60 times into 60 cups of milky water for adult family members, as I performed the emotional labour of smiling winsomely as I did so. By the time I was a Girl Guide, in 1986, I sussed something was up. Why was it that our weekend camp emphasized such surreal survival skills as constructing a washing-up stand and crockery-drying rack out of a selection of foraged sticks? Why was it necessary for me to learn how to fold hospital corners, pack a suitcase and make milky puddings for invalids? Why, moreover, didn't I get to stomp on bugs and sit in a bucket of gunge like my brother, Adam, was at Scouts? (Gunge-sitting was surprisingly big in the 1980s, and I've always wondered whether that doesn't explain the domestic mess Gen Xers are in.)

As we've seen, the presentation of such tasks as badges of feminine honour obscures a reality in which such tasks are, for the most part, shitwork. As a child this feminine myth-making both perplexed and reviled me. Cold, hard £1 coins were, however, something my inchoate feminism could grasp hold of. So it was unequal pay that inspired my first feminist direct action when, at the age of nine, I discovered that the Church of England church I attended paid the boys' choir my brother sang in £2 a head to sing in weddings, while girls in the mixed-voice choir received the ignoble sum of £1.50. In response, I did the only sensible thing. I wrote a cruel protest rap, inspired by Wham!. This work of questionable genius rhymed, I recall, 'unfair' with 'disgusting hair' (a swipe at the choirmaster's strange, wooden hairdo).* When it came to the crappy tasks that were presented to me as natural, fun and feminine – from those endless cuppas with a smile to sticking a few daffs in a pot – I simply didn't know where to start. For a lower-middle-class girl growing up in Solihull – a borough of which Felicity Kendal, our most famous former resident, once said 'no one ever finds themselves in Solihull' – those salient arguments of the 1960s and '70s Marxist feminists arrived half-baked. I knew that there was something wonky with the future that I was glimpsing in those unappetizing Domestic Science cookery lessons and Girl Guide badges, but if pressed I would probably have told you, simply, that housewifery was uncool. So I filed these anxieties – alongside concerns about how sex worked and how to get my hair to sit flat – in the binder marked 'things I'll deal with when I'm a grown-up' and I compliantly made those cups of milky tea. As a teenager, I learned to cook. In my twenties, I cleaned up after cohabiting boyfriends (most of whom were permanently stoned). I smiled and cooked and fucked. And I built up the resentments that would come back to bite me when, a couple of decades later, I decided to reproduce with a well-meaning liberal man.

Our Second Wave feminist sisters taught us that housework is power. Housework is not just the relationship between a

---

* In fact, I remember the 'Pay Gap Rap' word for word, but despite being asked, on several occasions, to perform this memorable piece, I have never been plied with sufficient amounts of wine to weaken my resolve, and so I leave its clumsy stanzas in the mid-1980s.

tired woman and a sink of unwashed pots; it also defines the relationships between human beings. To talk about housework – who does the housework, who is underpaid or not paid to do housework, and who shirks housework – is to talk about power. This is an insight that's as true today as it was in the 1970s, when the momentum of history seemed – for that brief and brilliant moment – to be on women's side.

In 1977, change was in the air: sisterhood was (or at least seemed to be) global, and women of colour, First Ladies, domestic workers, women who loved women, and white middle-class housewives stood shoulder to shoulder to speak out against the injustices that women experienced in both the public and private spheres. At the 1977 National Women's Conference poet Maya Angelou and civil rights campaigner Coretta Scott King joined First Lady Rosalyn Carter and former First Ladies Betty Ford and Lady Bird Johnson on stage in Texas as the crowd chanted: 'Every woman is a working woman. Every woman is a working woman!' The personal, as the mantra famously went, was political.

Home Is Where the Heart Is

For many working men in the 1970s, home had never been the sanctuary it was popularly supposed to be: an escape from their labours under capitalism. For women, these theorists and activists showed us, home was forever a troubled domain: a 'domestic factory' where their labour was both extracted and disavowed by patriarchal capitalism. This 'women's work' – the labour delegated to women on the basis of their biology – was erased: erased as an expression of male privilege, and erased as work. This work became, instead, love: natural, women-given, motherly, wifely, sisterly 'love'. No wonder life, for so many women, seemed thankless, soul-destroying and repetitious. Every woman was a working woman. Every woman was a housewife under capitalism. Every woman faced, to some extent, this dirty domestic double-bind.

The Second Wave feminists also saw an obvious solution to the injustices and degradations of this women's work. After all, homes founded on heterosexual unions already housed two able-bodied adults. Surely after a few squabbles and refusals, men would share work – if not graciously, then at least willingly? The fair families envisaged in the 1980s would, many feminists hoped, become the 21st-century norm. By 2020 – it was felt, and with no small sense of conviction – we would live in a world that had recognized domestic labour for what it is: essential and life-giving work that should be valued, shared and adequately remunerated.

Of course, we've seen how those hopes were viciously dashed. How men failed to step up, and how, as the middle classes and opinion-makers offloaded their shitwork down a raced and gendered pecking order, housework fell off the political agenda. Feminism was outwardly seen to triumph, as women joined the paid workforce in record numbers and a handful of these women moved into high-profile careers. On the home front, however, feminism suffered its 'micro-defeat': a death by small cuts that left it barely conscious on the kitchen floor.

There are changes from which we are chided to take heart: that the housework gap has closed since the 1970s, with British men, for example, almost doubling their contribution between 1971 and the present to an average of 16 hours of domestic labour a week, as British women pitch in three fewer hours a week than their 1970s counterparts. Indeed, some heterosexual couples enjoy almost-equal domestic unions, as men pitch in with household chores even if, for the most part, they renege on the third shifts of emotional labour and household management. Sadly, truly non-sexist unions remain the preserve of the privileged few, amongst them lesbian couples alive to the traps of gender socialization, conscious non-binary communalists, and childless heterosexual couples who strive to live by feminist principles and are not yet subject to the pressures and accommodations of the Parent Labour Trap. Almost equal isn't good enough. To what extent can we truly take comfort in a rising tide of social progress when advances in men's domestic contributions have stalled? At the current rate of progress, British men will pitch in equally at some point in the 2150s, if at all.

For many working women today, the situation is critical. Unsympathetic working practices such as lengthening work days and 'always on' digital culture (the fourth shift), paired with the demands of the second and third shifts, are leading to an epidemic of anxiety and depression in women. There are more than a million women of working age on long-term antidepressants in England,[119] and an estimated one in eight women in their middle working and childrearing years in the US are clinically depressed.[120] In the UK, women are 42 per cent more likely to take sick days than men, and more likely to cite mental health issues when they do so.[121] Health charity Mind talks of an 'epidemic' of stress in the British public sector, where women workers predominate. Despite news stories trumpeting the beneficial health effects of housework, the triple shift can, in fact, be deadly: a 2016 Canadian study found that women who took on an unequal burden of housework were more likely to die early than women in unions that were more egalitarian.[122] The high stress and diminished leisure time suffered by women putting in the long working hours of the Double Day also increases their risks of cancer, arthritis and diabetes.[123] The children of heterosexual parents, who argue about housework more frequently and exhibit 'resentment displaying' behaviours, are, as we've seen, at increased risk of anxiety and 'maladjusted childhood behaviours', compared to their counterparts who have gay, or single, primary carers.

In the face of rising workplace demands and change-resist-ant men, many women are voting with their wombs. In 2018, the US birth rate sank to a record low (1.8 per woman, from 2.08 in 1990), a drop that the *Economist* in part attributes to a lack of policies to help women deal with the demands of the Double Day,[124] and in European countries with the least egalitarian division of labour, birth rates are plummeting. Italy now has a birth rate of 1.35 (and men do on average 3.5 hours of housework to women's 24.5), its lowest rate for 150 years; and in Portugal, where men hold the ignoble distinction of being Southern Europe's top housework shirkers (men do 2.8 hours to women's 22), the birth rate of 1.3 has lawmakers rattled.

When I ask a 30-something Italian author why the Italian birth rate is falling so precipitously in her home nation, she puts it simply:

> Expensive childcare, a lack of affirmative action aimed at keeping women in the workplace when they have children, and, frankly and importantly, Italian men of my generation being on average rather crummy. They expect women to do all the heavy lifting and demand praise for even so much as washing the dishes after dinner.

The US, Italy and Portugal had, like many nations, presumptuously relied on religious family values to keep birth rates high in the face of inhospitable social realities. Until the 2010s, this approach had worked. Today, women are rebelling.

Shirking Men and the Devaluation of the Work of Care

There are pressing political reasons to put housework back on the agenda.

While we are sleeping on the job (or perhaps the hob?), patriarchy is busy updating itself. Blustering misogynists, assuming the leadership of national governments, are blaming uppity women – those who've abandoned their nature-ascribed roles as domestic workers and carers – for societal malaises ranging from fragmentation to male worklessness, and, yes, falling birth rates. Viktor Orbán's view that it is Hungarian women's patriotic duty to birth five-plus kids to counteract the scourge of immigration is, if we are not alive to these narratives, only the beginning. From Sweden's White Offended Men to Golden Ageist Brexiteers and social media sensation Mrs Hinch, a nationalist-nostalgic backlash – one that centres on women's allotted natural role in an idealized home – is on the march. Feminists need to address the grievances articulated by the anti-system parties and make them our own. Otherwise the gains we've made will be thrown under the bus and our causes positioned as petty (as history has so often shown) in the face of political crisis.

Women will also bear the brunt if the world – *we* – don't take rapid and concerted action against climate change and its impacts. Thanks to our disproportionate responsibility for the domestic, women are more likely to be at home when climate-induced disasters such as heatwaves, violent storms and hurricanes strike, and as caretakers for the young and elderly we are less able to evacuate. It's women who struggle to maintain homes on the flood-prone plains of Bangladesh, and women who are tasked with securing food and water. Women environmental activists are leading the global fight against erosion – from the First Nations oil pipeline activists to India's tree-preservation Chipko movement to Navdanya, a woman-led initiative to protect biodiversity – and this is to be celebrated. If men assumed an equal share of domestic labour, they, too, might feel the urgency of this task.

A Fresh Feminist Project

What will it take to renew the popular feminist project? To focus, as Barbara Ehrenreich put it, on the dropped socks as well as spiked heels? For a start, women and their allies* need to refuse and resist. As Wages for Housework's 1972 manifesto puts it: 'we need to reject this work and we need to reject this role'. We need to throw open the doors and windows of our homes to sunlight: to interrogate and illuminate, with its merciless rays, the heterosexist state we're in. We need to admit that we're coping with and accommodating for resistant patriarchal structures off our own backs (and on our knees). We need to remember that our problems, however intimate and unique they might seem, are common problems. And we need to acknowledge that every time we roll our eyes and stack the half-filled dishwasher our husband abandoned for the footie; every time we take on such anodyne-seeming gigs as sending Christmas cards to a male partner's family; every time we rely on a foreign-born woman to clean our bathrooms, we're reinforcing the unequal power structures that have led us to this domestic impasse. These are our home truths.

This will mean, for some of us, an uncomfortable process of letting go. Letting go of the retrograde and unfeminist beliefs that pose as comforts: that women are 'just better' with kids; that women are more able, thanks to their magical lady eyes, to spot dirt or mess; that men are, you know, *men* and that's Just the Way Things Are; that the natural dues of divorce should be that women have primary custody of children. We cannot have our cake and bake it.

But women have already done a lot of changing: we've learned to combine work with the persistent demands of home; we've made ground in traditionally male careers and smashed the straw-women of the Ideal Housewife and Having It All career woman. Feminism has a poor track record in changing male behaviour. But feminists can no longer ignore the fact that

---

* Here I include everyone who identifies as women, and also non-binary people and men alive to the negative effects of sex-role socialization in their own lives and homes.

housework inequality is the product of male volition. Future progress is going to require change on men's part. Men will have to develop a greater sense of responsibility and moral feeling towards the women they live with; and they will have to take this sense of responsibility and moral feeling and actually put it to use. Change will require men to dispense with heterosexist entitlements, and it will require them to assume the mental and emotional costs of householding as well as their full share of manual domestic labour. It will also demand that men are willing to enter traditionally 'feminine' professions and to fight, in allyship, for adequate and equal payment when they do.

To talk about housework is to talk about power: hierarchical and gendered power, but also as a capillary power that bleeds through political structures and society. To reboot the stalled feminist revolution we're going to need structural changes, too. To tackle the Parent Labour Gap we need to adopt the best and most progressive global policy models, such as the Nordic 'daddy quota' of earmarked parental leave, and Iceland's state-funded universal childcare. Half-assed policies such as Britain's Shared Parental Leave and flexible working[125] fall flat in the face of resistant social norms and the gender pay gap. We need to explore radical initiatives such as the four-day week: initiatives that will allow all of us to live human lives that accommodate the work of care whilst avoiding naturalizing this work as 'women's work'. We need, with some urgency, to challenge national governments' risible reliance on women's work to plug the funding gaps that have widened under austerity; and we need a new approach to measuring the societal value of work that captures its social, as well as its putatively economic, benefits.[126]

We also need to interrogate a welfare state that's based on the 1950s Breadwinner/Housewife model and rebuild it with the diversity and fluidity of modern life courses in view. Our new version welfare states should address not just the coming challenges proposed by automation, which are discussed ad nauseam, but also articulate and challenge inequalities in the private sphere. The right to well-funded care leave is a good start. As is the idea of a tax-funded universal care budget, as proposed by domestic worker activists the National Domestic Workers Alliance (NDWA) in the US. To be truly progressive, working-age transfers such as Universal Basic Income (UBI), heralded as a solution to future joblessness and an aid to women's emancipation,[127] need to be linked to the project of making visible the work that is erased by patriarchal capital: the work of caring for the young and elderly; the work of maintaining human lives and homes. This vaunted 'post-work' era that UBI seeks to address won't live up to its promise for many women without this progressive view. Indeed, it will do little more than entrench pre-existing injustices, especially if the political right uses UBI as a means of doing away with the welfare obligations of the state.

And this brings us to another point. Our job is not to make life slightly better for some white women. Or to feed a new rebellion with old slogans. Our job is to reach out in allyship across race, class and gender boundaries. And that means rediscovering the impetus that once led feminists of all classes, races and genders to stand shoulder to shoulder and articulate their intimate problems as all being one. In the 1980s, popular feminism lost this sense of allyship. White American feminists talked of the reproductive right to abortion and neglected the fact that black women were being sterilized by the state. Too few of us decried the social scapegoating of single mothers on benefits, or welfare moms – women at the sharp end of the injustices of patriarchal capital. Today, women of colour have talked of feeling jostled and unwelcome in women's rights marches. These failures shame feminism, and shame all of us who consider ourselves feminists.

Too few middle-class feminists speak up for the elderly and frail, who suffer the consequences of the lowly pay given to workers in the 'pink collar' care sector, or the breadline existence of the women who perform this vital work. The devaluation of women's work debases all of us, and we all need to speak out. Speak out for women who don't speak English and who are abused by cleaning and care work agencies. Speak out against the shameful pay and working conditions of those who take on our shitwork. Frankly, we don't have time for feminist fragmentations and failures of allyship, not least because our energies are being devoured by the succubi that are the second and third shifts.

Our pink-collar allies are beginning to fight this, our necessary fight. In 2018, Australian childcare workers staged three successive strikes to demand a 35 per cent rise in wages; in January 2019, German nursery workers joined that nation's teachers and social workers in a nationwide strike for improved pay and conditions. In January 2019, 50,000 women garment workers in Bangladesh staged a militant work stoppage for higher wages that lasted for nearly two weeks and was met by a violent police crackdown. Spanish domestic workers' unions, meanwhile, were one of the principal forces behind the 2018 Day Without Women in Spain. And in the US, the National Domestic Workers Alliance, formed in 2007, is busily organizing domestic workers across the States, calling for strikes and a new centrally funded care model to cover all forms of care and make domestic work a living-wage job. One of the NDWA's slogans, a member told me, is borrowed from Wages for Housework: 'Without Us, Nothing Moves'. Similarly, in 2018, Peruvian domestic workers walked out, with a rousing call to solidarity amongst all working women: 'A living wage for caring work – in your own home and other people's.'

You'll remember Josephine Hullett, the domestic worker from Ohio, who in 1973 told *Ms.* magazine: 'There's a sense in which *all* women are household workers. And unless we stop being turned against each other, unless we organize together, we're never going to make this country see housework for what it really is – human work, not just "woman's work".'

Housework is human work, not women's work. As late-capitalist creatures, we expend a lot of effort denying this fact. To admit that we need our arses wiped and our loos cleaned, that we're vulnerable if we don't have recourse to a clean, warm home supplied with nutritious edible foodstuffs, is to admit we're human – and, by extension, vulnerable; mortal. The most prized cleaners and workers are popularly held as those who allow us to forget this fact; who quietly go about their duties in the shadows and whose presence is barely felt, or who pretend to be chums that happened to have dropped in to sponge our loo, like cleaner Chris. This cultural denial of our vulnerability and mortality is one of the reasons the capitalist patriarchy has succeeded in its trick of repackaging our care and domestic work as 'nonwork'. If we don't need our arses wiped and our loos cleaned – goes the logic – we won't die. Yet none of us are autonomous or invulnerable, and none of us are individuals: we are all interdependent and we are all dependent on the processes of care. By erasing and disavowing these processes, we erase and disavow ourselves.

Here is perhaps a point of departure from which a new intersectional feminist mandate might be established: that we are all vulnerable, we are all a few steps away from illness, homelessness or joblessness. We are all in need of the nourishment of the work formerly known as 'women's work'. First proposed by the American ethicist and psychologist Carol Gilligan,[128] care ethics critiques the gendering of the work of care and instead proposes care as a human strength. Care in Gilligan's view is a fundamental aspect of human experience that should be taught to all and become the responsibility of all. We should *all* become capable adults who cook, clean and softly take the arm of a human in need. Care is, by its nature, alive to conditions of vulnerability and inequality.

Making care our defining social responsibility – a responsibility shared laterally, rather than down the chain of labour to lower-status women – is an important first step in according this work its proper value.

As Chris the London cleaner said: 'Home's private, and being able to wash your own plates and tidy your own stuff up and look after yourself – there's something in it, isn't there?' Caring for ourselves and others is what it is to be human.

Rebooting the stalled domestic revolution is not our only pressing feminist task. It is, however, a foundational one, whose effects will ripple through the public sphere and politics as it informs our stewardship of the environment.

If we make quality, non-sexist householding our project, we will enrich our parenting, our romantic unions and our world.

See you on the Home Stretch...

Postscript

How have things changed at Walnut Tree Road since Tim, Leo and I began to explore the intimate politics of housework? In some ways, profoundly. Inspired by the latte pappas, Tim took eight months' parental leave to look after Leo. He feels this has made him a more capable, feminist co-parent; and I, happily, agree.

We no longer have a domestic cleaner. After trying, initially, to pay a non-agency cleaner a figure commensurate with our own hourly incomes, we decided that this, too, wouldn't wash. We felt uncomfortable with this transaction in light of our new knowledge about the domestic labour sector, not to mention the feminist implications of handing our shitwork down a feminized labour line.

These days we make cleaning a weekend task: Tim and I pull on our hypoallergenic marigolds and put Radio 6 on full blast as Leo joins in with his 'racoon cleaner' (in fact, a yoga strap he imagines is a hose). But we don't glamorize the project. And we don't follow the hysterical advisories of either Mrs Beeton or Mrs Hinch.

Sometimes, when necessary for our sanity, we let hairs choke the plughole and dust settle on the blinds.

When I asked Tim if our research for this book had revolutionized our domestic division of labour, he was clearing out the organic scraps bin at our house-swap in the US and he told me, distractedly, that he didn't 'have time to massage your colossal eagle', which now ranks as one of my top-ten

Tim malapropisms. But after a few puns about bald heads and twitching, he became serious.

'Well, you still do most of the cooking,' he said. 'But I do most of the tidying, I think, and I clean up those awful white toothpaste dribbles you leave all over the bathroom. Only yesterday, for example, I wiped up a Hall of Shame of toothpaste dribbles. But I digress. I certainly think we're more aware of the politics of all of this now; or I am.'

Then he turned to me. 'And I am going to try to cook meals without a recipe. Though you know it's not my style.'

In truth, Tim's eight-month paternity leave was a game-changer. During this period he assumed primary responsibility for household management and food shopping* and I stepped back, resetting our domestic dynamics. Part of this process was letting go. Letting go, in particular, of my comforting delusions around the primacy of motherhood. This was a challenge, especially when Leo switched parental allegiances and began to call out for 'daddy, daddy' at night. Today, however, Tim and I are much closer to our dream of being quality, non-sexist co-parents and householders. But we realize how fortunate we have been to take this 'feminist pause' when so few can afford to do so.

For my part, I've become more inquisitive about the women I see out and about in London: women apologetically sweeping under my feet in restaurants; the harried-looking care workers who visit the elderly man three doors down; the legion of pink-collar workers in the shadows that make a 21st-century city run smoothly and whose work we should celebrate as we give them their due.

I also refrain from mumsplaining Tim's parenting. A couple of days ago, for example, I noticed that as Tim was changing

---

* Tim, in keeping with his tech suspicions, has unilaterally cancelled the household's 'robot food' online food deliveries and resumed his trips to the supermarket for the weekly shop.

Leo's nappy, he'd tucked our son's penis outside one of the gathered leg-holes like a mini urine hose. With effort, I kept my own counsel.

In further news, Tim is now on WhatsApp, so assumes some of the emotional labour of messaging family and arranging Leo's social life. In the run-up to Christmas 2019 he wrote family addresses on Christmas card envelopes I had bought and stamped for him. Christmas 2020, I hope, will see a final breakthrough when it comes to sharing the seasonal mental load.

You'll be happy to hear I'm still festooning my knickers around the bedroom furniture.

These days I see it as my small act of feminist resistance.

Acknowledgements

Thanks are due to my agent Imogen Pelham at Marjacq and my editor Clare Drysdale, copyeditor Gemma Wain and the team at Atlantic Books, whose enthusiasm for The Home Stretch was matched by their eagerness to share their own accounts of navigating the 'double day'.

Thanks to everyone in the Gender Studies department at the University of London's School of Oriental and African Studies, and especially Dr Gina Heathcote and Dr Katherine Natanel, who provided the grounding in material, intersectional and postcolonial feminist theory which, I hope, informs this book.

Thanks to Arlie Hochschild and Silvia Federici for sparing time for the latest in a long line of researchers inquiring into their seminal 1970s explorations of gender and domestic labour; this book owes much to your work, as it does to Wages for Housework's Selma James, Brigitte Galtier and Mariarosa Dalla Costa, and German socialist feminist theorist Maria Mies.

Thanks to Cléo Chassonnery-Zaïgouche at the University of Cambridge for casting an eye over my laywoman's history of economic theory and to Dr Leah DeVun at Rutgers University for the insights into the land-dyke and queerlands communities in the USA. Thanks, too, to Caroline Davidson, whose peerless 1987 history of housework in the British Isles was indispensable in fleshing out the historical practices of housekeeping. Thanks also to Professor Kirsten Swinth for her excavations of the Second Wave feminist battles around care work. Thanks to Sarah Costley for her thankless assistance in tabulating the survey data gathered for this book.

Additionally, thanks to Jurate for taking undoubted risks

in inviting me into the homes of her London cleaning clients as well as cleaner Chris, for his candid disclosures of the dirty truths of the London domestic cleaning industry. (Chris: you're a shoo-in for *Queer Eye*.)

Thanks too to the thousands of individuals – from my Nineties student housemates to journalist friends across the globe and acquaintances in London parenting groups – who shared their anecdotes and intimate experiences of domestic labour in their own homes, as well as responding to the survey that provides data for this book. It would have been a grey thing indeed without your thoughtful, and often hilarious, contributions.

Thanks to my mum Anne for putting up with having her life picked over in print, and my brother Adam for the Breville toasted sandwiches (1984-1989, Breville sandwich maker RIP).

Thanks to Sylvia and Charles for the many days of childcare that meant I could put in the hours to complete the manuscript for this book (an irony not lost to me).

And, of course, to Tim and Leo, for joining me on this adventure: for the mopping and 'racooning' (vacuuming), the laughter and love and everything, absolutely everything, else.

Picture Credits

p. 17 Author's photo

p. 28 'We Can Do It!' by J. Howard Miller, 1943; *Modern Homemaker* Home Canning Cookbook by KERR, 1945.

p. 35 'It Needn't Be a Chore', *Spare Rib*, March 1972.

p. 46 'Ban the Garbage Can', Emerson Electric Co., 1969; 'Get the Power', Clorox Cleaning Company, 1979.

p. 57 Scold's Bridle, *The Strand Magazine*, 1894.

p. 60 *Mornings at Bow Street* by J. Wight, 1824

p. 101 Samsung Modern Masterpieces Campaign, Taylor Herring, 2018.

p. 129 Istanbul graffiti photographed by Selin Çağatay, 2019.

p. 133 Roberto Peri, Corbis, 2014.

p. 196 The 'mechanical maid of the future', Arthur Radebaugh, 1958.

p. 200 The 'Maid Without Tears' by J.P. Rutland,1978.

p. 205 Electrical Association of Women examining a model kitchen for 'working class flats', Electrical Association of Women, 1931.

p. 242 Oregon Women's Land Trust Meeting, Ruth Mountaingrove, 1970.

p. 249 Author's photo.

p. 254 'Scotch washing', Isaac Cruikshank, 1810.

p. 256 The Three Magnets from *Garden Cities of To-morrow*, Ebenezer Howard, 1902.

p. 277 Aprons hang from balconies in Galicia, AFP, 2018.

p. 279 'My Mum's is On Strike', Women's Strike, 2019.

p. 293 'Fuck Housework', Shirley Boccaccio, 1971.

p. 294 *Who's Holding the Baby?*, Hackney Flashers, 1978.

Endnotes

1   http://www.columbia.edu/~sss31/rainbow/wife.html.
2   I have sympathy with Professor Guy Standing's broad argument for a distinction between the terms 'work' and 'labour'. In our context I use the terms interchangeably to refer to the discrete tasks performed in the home, with 'domestic labour' also performing the function of elevating this labour to an economic category that should be 'accounted for' in financial terms, as it is 'counted' by society.
3   Silvia Federici, *Revolution at Point Zero: Housework, Reproduction, and the Feminist Struggle*, PM Press, 2012.
4   https://www.ons.gov.uk/peoplepopulationandcommunity/wellbeing/articles/menenjoyfivehoursmoreleisuretimeperweek-thanwomen/2018-01-09.
5   https://www.demographic-research.org/volumes/vol35/16/35-16.pdf.
6   In the US, men are doing proportionally more childcare. In fact, more recent data, from the 2010 American Time Use Survey and using time diaries, finds that although married fathers are doing slightly less housework (as are mothers) than in 1995, fathers seem to have shifted into doing more childcare. According to Bianchi and her colleagues, the gender gap in childcare declined over the period from 1995 to 2010. The ratio of married mothers' to fathers' childcare time declined from 2.5 in 1995 to 1.9 in 2010. Thus, research using the 1993 survey is problematic because it is 20 years old, and data on childcare contributions is not included in the Kornich et al or my research.
7   https://contemporaryfamilies.org/3-cassino-men-compensate-for-income-to-women/.
8   We should here point out that these figures are from low bases: from 1 to 8 per cent US Fortune 500 CEOs; gender pay gap now 85 per cent compared to 64; and female parliamentarians in the West limping from 11 per cent in 1995 to 24 per cent today.
9   https://docs.google.com/forms/d/1dxFCXucuZTBQYl2Z61sgt4Ta5w8AqmVGFfLrc0RpSUQ/edit?usp=drive_web.
10 These figures are a little misleading as it was more common for women and men to remain childless and unmarried than we might think in the early 20th century (30 per cent of adults were childless and unmarried in the 1900s, for example). It was only

with the wealth of the post-war period that most adults married and reproduced.

11 Virginia Nicholson, *Perfect Wives in Ideal Homes: The Story of Women in the 1950s*, Penguin, 2016.

12 https://dspace.lboro.ac.uk/dspace-jspui/bitstream/2134/5286/3/EngyBld08%2040%28%29Firth.pdf; https://www.theguardian.com/environment/datablog/2011/jul/21/uk-household-energy-use

13 http://press.uchicago.edu/ucp/books/book/chicago/F/bo3684531.html.

14 A 2019 study disproved this prevailing lie, finding that women aren't better at multitasking and that in fact no humans are adept at rapidly toggling between tasks. Women just do more work. https://journals.plos.org/plosone/article?id=10.1371/journal.pone.0220150.

15 Email, Women's Aid March, 2017.

16 http://journals.sagepub.com/doi/abs/10.1177/026101839001002914?journalCode=cspa.

17 BBC People's History.

18 David Kynaston, *Austerity Britain*, Bloomsbury, 2008, p. 209.

19 Nicholson, *Perfect Wives in Ideal Homes*, p. 13.

20 https://data.journalarchives.jisc.ac.uk/britishlibrary/sparerib/view?publd=P523_344_Issue5PDFP523_344_Issue5_0010-0013_19pdf.

21 Brigid Schulte points out that the revolutionary theorist's wife Jenny toiled in squalor with the surviving three of their six children while Marx spent his days writing at the British Museum.

22 It's not strictly true that early Marxism elided women. In 1884's *The Origin of the Family, Private Property, and the State*, Marx's collaborator Friedrich Engels adapted Marx's theory to account for the fate of women under capitalism. To Engels, the advent of private property created an obsession with women's chastity as a means of guaranteeing the inheritance of private property by landowners' offspring. The monogamous nuclear family, in this view, institutionalized these forces, guaranteeing men's control of women's sexual facilities and labour through their reliance on the male wage. Engels saw relations between women and men – the gendered haves and have-nots – under capitalism as similar to those between the classed haves and have-nots, a system maintained to serve the interests of capital and the ruling class. In Engels's view, the nuclear family was also part of a compact made by the ruling class with the proletariat male. By giving working-class men power over working-class women, the ruling class secured these men's support for the capitalist system (which in turn oppressed them). Engels was scathing about the heterosexual nuclear family, seeing it at best as 'a conjugal partnership of leaden boredom, known as

"domestic bliss"'. He saw women's emancipation as possible only through the dissolution of capitalism and the transformation of the private work conducted within the family into public industry, with children raised as a 'public affair'. It was theories such as this that influenced the rollout of public nurseries and canteens under communism in Mao's China and the USSR.

23 On the timeline of feminist interventions into Marxist theory, see Lisa Vogel's *Marxism and the Oppression of Women: Toward a Unitary Theory*, Rutgers University Press, 1983.

24 Kirsten Swinth, *Feminism's Forgotten Fight: The Unfinished Struggle for Work and Family*, Harvard University Press, 2018.

25 Ibid., p. 112.

26 See, for example, http://www.legislation.gov.uk/ukpga/1975/65/pdfs/ukpga_19750065_en.pdf.

27 Ellen Malos, ed., *The Politics of Housework*, Allison and Busby, 1980.

28 Quote from Louise Howe, *Pink Collar Workers*, Putnam, 1977.

29 A note on feminism's 'waves': Avtar Brah and the LSE's Clare Hemmings are not alone in pointing to the peril of interpreting the history of feminism in discrete waves. The consensus view is that we're now in the Fourth Wave of a herstory that began with the First Wave of the late 19th and early 20th centuries, which focused on legal issues such as achieving suffrage and in the US was intertwined with the abolitionist movement; the Second Wave, or 'big bang' of the 1960s to 1980s, which focused on women's labour and sexual violence and saw the first awareness of the erasure of women of colour and working-class women in earlier feminisms; the Third Wave, beginning in the late 1980s, which disavowed some of the ideas of the First and Second Waves and concerned itself with cultural representations, beauty, sexuality and postmodernist deconstruction of the category of 'woman'; and the Fourth Wave, beginning in recent years, in which transgender and transnational issues and an intersectional view of the oppressions of class, gender and race are paramount.

30 Jonathan Gershuny et al, 'Gender Convergence in Domestic Work', *Sociology*, 45(2), 2011, pp. 234–51.

31 http://journals.sagepub.com/doi/abs/10.1177/1060826515600880.

32 https://journals.sagepub.com/doi/10.1177/002214650404500201.

33 Arnstein Aassve, 'Desperate Housework: Relative Resources, Time Availability, Economic Dependency, and Gender Ideology Across Europe', *Journal of Family Issues*, 35(8), 2014, pp. 1000–1022.

34 https://pdfs.semanticscholar.org/90da/05bd9e11bb2e764969b1a980ff8620729b71.pdf.

35 https://link.springer.com/article/10.1007/s11199-019-01061-9.

36 The National Childbirth Trust, a British organization founded in 1956 that offers paid-for prenatal birthing lessons that many

middle-class British parents principally attend to forge a social group of fellow parents with similarly aged children.

37 Judith Butler, 'Performative Acts and Gender Constitution: An Essay in Phenomenology and Feminist Theory', *Theatre Journal*, 40(4), 1988, pp. 519–31.

38 Candace West and Don H. Zimmerman, 'Doing Gender', *Gender and Society*, 1(2), 1987, pp. 125–51.

39 https://www.umass.edu/newsoffice/article/umass-amherst-study-raising-adopted-children-how-parents-work-together-more-important-their.

40 https://journals.sagepub.com/doi/abs/10.1177/0049124119852395; https://www.ncbi.nlm.nih.gov/pubmed/19934011.

41 A 2019 LSE study has found that men respond to women moving into masculinized fields such as construction and engineering by selecting male-typed jobs with greater frequency, despite the fact that men in 'pink-collar' jobs ride what Barbara Risman refers to as the promotion 'glass elevator'.

42 The Smith–Lever Act of 1914 and the Smith–Hughes National Vocational Education Act of 1917.

43 https://www.pewsocialtrends.org/2017/12/05/gender-genera-tion-and-partisanship-come-into-play-in-attitudes-about-raising-boys-and-girls/.

44 https://www.pewresearch.org/fact-tank/2019/02/20/the-way-u-s-teens-spend-their-time-is-changing-but-differences-between-boys-and-girls-persist/.

45 Giuliana Pompei, *Wages for Housework*, trans. Joan Hall, 1972.

46 See Michelle J. Budig, 'The Fatherhood Bonus and the Motherhood Penalty: Parenthood and the Gender Gap in Pay', 2014, https://www.thirdway.org/report/the-fatherhood-bonus-and-the-mother-hood-penalty-parenthood-and-the-gender-gap-in-pay.

47 https://www.11alive.com/video/life/millennial-women-working-more-and-doing-most-of-the-housework-research-shows/85-1f367e0f-2d0c-41e3-b080-21e48901da51.

48 https://www.sciencedirect.com/science/article/abs/pii/S0927537100000208.

49 https://www.mitpressjournals.org/doi/abs/10.1162/003465302317411514.

50 Twice as many British women as men are on antidepressants, in all age groups. See https://www.theguardian.com/society/2018/aug/10/four-million-people-in-england-are-long-term-users-of-antidepressants.

51 https://www.bbc.co.uk/news/business-46558944.

52 Alongside Cyprus, Ireland, Switzerland and Greece. See https://www.thelocal.se/20190614/sweden-ranked-among-worlds-best-places-raise-a-family-unicef-report.

53 https://www.dss.gov.au/our-responsibilities/families-and-children/programmes-services/paid-parental-leave-scheme.
54 https://www.dol.gov/sites/dolgov/files/OASP/legacy/files/PaternityBrief.pdf.
55 Termed 'partner pay', see https://www.dss.gov.au/publications-articles-corporate-publications-annual-reports/department-of-social-services-annual-report-2017-18.
56 https://aifs.gov.au/aifs-conference/fathers-and-parental-leave
57 https://www.gov.uk/shared-parental-leave-and-pay
58 Report by EMW, the commercial law firm, from FOI requests, August 2019.
59 Parental leave also shifts male attitudes. Economists who studied the effect of the introduction of paternity leave in Spain in 2007 found that fathers who took paternity leave were less likely to have a subsequent child. See https://qz.com/work/1614893/after-men-in-spain-got-paternity-leave-they-wanted-fewer-kids/.
60 Andelin's relationship with Second Wave feminism and its exponents was, in fact, complicated. In *Helen Andelin and the Fascinating Womanhood Movement* (University of Utah Press, 2014), historian Julie Neuffer notes that at first Andelin thought of the feminists as misguided women who, once they heard the truth of her message, would come around to the right way of thinking, and referred to them as her sisters. In time, however, she began to see them as her enemies and dubbed them 'sick and confused individuals' who had 'failed at being women'. Thus, she claimed, they were not qualified to speak for other women. Friedan was just as surprised to learn that there was a whole population of American women who didn't care about equal rights and did not want to be liberated.
61 https://www.ons.gov.uk/employmentandlabourmarket/peopleinwork/employmentandemployeetypes/bulletins/uklabourmarket/august2017.
62 In her book *Where the Millennials Will Take Us: A New Generation Wrestles with the Gender Structure*, Oxford University Press, 2018.
63 http://www.vatican.va/roman_curia/congregations/cfaith/documents/rc_con_cfaith_doc_20040731_collaboration_en.html. 'The obscuring of the difference or duality of the sexes has enormous consequences on a variety of levels. This theory of the human person, intended to promote prospects for equality of women through liberation from biological determinism, has in reality inspired ideologies which, for example, call into question the family, in its natural two-parent structure of mother and father, and make homosexuality and heterosexuality virtually equivalent, in a new model of polymorphous sexuality.'
64 Removing requirements for proof of income and permission to remarry from a groom's first wife, https://assets.publishing.service.

gov.uk/government/uploads/system/uploads/attachment_data/
file/677541/Libya_-_Women_-_CPIN_-_v2_0.pdf.

65   In his forthcoming book, *Anti-System Politics: The Crisis of Market Liberalism in Rich Democracies*, Oxford University Press, 2020.

66   https://www.economist.com/leaders/2018/10/11/londons-financial-flows-are-polluted-by-laundered-money.

67   https://www.opendemocracy.net/5050/yasmin-gunaratnam/sick-and-tired-sri-lankan-domestic-workers-fight-back-against-violence.

68   Taken from the pay differential at the law firm where Tim trained, the yawning pay gap of the male–female partner divide, and the fact that women disappear from law firms before they make partner-grade. Six months after reporting this pay gap, the law firm in question appointed a woman as London managing partner, one of a handful of women in senior managerial roles in the magic circle.

69   In an address made by Betty Friedan at the 1970 Strike for Equality in New York.

70   This was before I read the Irish Human Rights and Equality Commission's 2019 study, which found that women in Ireland put in over twice as much housework as men, commensurate with the picture in the rest of the UK.

71   Liliana E. Pezzin and Barbara Steinberg Schone, 'Intergenerational Household Formation, Female Labor Supply and Informal Caregiving: A Bargaining Approach', *Journal of Human Resources*, 34(3), 1999, pp. 475–503.

72   'Gender deviance neutralization' is the jargony academic term for the mechanism by which men and women correct for behaving contrary to gender norms in one area of their lives ('I'm a female engineer!') by overcompensating in another ('BUT I wash all the dishes!').

73   https://www.aquinas.edu/sites/default/files/Gender_deviance_Schneider.pdf.

74   Counting both the formal and informal economy. See https://www.economist.com/leaders/2018/07/05/why-india-needs-women-to-work.

75   https://onlinelibrary.wiley.com/doi/abs/10.1111/jomf.12381.

76   https://ro.uow.edu.au/cgi/viewcontent.cgi?referer=http://scholar.google.co.uk/&httpsredir=1&article=1088&context=artspapers.

77   https://www.dailymail.co.uk/news/article-3516617/One-three-families-pay-cleaner-35s-drive-trend-hiring-domestic-help.html.

78   For more on intersectionality and intersectional feminism, see this backgrounder from Kimberlé Crenshaw, https://www.youtube.com/watch?v=ViDtnfQ9FHc.

79   Kalayaan's figures, by email, April 2019.

80   https://www.theguardian.com/global-development/2017/oct/19/

absolutely-unacceptable-uk-accused-of-failing-to-protect-domestic-workers.

81 https://migrationobservatory.ox.ac.uk/resources/briefings/migrants-in-the-uk-labour-market-an-overview/.

82 https://www.dailymail.co.uk/news/article-5630353/Jobs-available-Buckingham-Palace-Queens-cleaners-paid-2-03-London-Living-Wage.html.

83 Bridget Anderson, *Britain's Secret Slaves: An investigation into the plight of overseas domestic workers in the United Kingdom*, Human Rights series, Anti-Slavery International, 1993. A landmark British case.

84 https://www.theglobaleconomy.com/Philippines/remittances_percent_GDP/.

85 https://www.tandfonline.com/doi/pdf/10.1080/09612020400200381.

86 As quoted in Swinth, *Feminism's Forgotten Fight*.

87 https://www.theguardian.com/global-development/2019/apr/07/violence-sexual-abuse-vietnam-garment-factory.

88 Kristi Rowan Humphreys, *Housework and Gender in American Television*, Lexington Books, 2015.

89 J. P. Rutland, *Exploring the World of Robots*, Piccolo Books, 1978.

90 *Real Humans* (2012).

91 Davidson, p. 198.

92 The US figures encompass single mothers as well as cohabiting or married women with partners/husbands who do not work. But, with caveats, we can speak of a reversion to breadwinner/stay-at-home modes of living amongst the upper-middle and middle classes in the US, and amongst the wealthiest in the UK.

93 Shani Orgad, *Heading Home: Motherhood, Work and the Failed Promise of Equality*, Columbia University Press, 2019.

94 Kynaston, *Austerity Britain*, p. 208.

95 Angela McRobbie, 'Illegible Rage: Post-Feminist Disorders', in *The Aftermath of Feminism: Gender, Culture, and Social Change*, SAGE, 2009.

96 In 2017, consumer advocacy group Truth in Advertising filed a complaint with the US government regulatory agency regarding over 50 health claims made by Paltrow's site, which it claimed were 'dangerous and false'; and in 2018 it was reported that Goop Inc. had agreed to pay $145,000 to settle allegations it made unscientific claims about the benefits of three products including vaginally inserted eggs, which Goop claimed had the effect of balancing hormones and improving users' bladder control. Despite these criticisms and setbacks, Goop has several million active users, a staff of 30 in its slick Feng Shui'd offices in Los Angeles, and in 2017 launched a glossy news-stand magazine.

97 On Instagram and Twitter, webscraped data.

98 The word 'womyn' is one of several alternative spellings of the English word 'women' used by some feminists as a repudiation of the traditions that define women by reference to a male norm. It first appeared in print in the US in 1976, referring to the first Michigan Womyn's Music Festival. Competing constructions include 'womban'; (a reference to the womb) or 'womon' (singular) and 'wimmin' (plural). 'Womxn' is now more common, intended by its users to indicate explicit inclusion of transgender women and women of colour.

99 'The back-to-the-land movement appears to recur throughout American history in cyclical waves, most of its adherents longing for a romanticized version of an early America, which in reality never existed. The two largest back-to-the-land movements, occurring in the 1900s and 1970s, idealized farm labor and the rural community of the past. The 1900s back-to-the-land movement, which peaked around 1910, focused on labor and a man's right to labor, whereas the 1970s movement sought to maximize the fruits of one's labor.' https://pdxscholar.library.pdx.edu/cgi/viewcontent.cgi?article=2079&context=open_access_etds.

100 Sue Deevy, Nelly Kaufer, Dian Wagner, Carol Newhouse, Billie Miracle, Country Lesbians: The Story of the WomanShare Collective, WomanShare Books, 1976.

101 Quoted in http://clgbthistory.org/wp-content/uploads/2010/11/NestlePrize2011_Grosjean_WomynsWork.pdf.

102 'Radical feminism' is a slippery term, but is usually used to apply to the branch of feminism which emerged in the Second Wave and which proscribed radical separation from men (and that, for example, all sex with males within the structure of patriarchy and male power was an act of sexual violence). Its poster-women were Andrea Dworkin and Catharine MacKinnon.

103 Quoted in Rae André, Homemakers: The Forgotten Workers, University of Chicago Press, 1981, p. 171.

104 Author of The Last Utopians: Four Late Nineteenth-Century Visionaries and Their Legacy, Princeton University Press, 2018.

105 I use the term 'suffragette' as this was used by the women themselves. I do so acknowledging the point, made by many theorists, that 'suffragists' should now be the preferred term, as 'suffragette' was a derogatory term applied by the contemporary press; also other positions that suffragists and suffragettes are two distinct groups (sympathizers and activists, respectively).

106 https://www.timebanking.org/what-is-timebanking/.

107 https://trashnothing.com/help/what-is-freecycling-and-how-does-it-work.

108 http://www3.weforum.org/docs/WEF_GGGR_2018.pdf.

109 https://www.tuc.org.uk/blogs/womens-pay-time-government-action-close-gender-pay-gap.

110 Iceland has a nine-month shared parental leave allocation on 80

per cent pay, with three months earmarked for the mother, three for the father, and three shared.

111 See state-by-state data here: https://www.epi.org/child-care-costs-in-the-united-states/.

112 Including childcare. National Institute of Statistics (INE), 2018.

113 The Women's Strike Assembly 'reject the far-right's insidious claims that their racism and xenophobia is motivated by a concern for protecting "our" women'.

114 Switzerland lags behind many of its European neighbours in gender equality: Swiss women only got the vote in federal elections in 1971, decades after most of the Western world; professional women earn on average nearly 19 per cent less than men; and 59 per cent of Swiss women say they had experienced sexual harassment in a 2019 Amnesty International survey.

115 As quoted in Swinth, *Feminism's Forgotten Fight*.

116 We can see echoes of this construction in Spanish feminist Esther Vivas's feminist call for the rise of the 'disobedient mother' in *Una mirada feminista a la maternidad (Disobedient Mum: A Feminist Perspective on Motherhood)*, published by Capitán Swing in 2019.

117 http://www.freilassung.de/otherl/arm/rzora84.htm.

118 https://www.youtube.com/watch?v=wCNWUSj46PU&fbclid=IwA R3DN7aXBPZrtwbRwq_s48pGlZLjlfcqxSXF8AyDRroHQWpsXSx-D4OWyAJw.

119 theguardian.com/society/2018/aug/10/four-million-people-in-england-are-long-term-users-of-antidepressants.

120 cdc.gov/reproductivehealth/depression.

121 https://www.ons.gov.uk/employmentandlabourmarket/peopleinwork/labourproductivity/articles/sicknessabsenceinthelabourmarket/2016.

122 With pre-existing health conditions: https://www.theguardian.com/commentisfree/2016/apr/23/women-housework-research-health-problems-chance-death-increases.

123 Conversely, a 2019 study conducted in Sweden found that in families with small children where fathers were given flexible paid leave, there was a 26 per cent decrease in women being given prescriptions for anti-anxiety medications, nber.org/papers/w25902.

124 https://www.economist.com/democracy-in-america/2018/10/31/americas-fertility-rate-continues-its-deep-decline.

125 Flexible working often re-inscribes women's responsibility for the reproductive sphere. Further, the current UK policy only legally allows individuals to *ask* for flexible working. No responsibility is placed on employers to actually provide flexible working.

126 When leftist economic think tank the New Economics Foundation proposed such a model, they found that hospital cleaners generate £10 in social value for every £1 they are paid, and that top

advertising executives destroy £11 of value for every pound in value they generate. See https://neweconomics.org/2009/12/a-bit-rich.

127 Pilots have found that Universal Basic Income leads to a rise in rates of divorce, as women are able to afford to exit unhappy unions. Advocates argue that UBI removes a barrier to leaving an abusive partner.

128 Gilligan's book, *In a Different Voice: Psychological Theory and Women's Development,* was released in 1982 and attracted criticism for reifying a naturalized mother's role. This is perhaps one reason the ethics of care has remained a marginal feminist concern.